I0812751

IMAGES
of America

BUXTON, HOLLIS, AND LIMINGTON

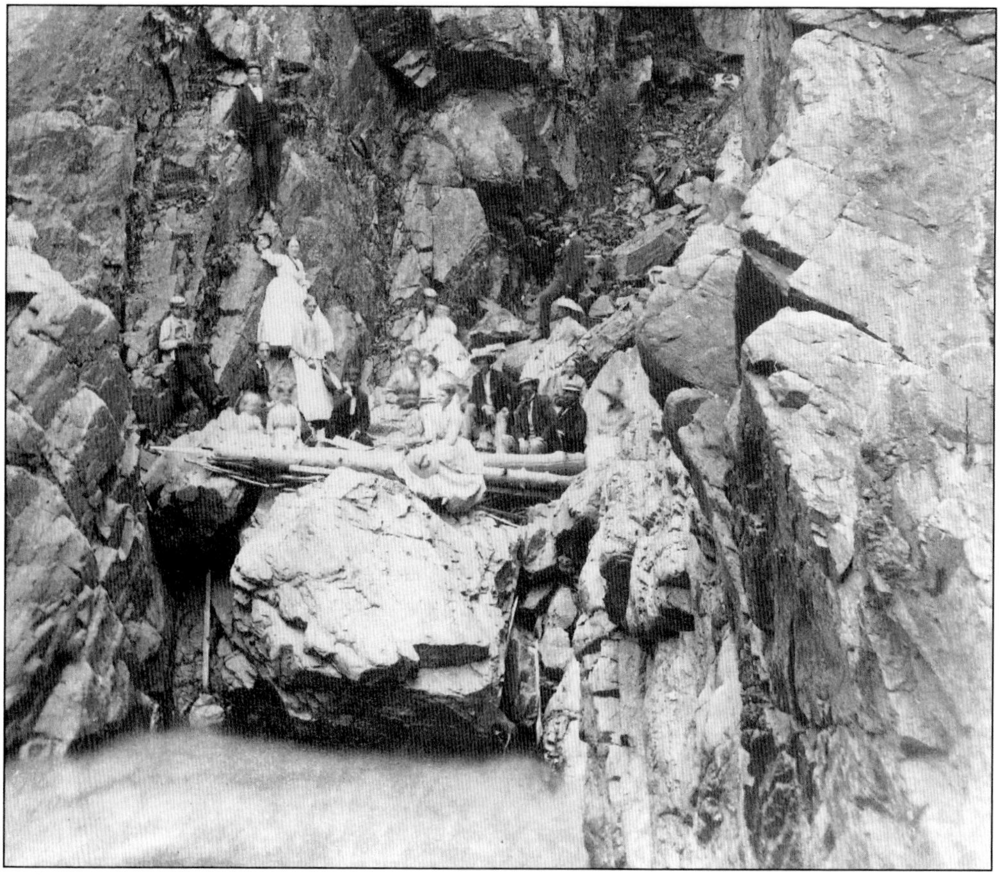

Indian Cellar on the Saco River in Hollis, 1870s. This is one of the recreational spots that flooded out when the electric power company dams were built on the Saco.

IMAGES
of America

BUXTON, HOLLIS, AND LIMINGTON

Frank H. Sleeper

ARCADIA
PUBLISHING

Copyright © 1997 by Frank H. Sleeper
ISBN 978-0-7385-3886-0

Published by Arcadia Publishing
Charleston, South Carolina

Printed in the United States of America

For all general information, please contact Arcadia Publishing:
Telephone 843-853-2070
Fax 843-853-0044
E-mail sales@arcadiapublishing.com
For customer service and orders:
Toll-Free 1-888-313-2665

Visit us on the Internet at www.arcadiapublishing.com

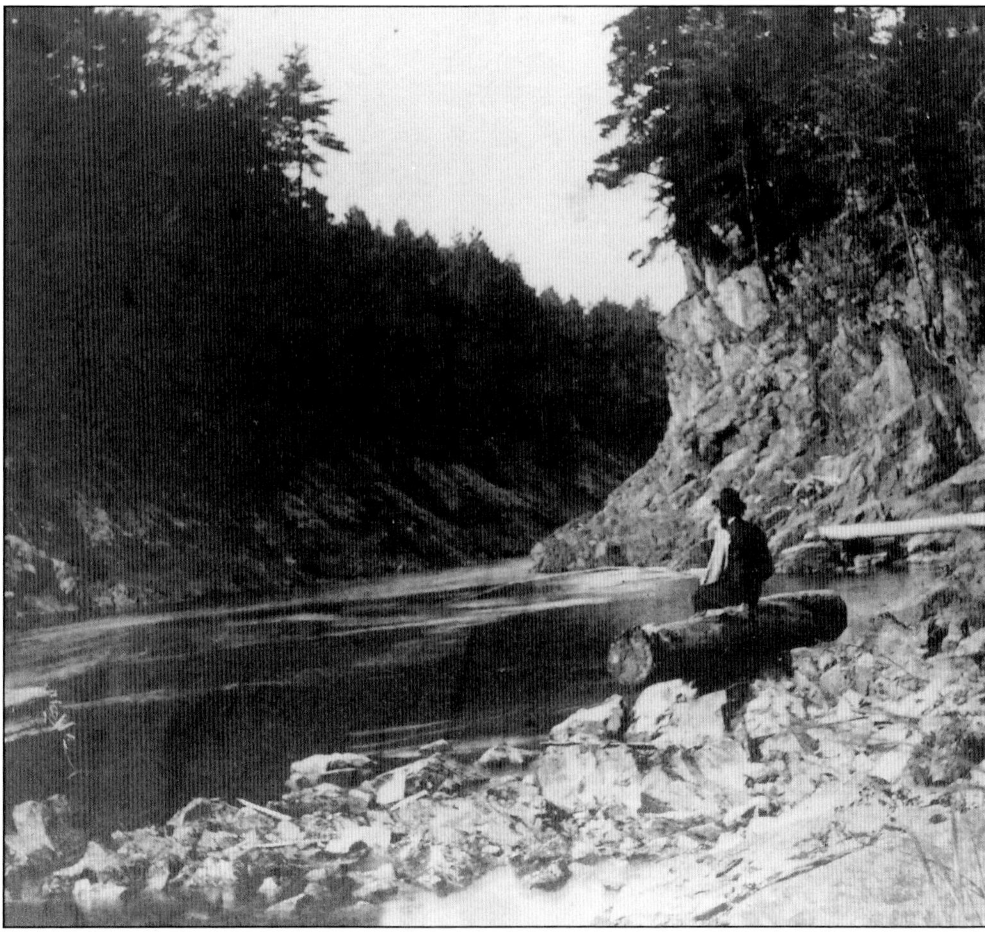

An unknown man sits on a log on the bank of the Saco River in Hollis, *c.* 1879. There were many sawmills along the river by then; as a result, at times, there were many logs in the river.

Contents

Introduction

Maine cities and towns grew up first along the seacoast and along the rivers. The Saco River water system is farthest south, and the area would have become populated even more rapidly than it did if it were not for the French and Indian Wars.

It was the Saco River's water power for the sawmills and gristmills that brought settlers to the three towns of Buxton, Hollis, and Limington. Hollis and Buxton grew across from each other on the Saco. Unlike the towns (now cities) of Lewiston and Auburn, separated by the Androscoggin River, Hollis and Buxton have always seemed to get along with each other. Limington lies north of these two communities and also has the Little Ossipee River running into the Saco River within its town limits.

There were mills; there were farms; there were stores—and the population grew for a time. But it was a tough living and large families brought too many people to support. From the 1849 Gold Rush until at least the turn of the century, people left these three towns for other parts of the United States. That outflow gradually slowed. By the 1960s and perhaps even earlier, the tide turned. Buxton first, then Hollis, and now Limington have become bedroom towns for Portland and perhaps Portsmouth, New Hampshire. Buxton is now believed to have more than 10,000 people, more than it ever did in the good old days. And Limington, with fifty new homes built last year, is considering a no-growth policy. The function of the three communities has changed. However, many of the families who have been there for generations still remain in spite of all the outflow and inflow.

I have found the ethnic makeup of the communities to be fairly homogenous. A core of people have survived here who go back to the Pilgrims and Puritans. Partly as a result, there is a strong sense of history and genealogy here. A look of history still remains about these places, with their many old homes scattered throughout the community. This rustic atmosphere has survived in spite of the change from mill towns with farms to bedroom communities with farms. These towns have also witnessed the river change from a place littered with logs to its present clearness, from a waterway spotted with small dams to one supporting large dam power stations.

The three towns are in the same school district, joined with Standish, which has been covered in another book in the Images of America series. They continue to have the interest in school and church they have always had. And, in spite of their Puritan forebears, they have maintained their interest in leisure time activities and recreation over the past centuries.

One true celebrity has emerged in the 250 years or so of settlement in the area covered by the three towns. This was Kate Douglas Wiggin Riggs, author of those American standard novels *Rebecca of Sunnybrook Farm* and *Mother Carey's Chickens*. Although not born in the area, she grew up in Hollis and then summered in that town for years until her death. Any book covering these communities must include Mrs. Riggs, who did as much for the community as anyone who ever lived there. Perhaps only Stephen and Tabitha King's gifts to Bangor can match her gifts to Hollis. Like King, Wiggin's novels were made into movies, and like King, her love for Maine was great.

From the three communities' only celebrity, we move in this book to one of its leading families, the Bradburys of Buxton and Hollis. They were everywhere. In J.M. Marshall's 1874 book *Buxton Centennial, 1772–1872*, about sixty-five Bradburys are listed in the index. There is still a large number in the area. Elizabeth Ring, eminent Maine historian, wrote a volume called the *McArthurs of Limington*. A similar work could easily be done about the Bradburys. Because Elizabeth's book is fairly recent, I've left out the McArthurs deliberately here. I hope there's no objection to that omission.

Finally, this book ends with a chapter on the doers and shakers in the area. As I have done in other books, I've included some well-known people in the area and some who were not so well-known. I have a firm belief that everyone contributes something, at least some of it good and benefiting others. Who knows the relatives that may feel good when these lesser-known persons appear?

Those in Buxton, Hollis, and Limington who have survived through the out-migrations and the in-migrations are good, solid people, the kind that Maine can be proud of. They have often gone out of their way to help in the compilation of this book.

As with the other seven books I've done in the Images of America series, I want to dedicate this small volume to the children and younger people of the three communities. It will give them a quick look at some pieces of the area's history. I hope, because of the photos included in it, it will take those folks away from their television sets for an hour or so. This is not a definitive history by any means, but I hope it will open doors to more interest in the area's history among its young people.

There should be much to interest them. Excellent family values, hard work conquering a tough environment, and basic straightforwardness are often found over the years in the three towns. I just hope that some of these attributes come through in the photos and the faces of these people. There's a lot of character here.

Frank H. Sleeper

One

The River Giveth

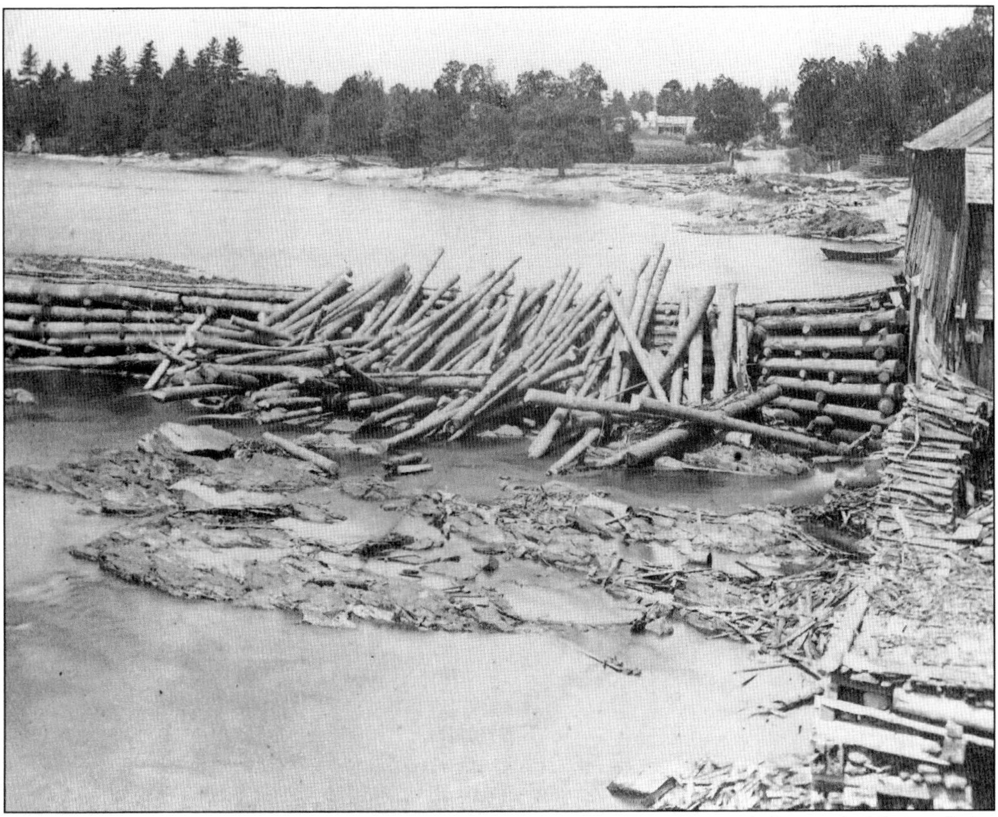

Scene on the Saco River at Bar Mills between Buxton and Hollis with logs piled behind the dam, 1870s. The logs are no longer in the river due to regulations. They went into the sawmills of the area.

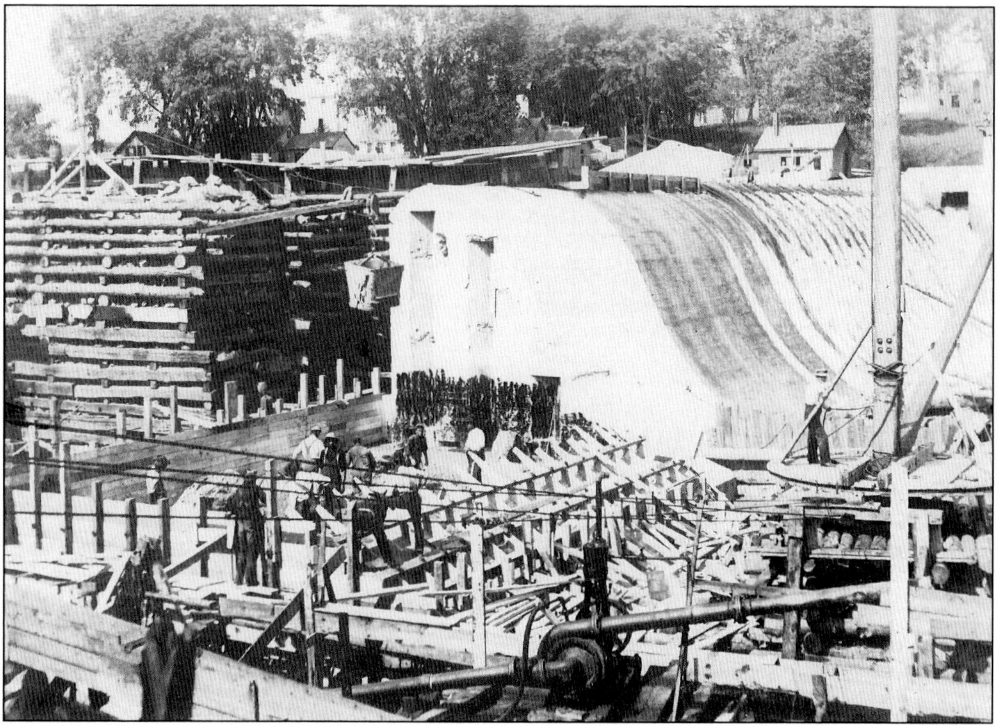

The dam being built in West Buxton, *c.* 1906. The dam was at the sites of falls, from which the power to run the mills was taken. The rivers were the roadways that brought many of the logs to the mills.

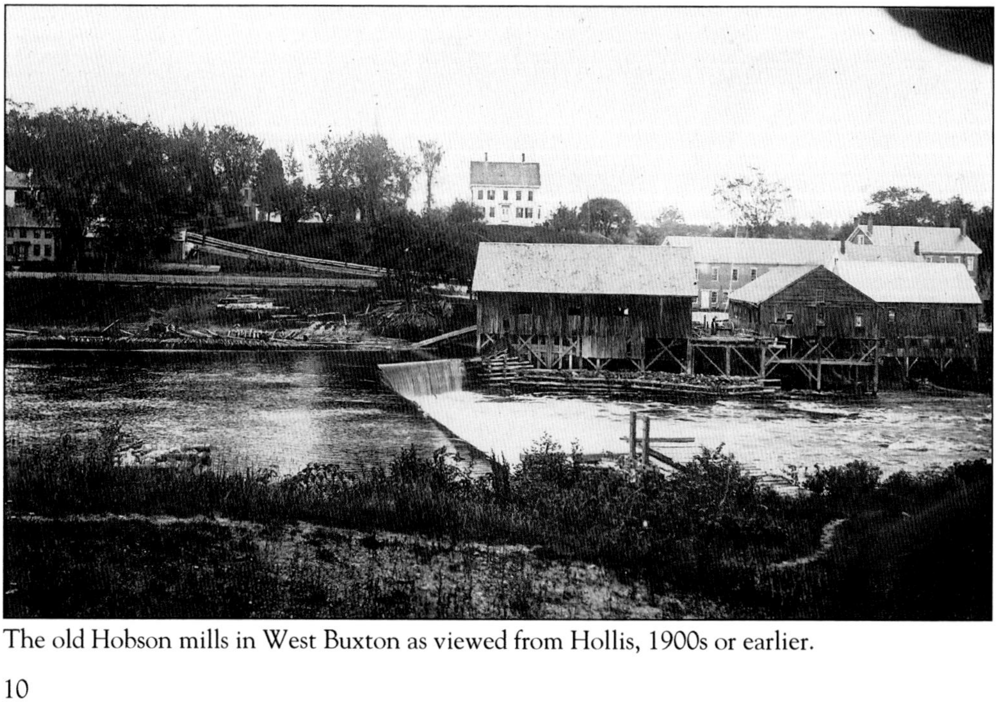

The old Hobson mills in West Buxton as viewed from Hollis, 1900s or earlier.

Winfield Scott McCorrison at the West Buxton dam. Winfield lived in Buxton, not far from the dam.

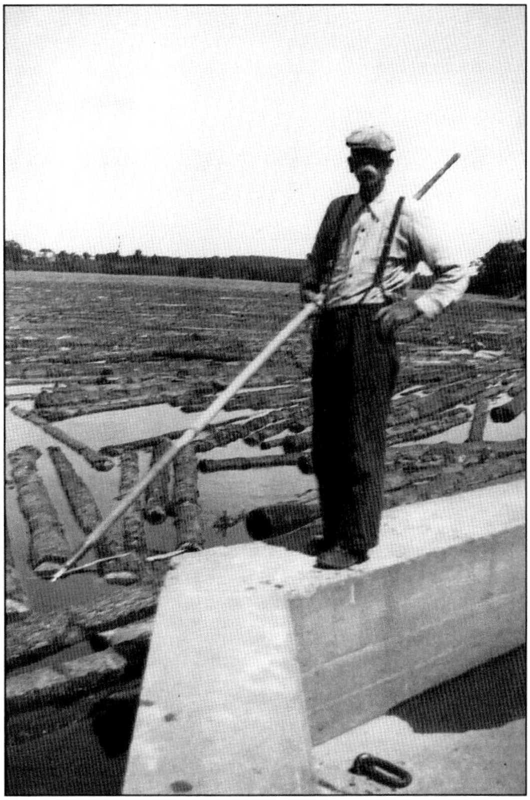

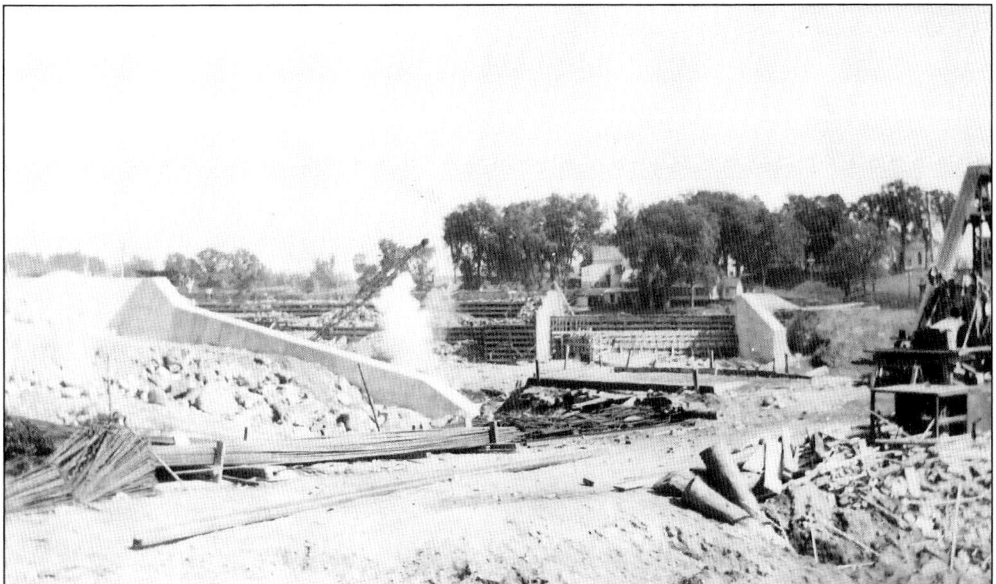

A cloud of dust where dynamite was being discharged in the bed of the Saco River at West Buxton. The date is September 16, 1937. This demolition was preparation for the westerly half of the present West Buxton dam, located in the area where land and buildings were lost during the March 1936 flood. The river bed is solid granite and mica schist.

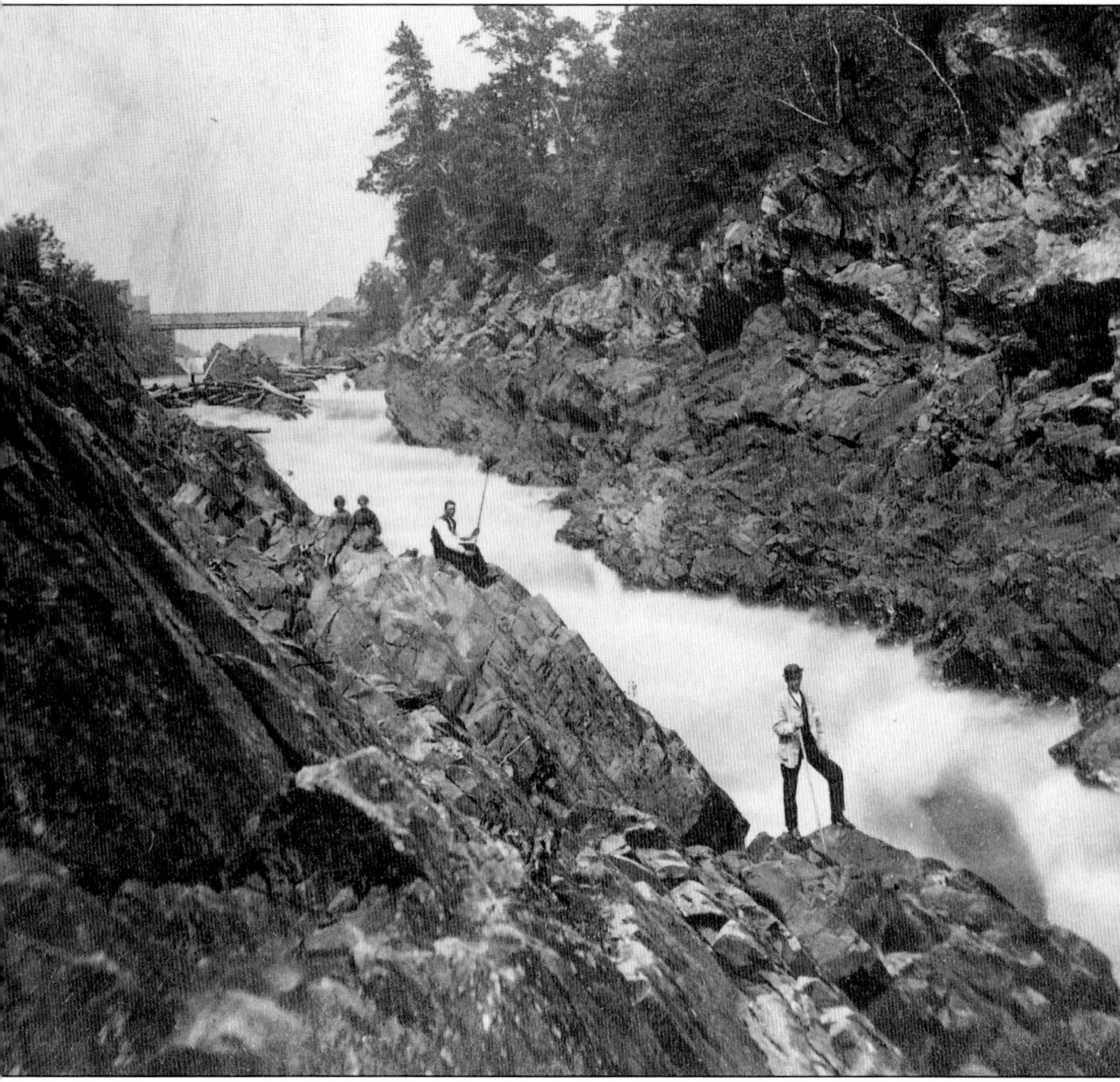

Men fishing in the gorge of the Saco River at Hollis and Buxton in this 1868 photo. Dams eventually flooded the scenic gorge. The same scenario played out on other Maine rivers as electrical power became more important,and hydro power from the rivers became more valuable.

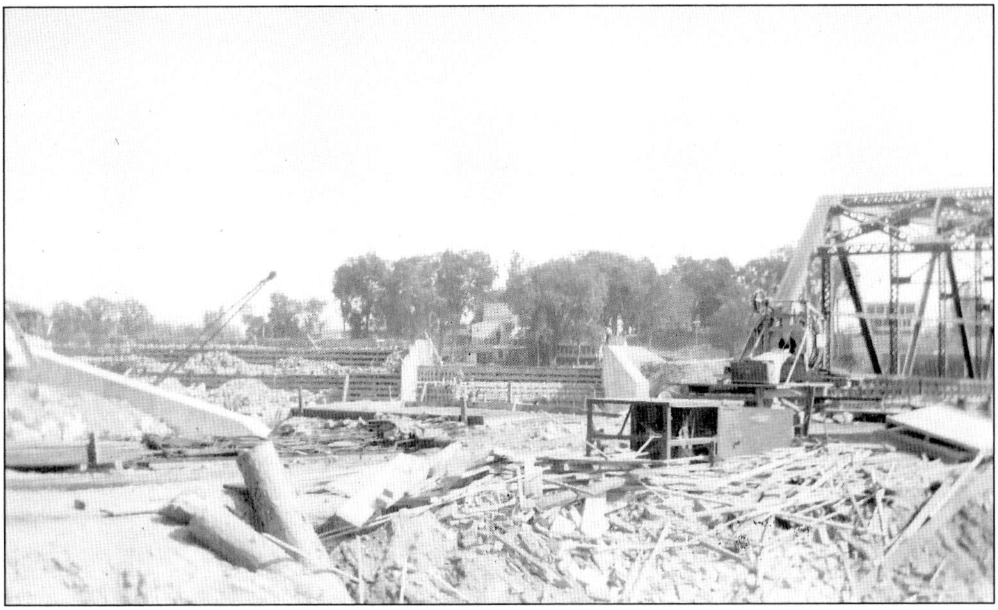

Two important pieces of construction underway at the West Buxton dam on the Saco River on September 16, 1937 (see p. 11). The dam was being built by what was then the Cumberland Power and Light Company, and the bridge, which was taken out by the flood, was being constructed by the Works Progress Administration (WPA).

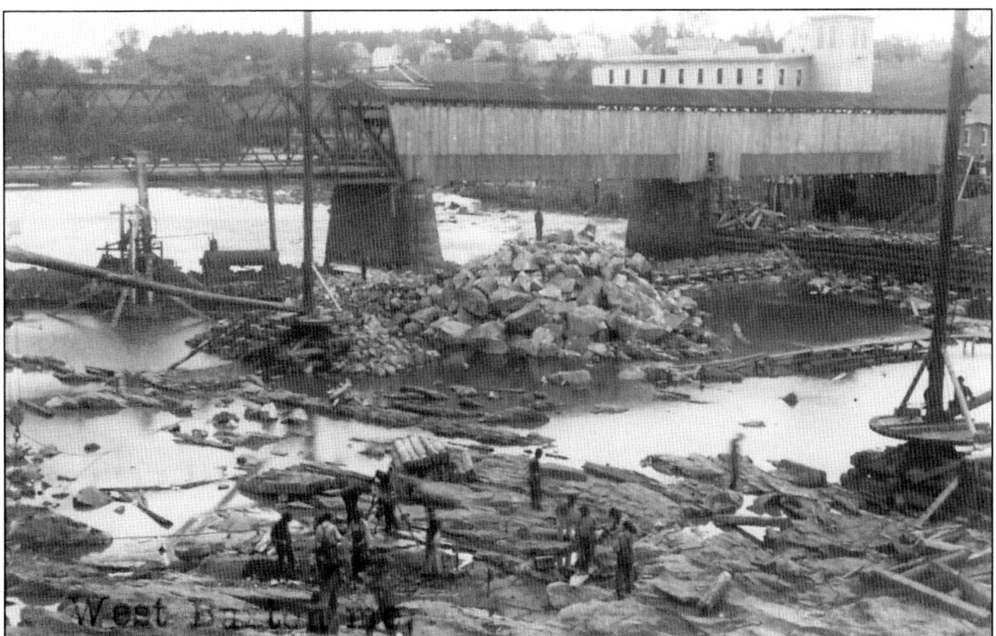

The construction of the new dam and power house on the Saco River, *c.* 1906. The photograph was taken in Buxton looking toward Hollis at West Buxton.

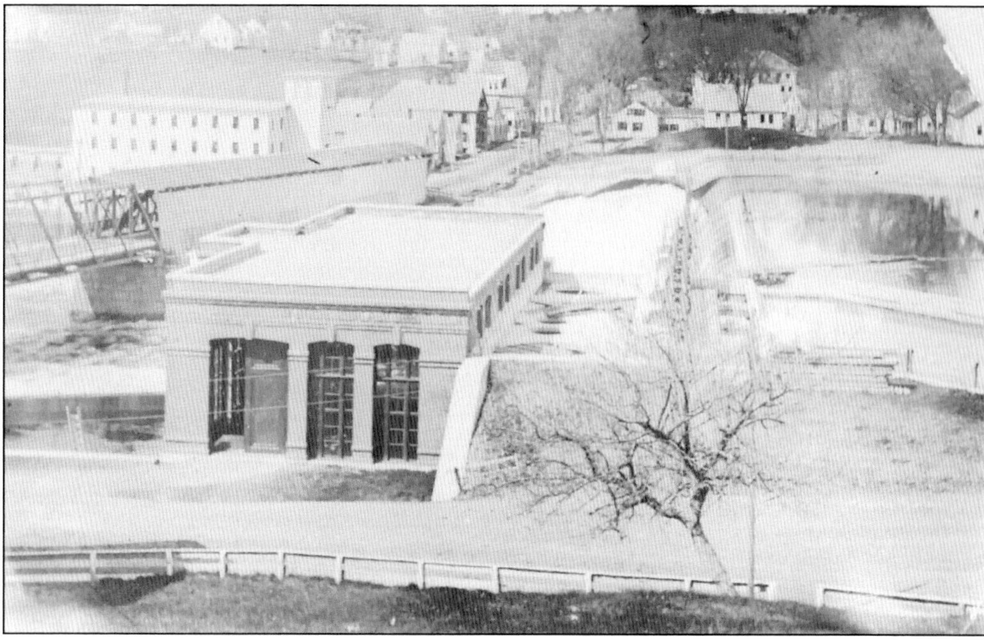

The power house built in 1906 on the Saco River at West Buxton. This photograph, like the preceeding one, was taken in Buxton looking toward Hollis at West Buxton.

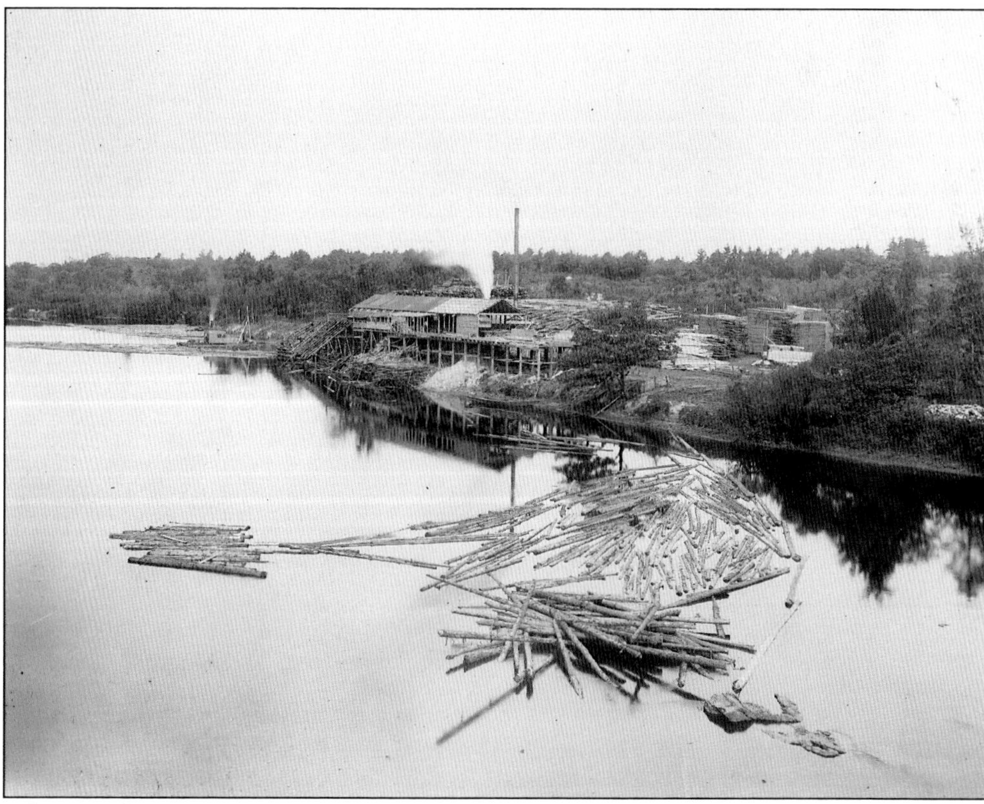

What was then a new sawmill at Bar Mills in the 1900s or 1910s.

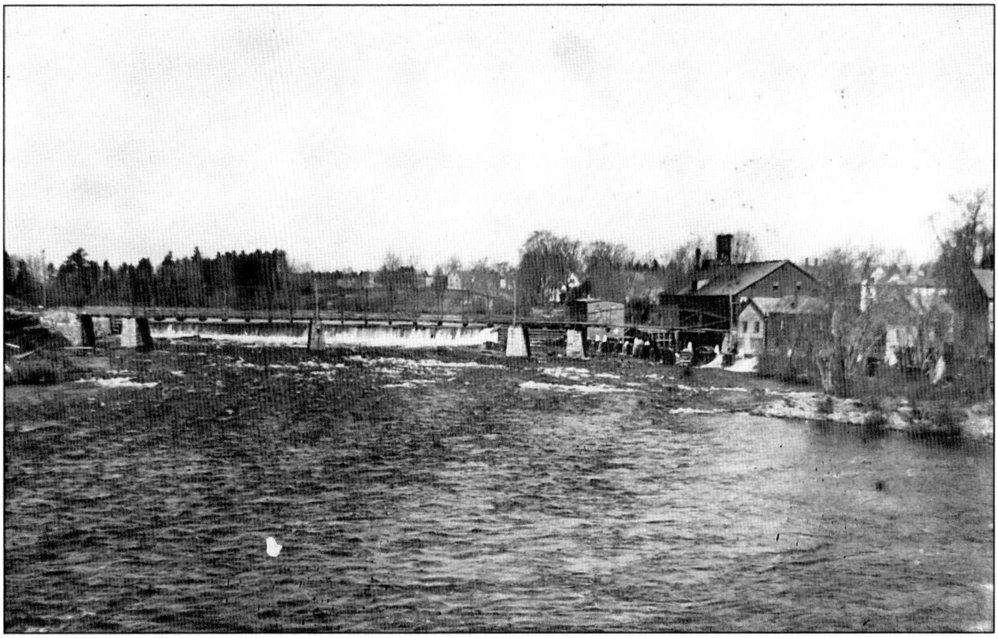

The dam at Bar Mills on the Saco River in the 1920s. Bar Mills is part of both Hollis and Buxton.

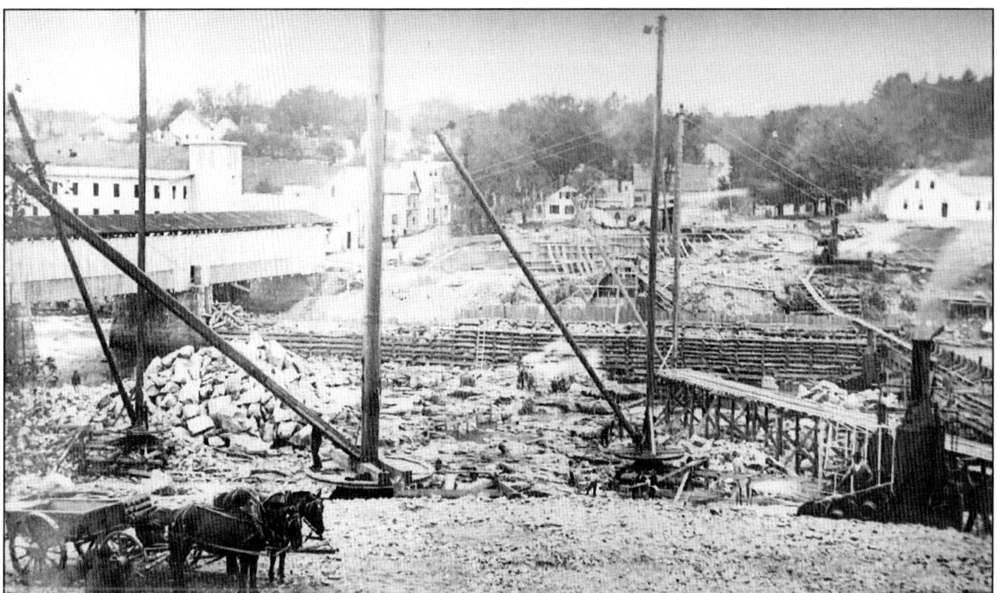

Demolishing the mills at West Buxton and building the power station, early 1900s. Those were Guy Smith's horses.

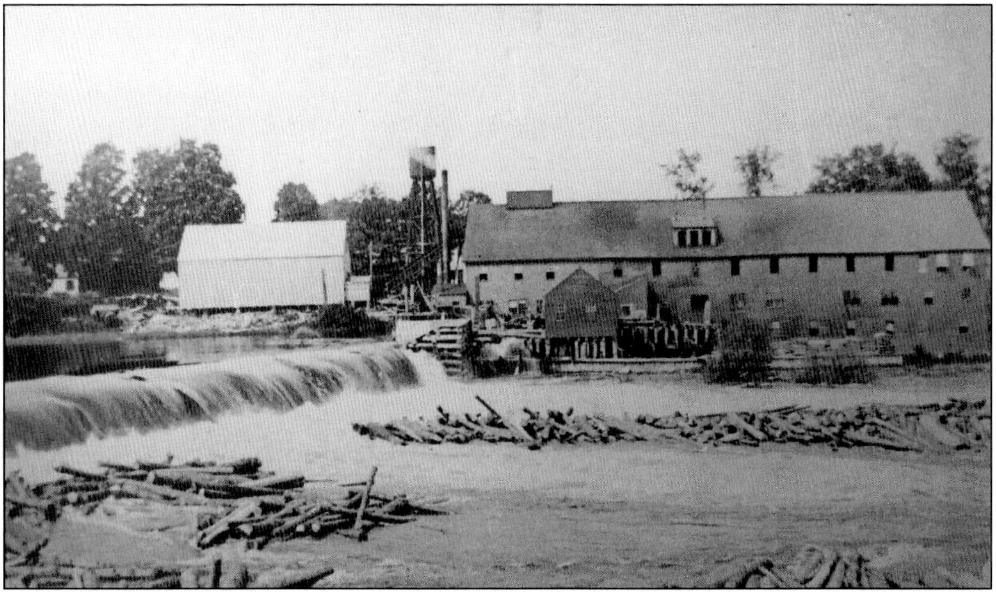

The furniture factory at Bar Mills, 1910s. This was later to become the Rogers Fiber Company plant.

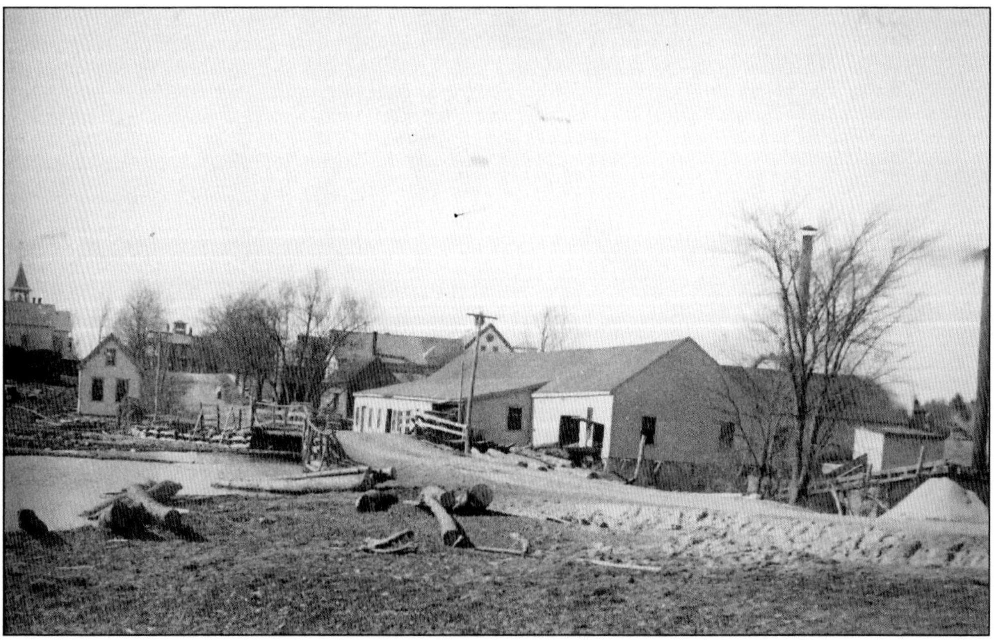

An early 1900s photograph showing Clark's Mills on Cooks Brook. This view was taken in Dayton looking toward Hollis. A small office building is on the left side of the road. The big door is the entrance to the sawmill, and the windowed part of the structure further on was the box shop. This was a steam powered mill, using slab and sawdust as fuel.

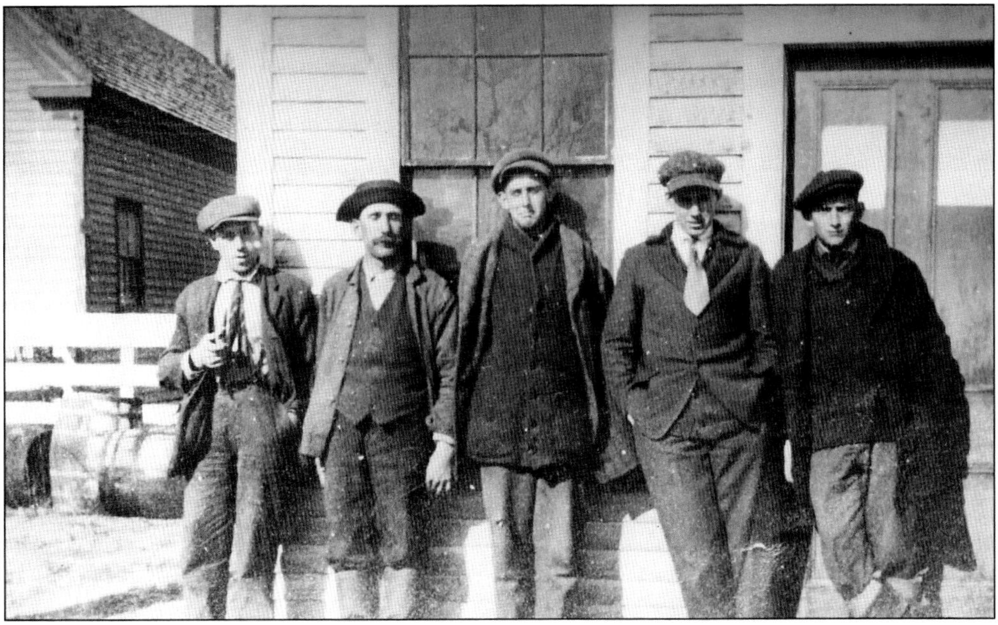

Clark's Mills again with Freeman Dennett in the center and Joe Dennett at the far right. Clark's Mills, located on Route 35 in Hollis, was at a point on Cooks Brook where there were falls.

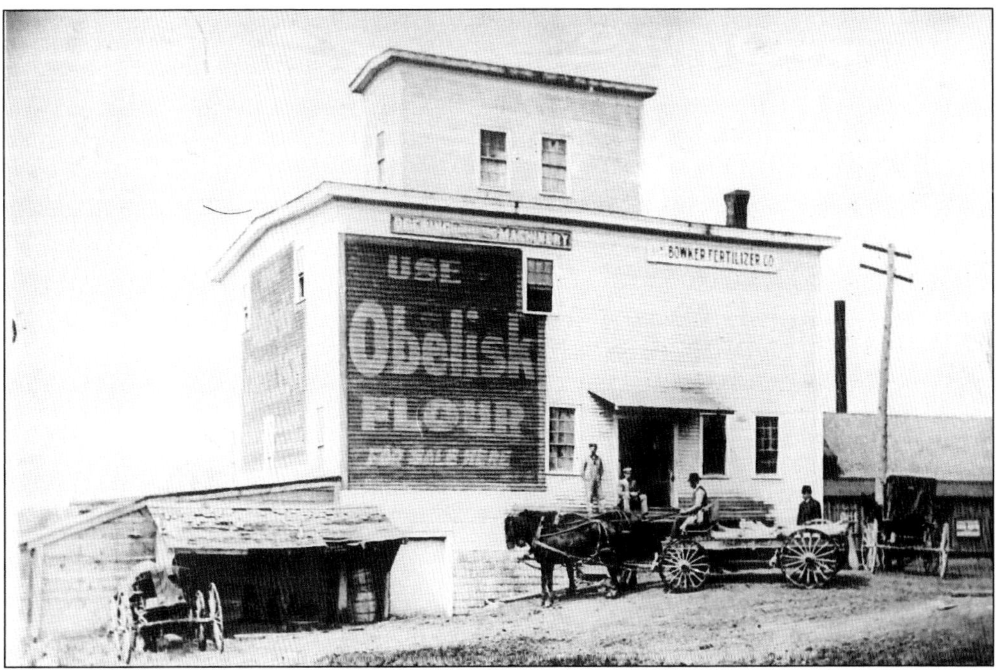

The grist mill at Hollis Center, operated by the Moulton brothers. In the background is the corn shop, and the railroad track was between the two. Later, there was an addition to the mill, and it became the Farmers' Union, 1910s.

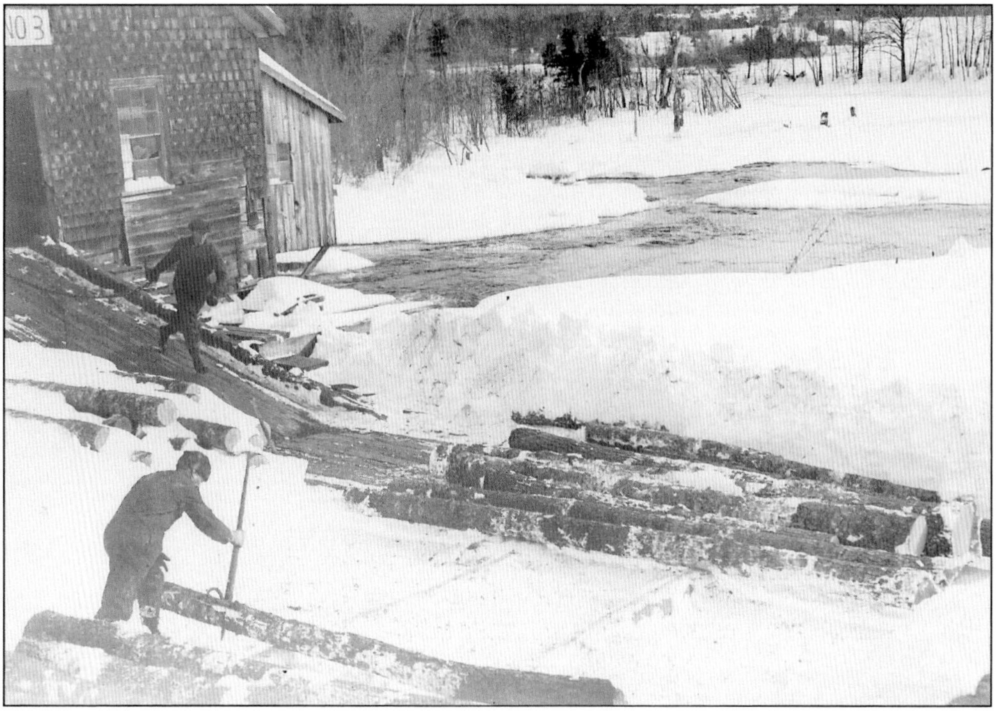

Wellington Hubbard front left with his peavey on a log while Harry Chick is running at mid-left. That Number 3 at the left on the Hubbard Mill on the Little Ossipee River in Limington was left over from a movie made there in the 1920s. The movie was a thriller with many Portland people in it.

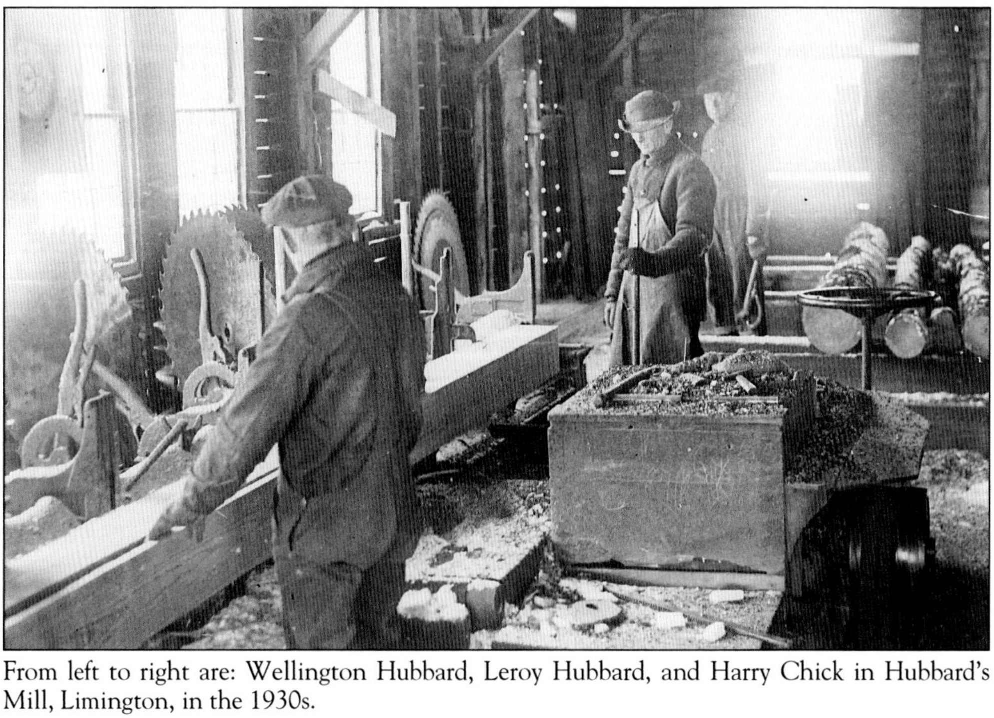

From left to right are: Wellington Hubbard, Leroy Hubbard, and Harry Chick in Hubbard's Mill, Limington, in the 1930s.

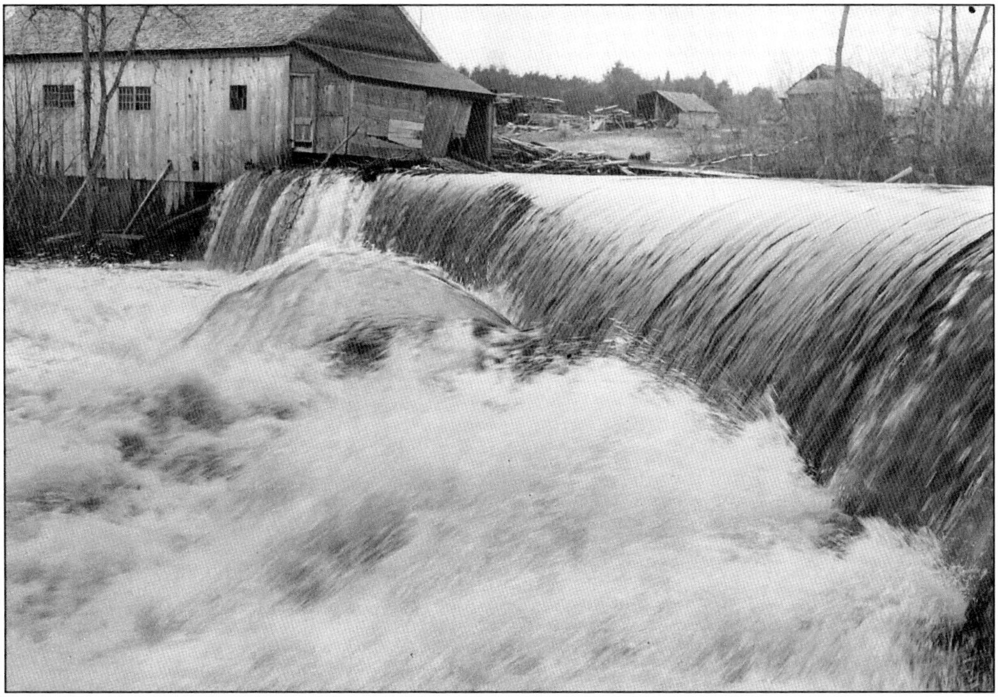

The dam between Chase's Mill and Hubbard's Mill on the Little Ossipee River, Limington, in the spring in the 1920s or 1930s. Chase's Mill is at the left rear.

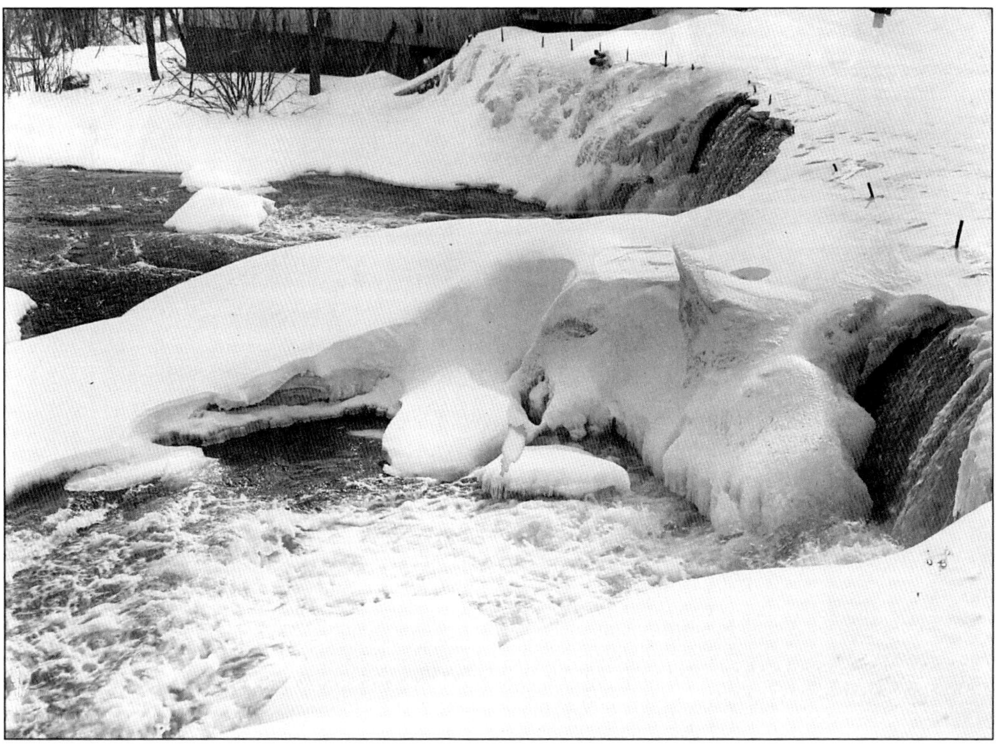

The same dam in the winter. It's a look the author hasn't often seen.

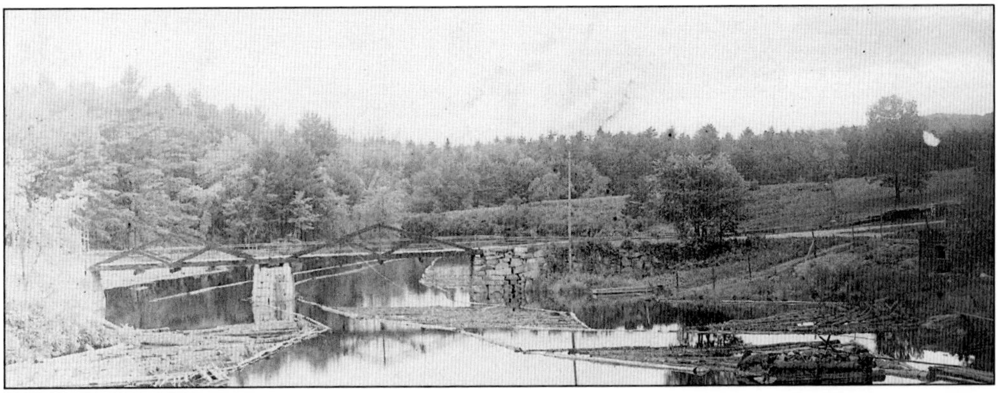

An all-wooden bridge over the Little Ossipee River in East Limington in the 1910s or 1920s. The structure was later replaced by a metal bridge in 1935.

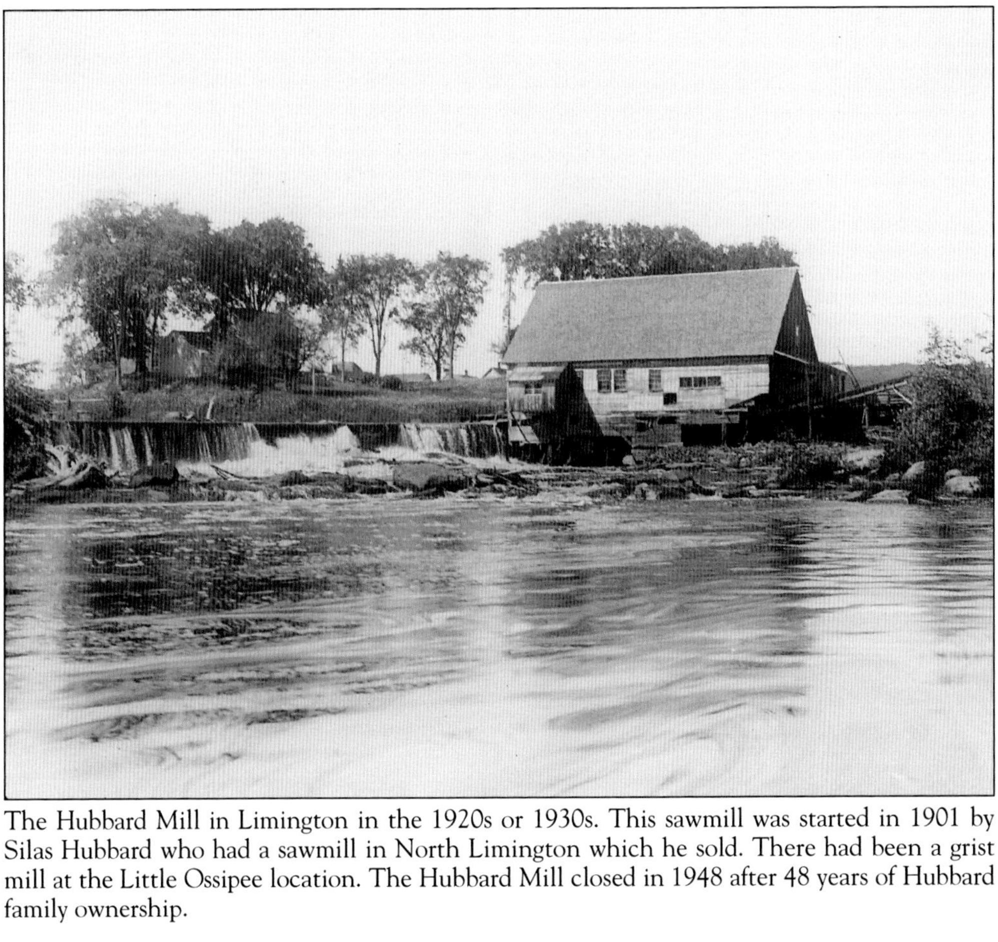

The Hubbard Mill in Limington in the 1920s or 1930s. This sawmill was started in 1901 by Silas Hubbard who had a sawmill in North Limington which he sold. There had been a grist mill at the Little Ossipee location. The Hubbard Mill closed in 1948 after 48 years of Hubbard family ownership.

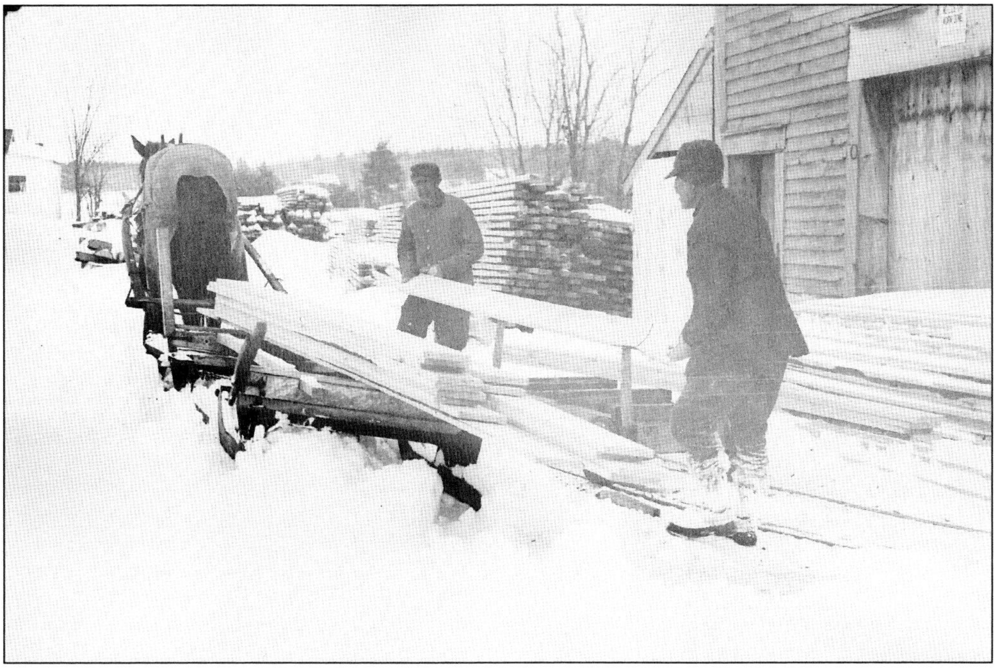

Leonard Buzzell, left, and Will Nason loading boards at the Hubbard Mill, around 1910 or 1912.

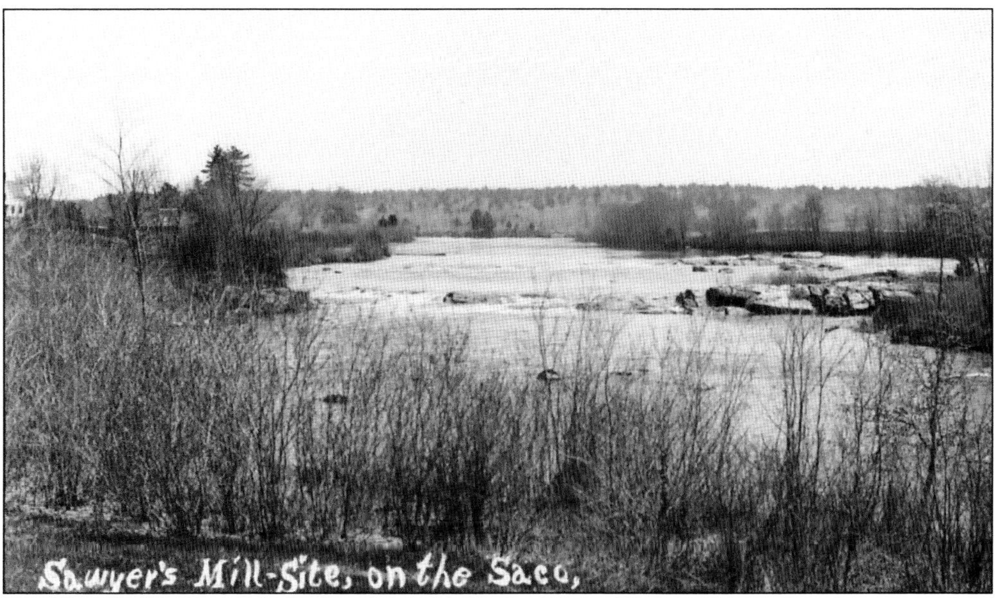

Sawyer's Mill site on the Saco River in East Limington around the 1910s.

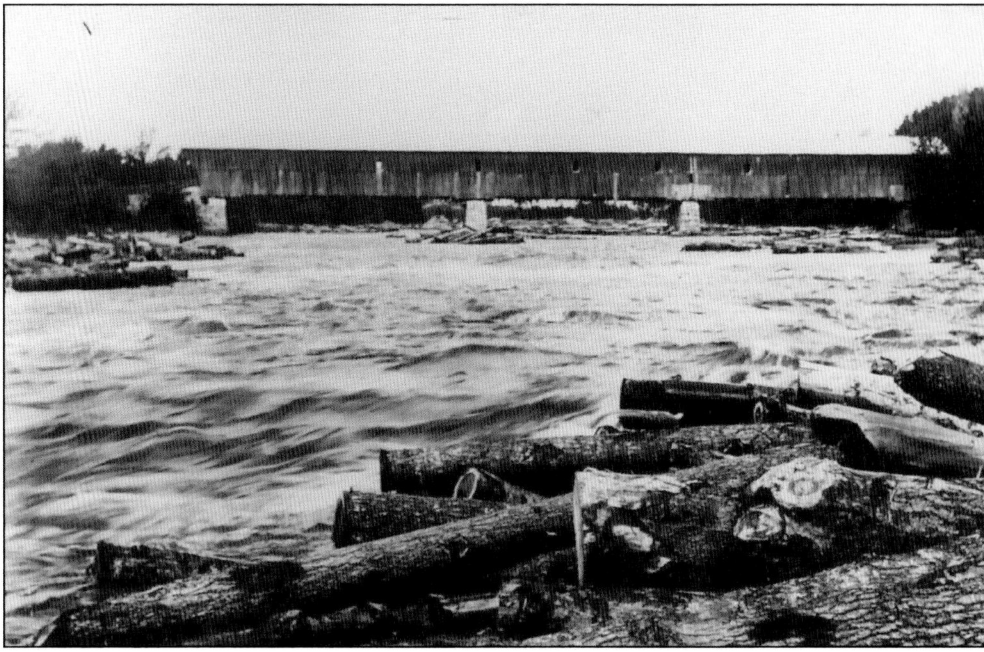

The East Limington covered bridge, 1910s. The bridge was erected in 1896 and taken out in 1928.

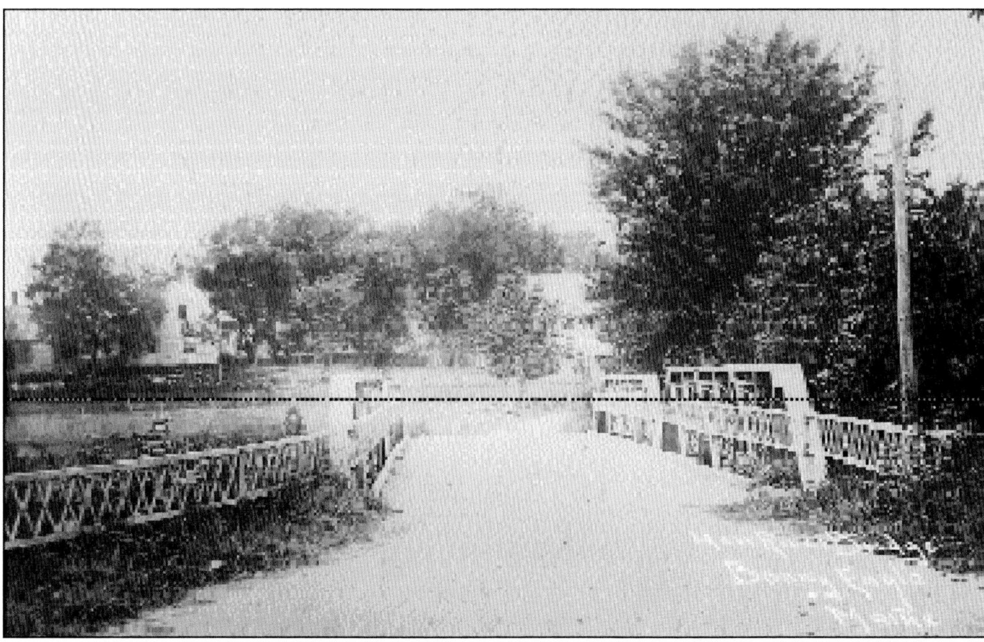

New river bridge over the Saco River in the early 1900s.

Two

The River Taketh Away

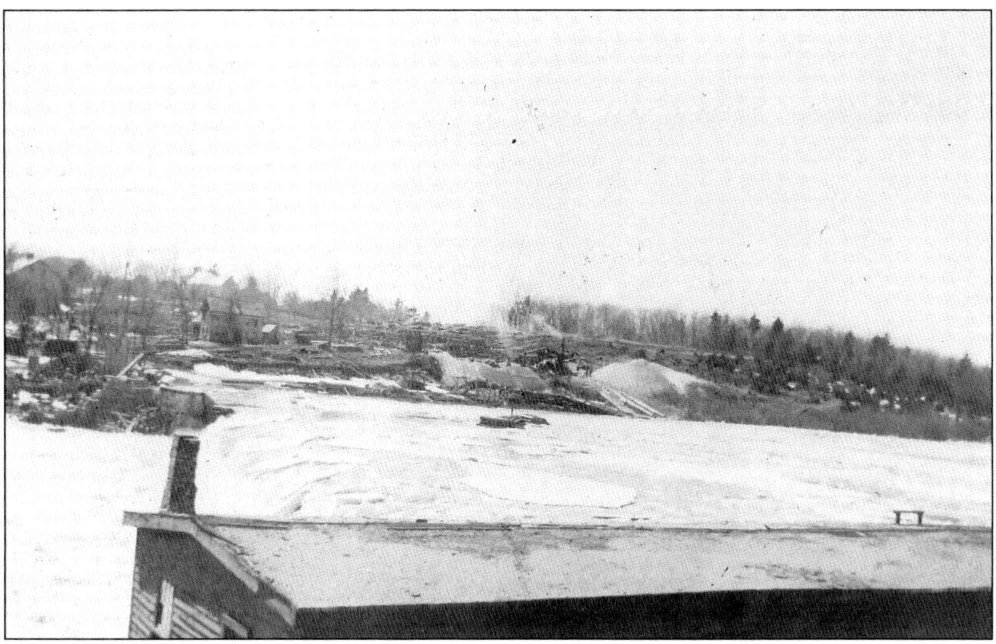

Saco River at Bar Mills during an early spring freshet in the early 1900s.

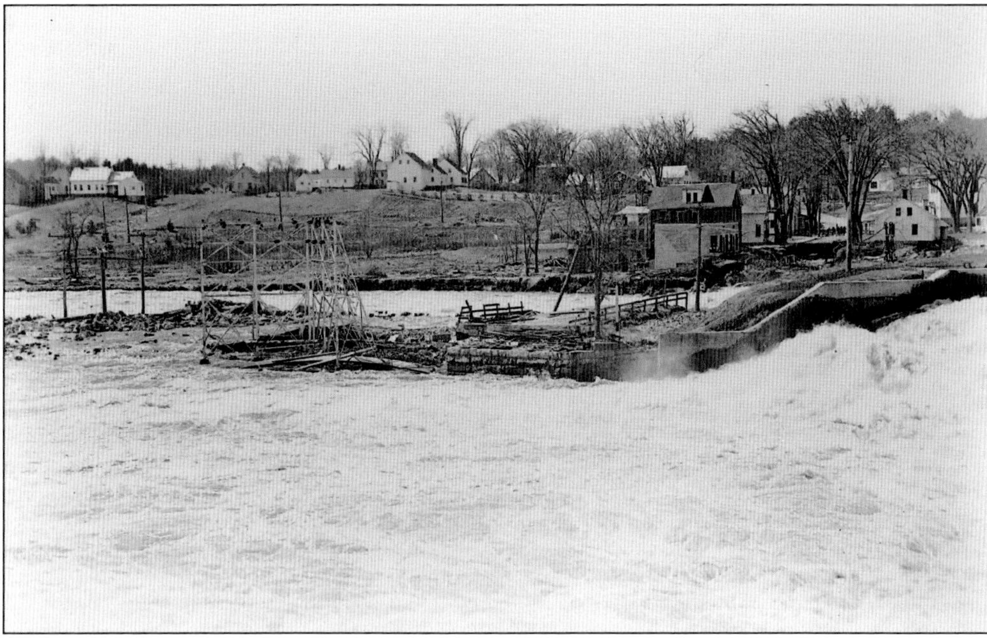

High water on the Saco River during the March 1936 flood. This photograph was taken in Buxton, looking toward Hollis at West Buxton. Note that the covered bridge is gone and the river has broken through beyond the road and transmission towers.

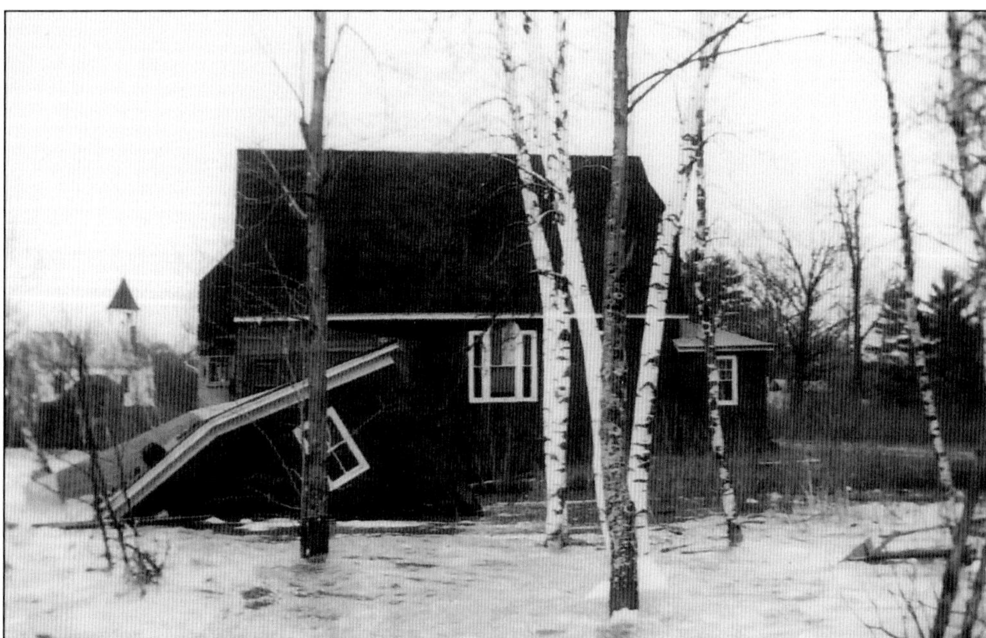

Part of the Saco River Grange Hall on the Salmon Falls Road at Bar Mills is carried away in the flood of March 1936.

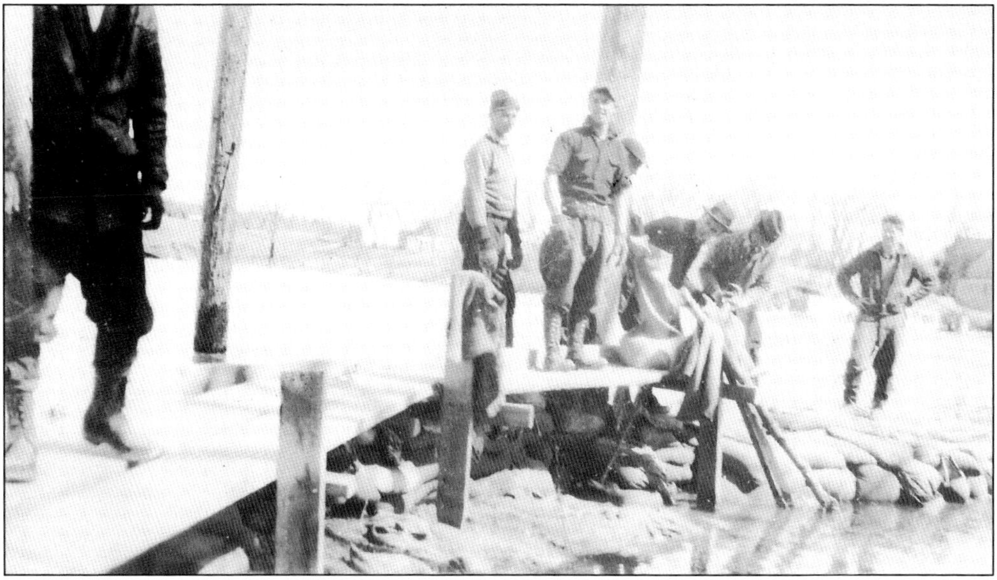

Men on a sand bag coffer, probably in Hollis, about noon on March 23, 1936.

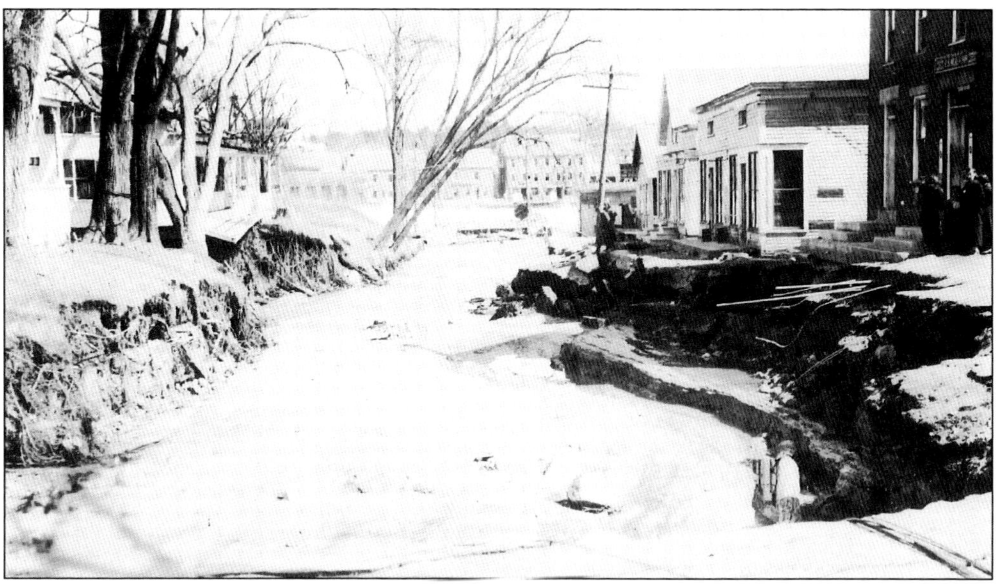

Looking east along High Street in Hollis towards West Buxton with the York Mutual Insurance building and the Masonic Hall in the distance at the upper center of the photo. This was again about noon on March 23, 1936.

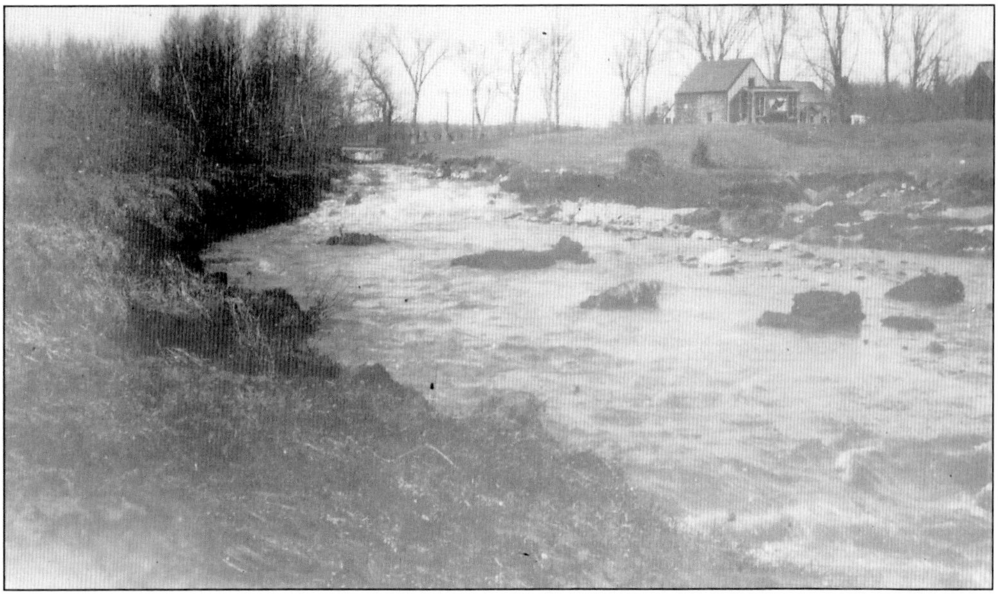

Water from a dike with Mr. Hobson and Dudley Field at noon on March 23, 1936.

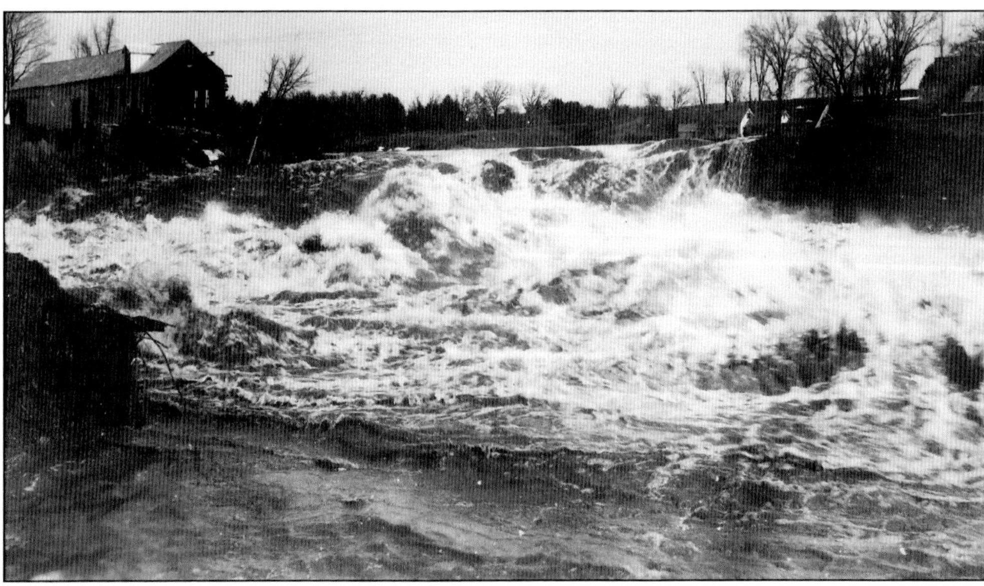

A break at the end of the wing wall in the dam March 24, 1936. This is the area where land and buildings were washed out and where the westerly portion of the West Buxton dam, with the gates, is now located.

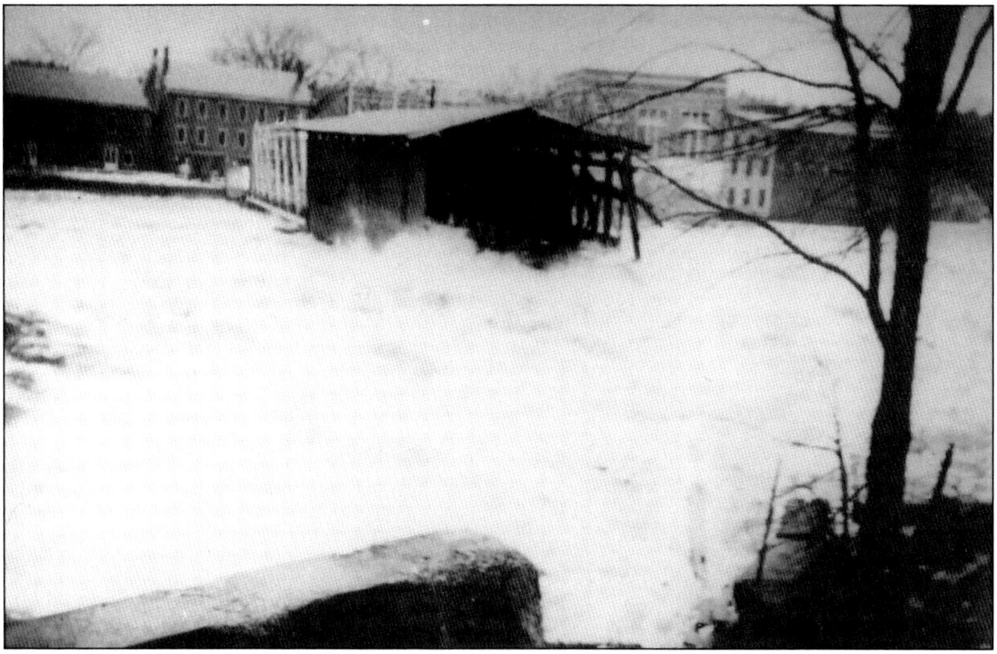

One span of the West Buxton-Hollis covered bridge was gone and the other was soon to go in the flood of March 1936.

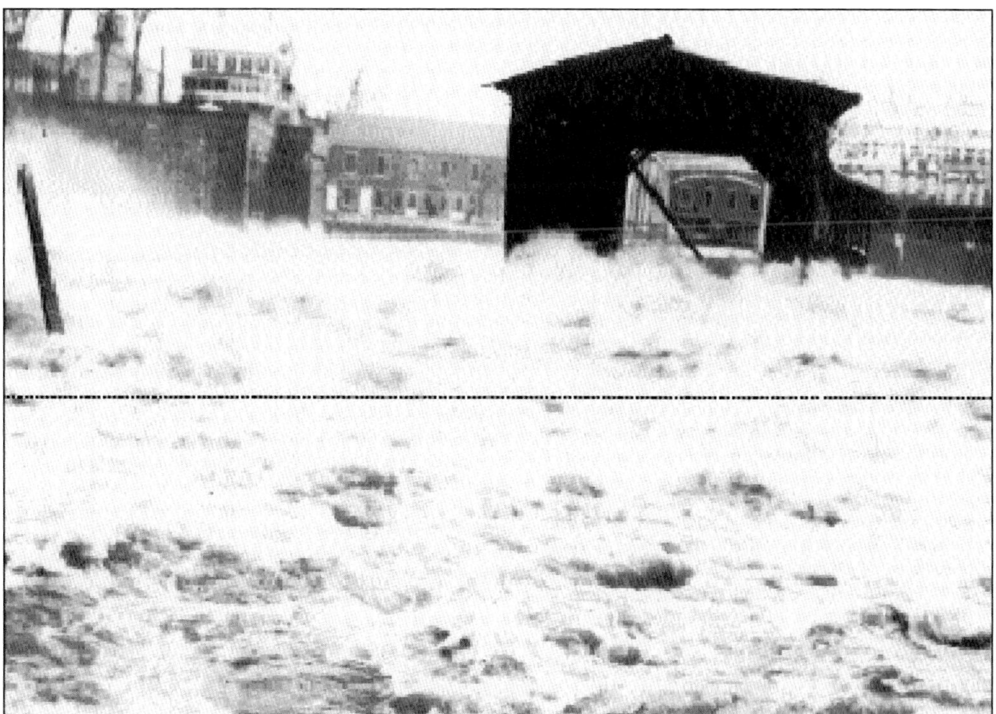

Looking from Hollis to West Buxton as the covered bridge goes out in the March 1936 flood. Note the store that can be seen through the bridge.

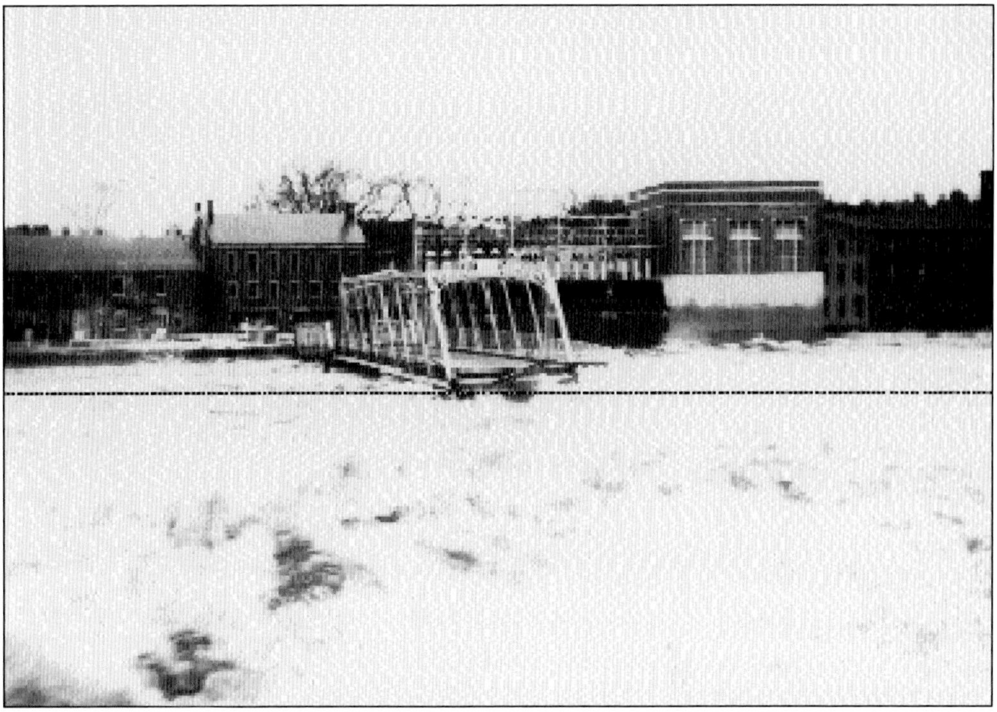

The metal section of the bridge between West Buxton and Hollis which remained for a short time after the two sections of covered wooden bridge were swept away between March 23–24, 1936. The metal part eventually was also pulled into the raging Saco River.

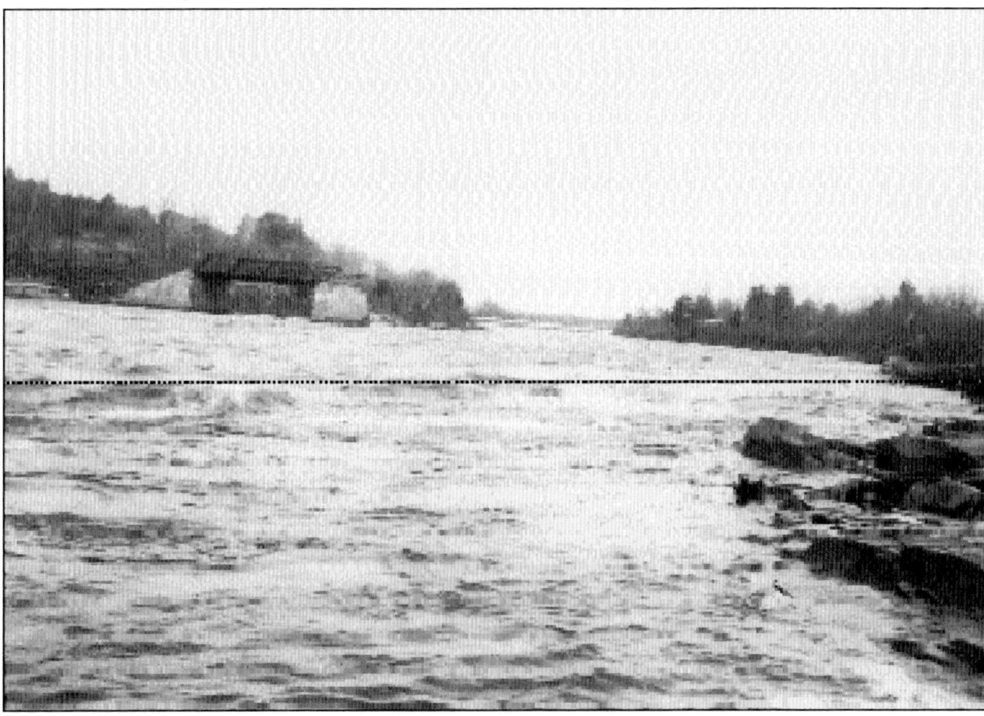

The railroad bridge at Bar Mills, more than half swept away by the March 1936 flood.

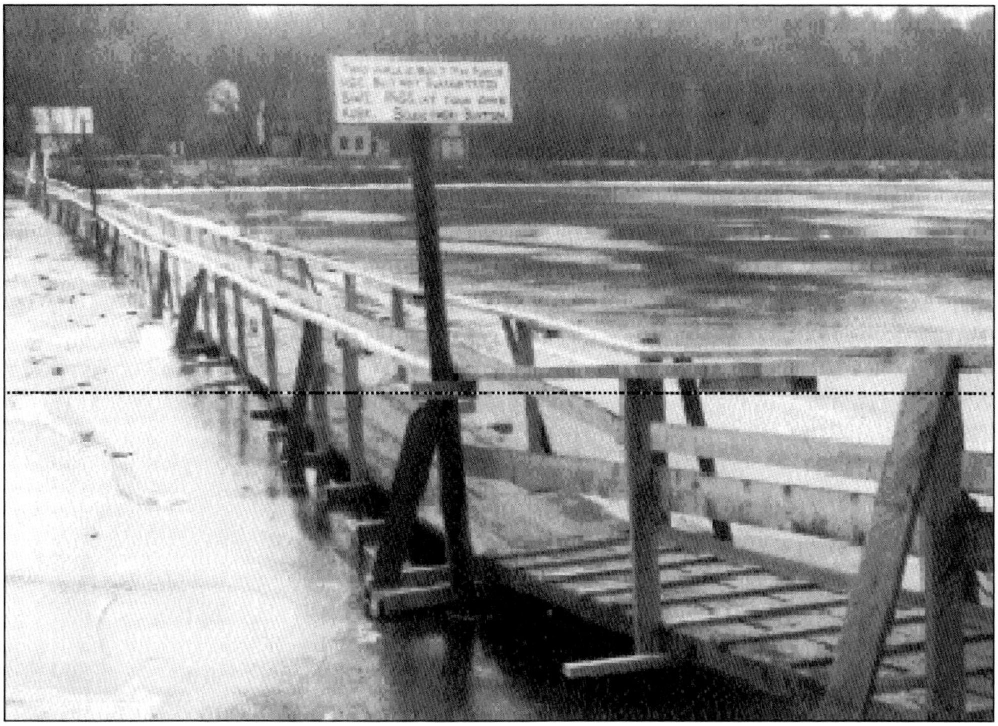

A foot bridge over the Saco River between Hollis and West Buxton. This bridge was probably built soon after the March 1936 flood.

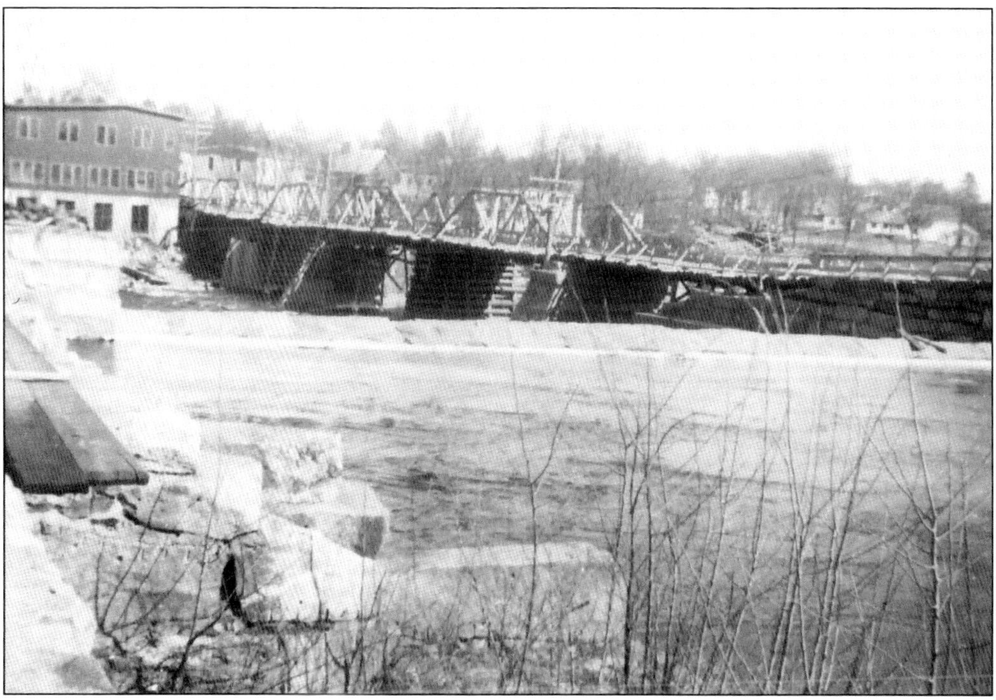

The temporary bridge built in the summer of 1936 at Bar Mills to replace the one swept away by the flood of March 1936.

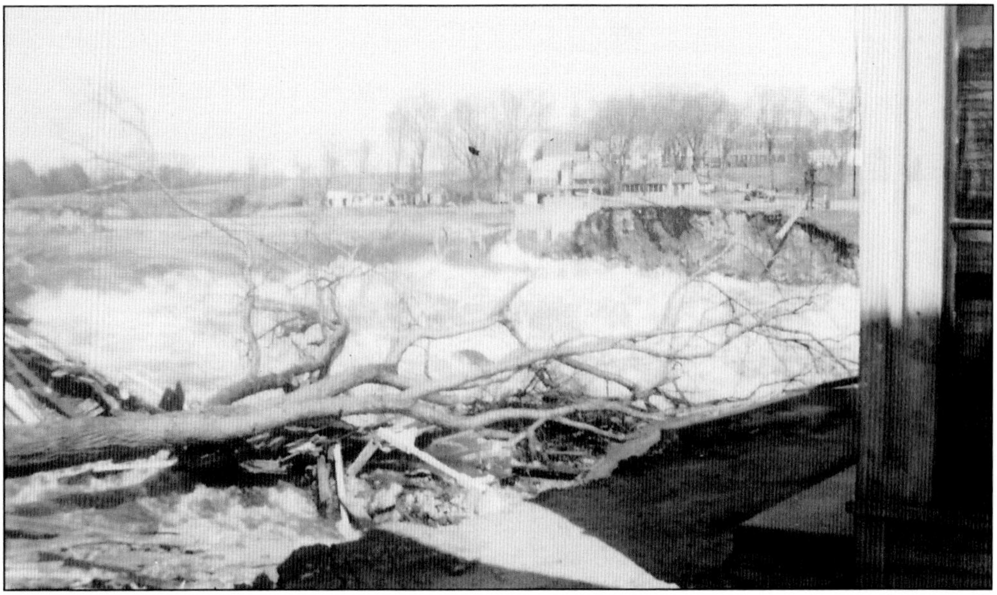

Another view taken in Hollis looking towards Buxton at West Buxton during the March 1936 flood.

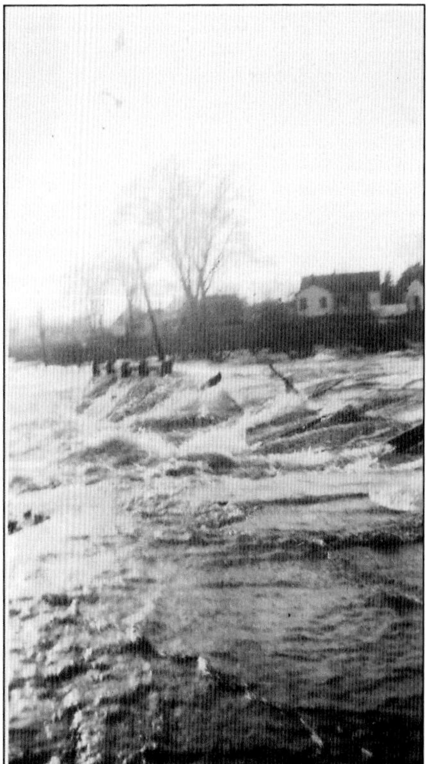

The 1936 flood on the Little Ossipee River in Limington.

Three

The Towns

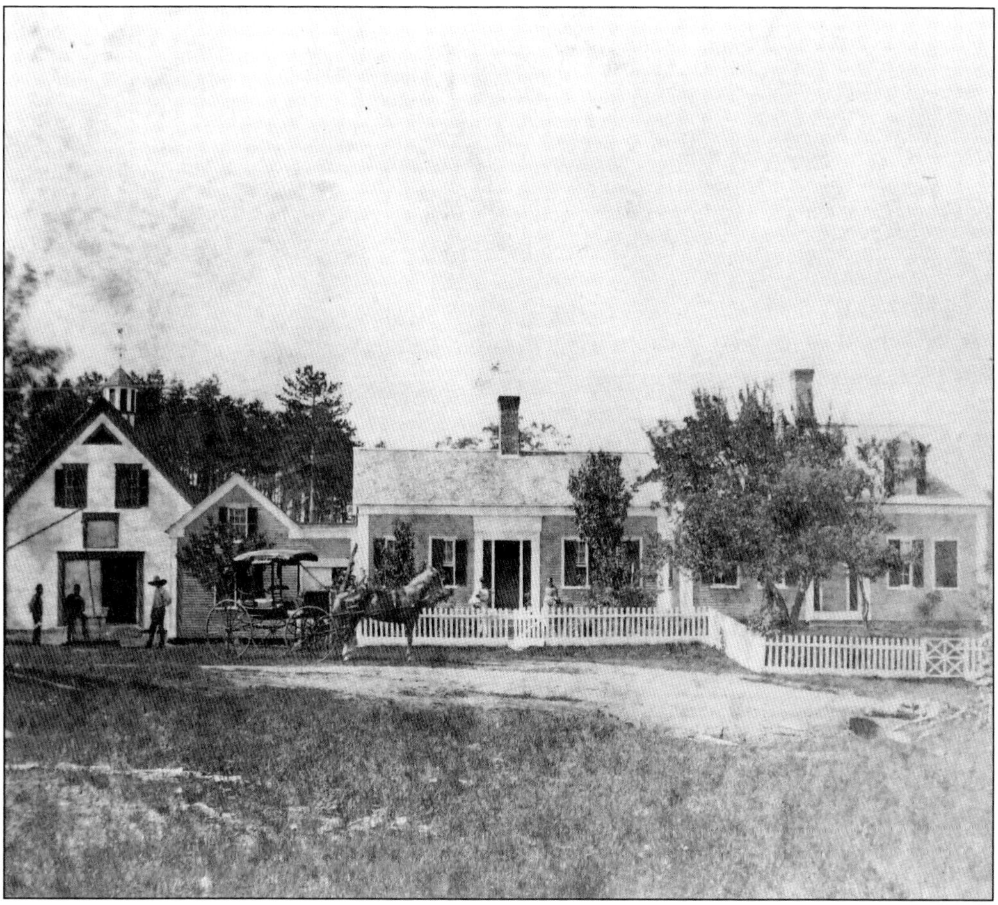

A house, barn, and horse-and-buggy in South Hollis, *c*. 1870s.

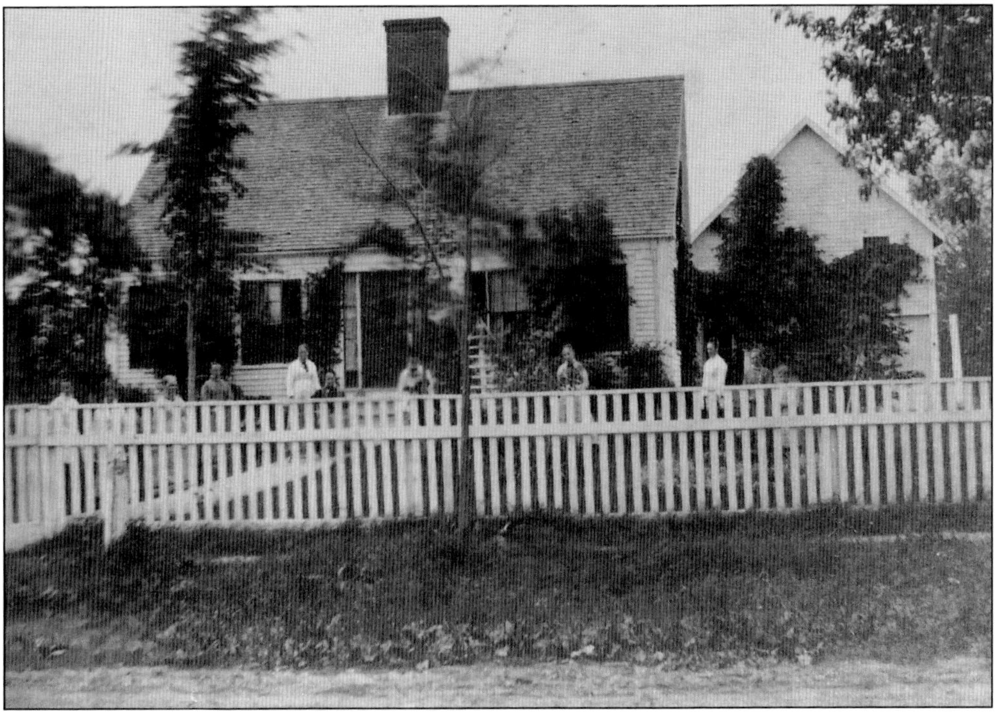

A view of South Hollis on August 22, 1879.

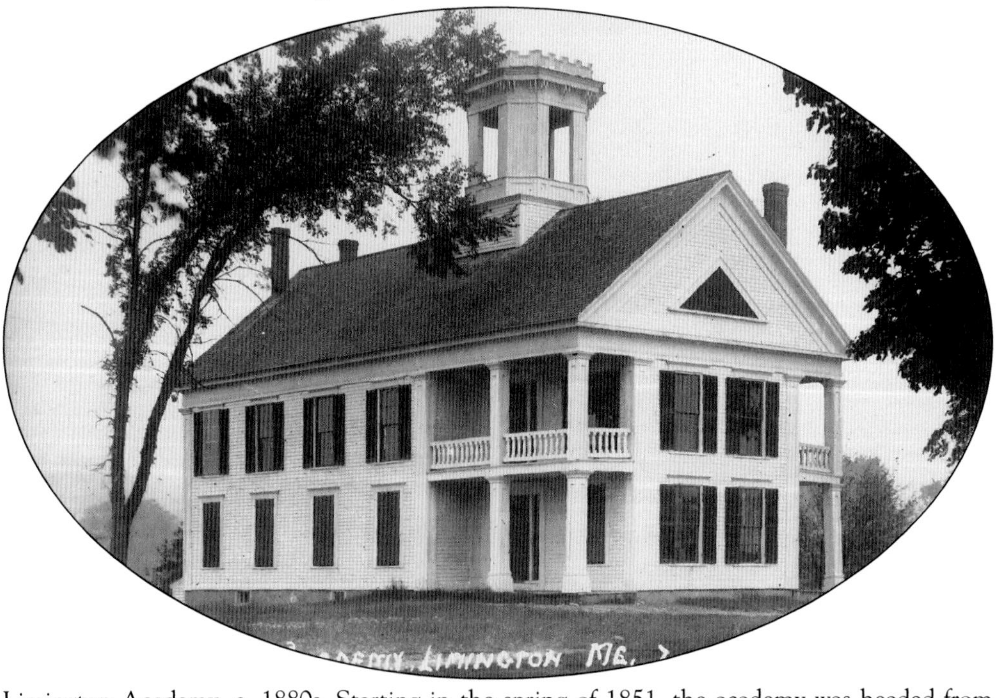

Limington Academy, *c.* 1880s. Starting in the spring of 1851, the academy was headed from 1851 to 1894 by William G. Lord. There were no grades. Pupils attended until it was felt they were ready to go to college, ready to teach, or able to take up some other occupation. The academy no longer exists.

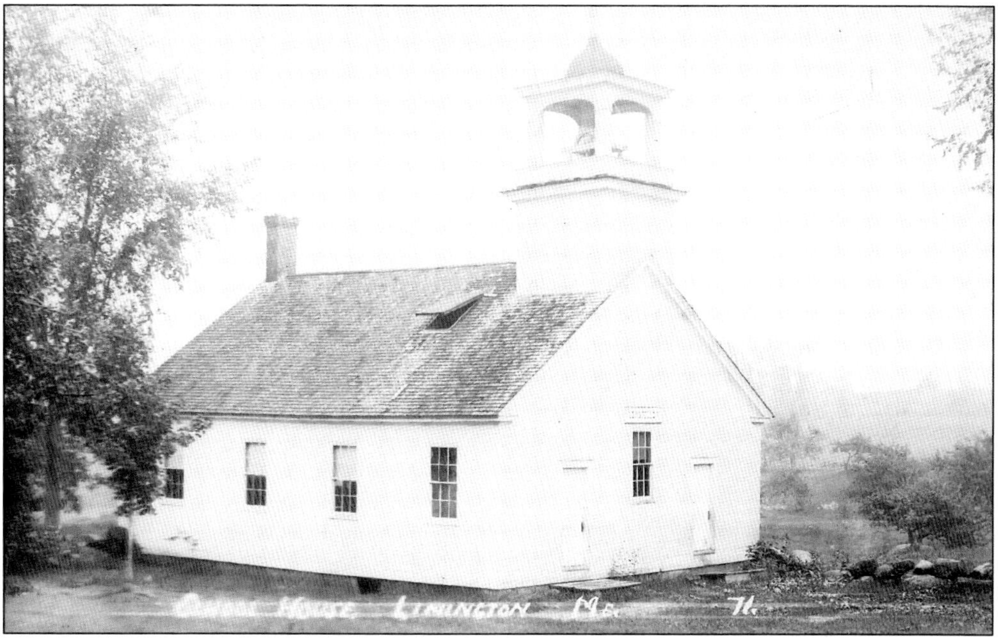

A Limington schoolhouse in the 1900s or 1910s. On the postcard to Miss Allie Shaw, Stevens Avenue, Ridgewood, New Jersey, are these words: "This is where mother fell asleep and was locked in so long ago. When she came to, she pulled the bell and the town turned out to see what was the matter."

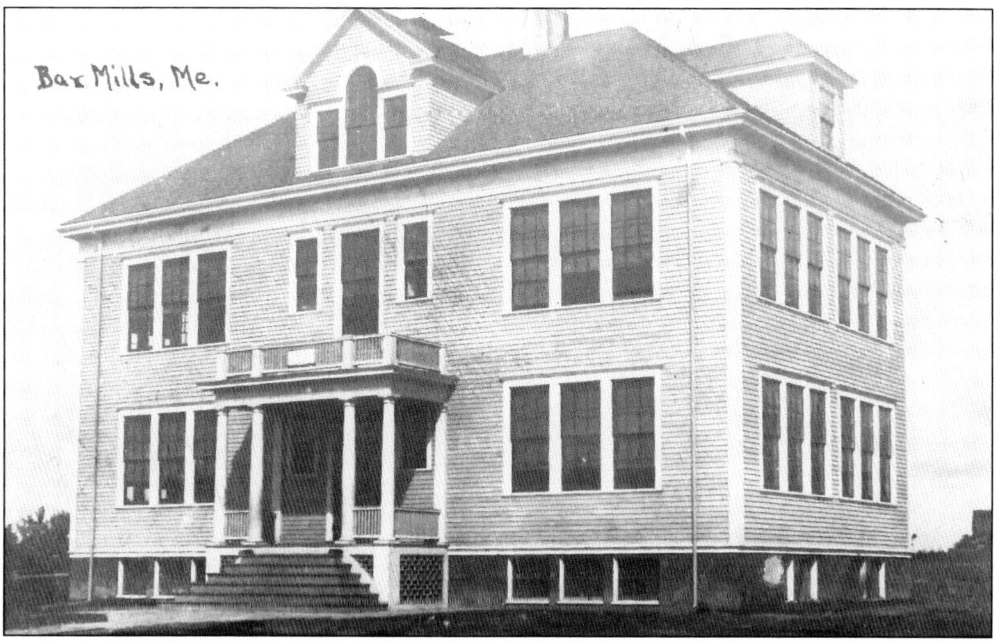

Grammar school at Bar Mills in the 1910s.

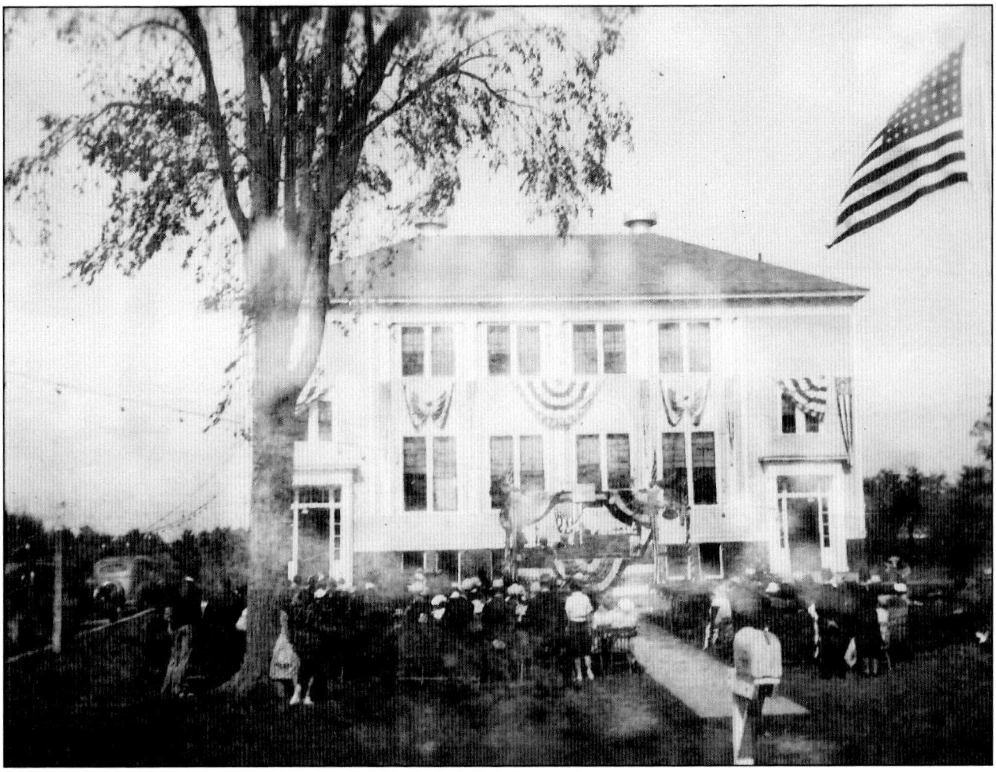

Dedication in 1930 of a school at Buxton Center. There were once as many as eighteen or twenty different schools in the town.

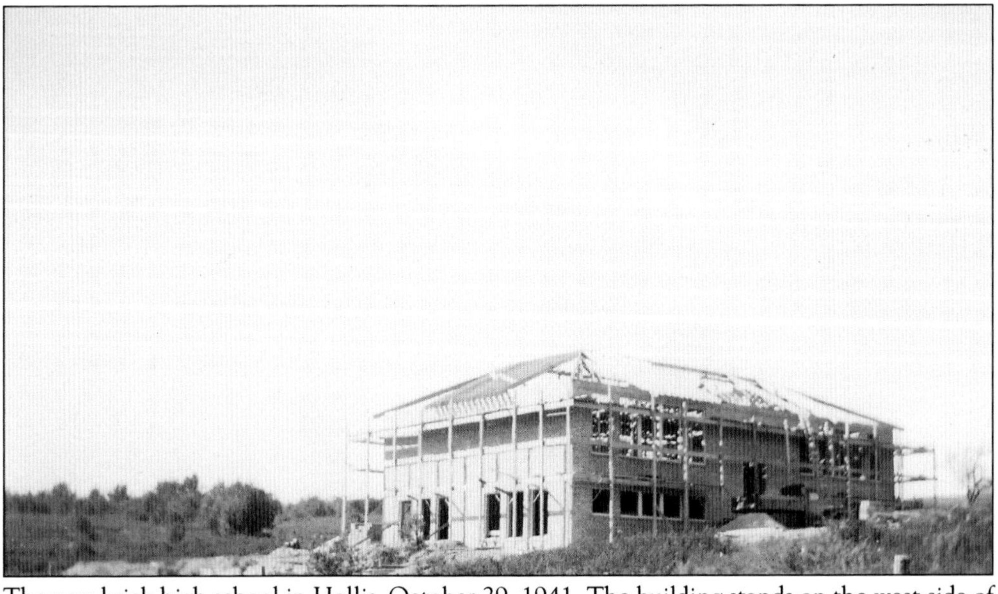

The new brick high school in Hollis, October 29, 1941. The building stands on the west side of the highway along the Saco River. It was paid for by proceeds from the town-owned wood lot.

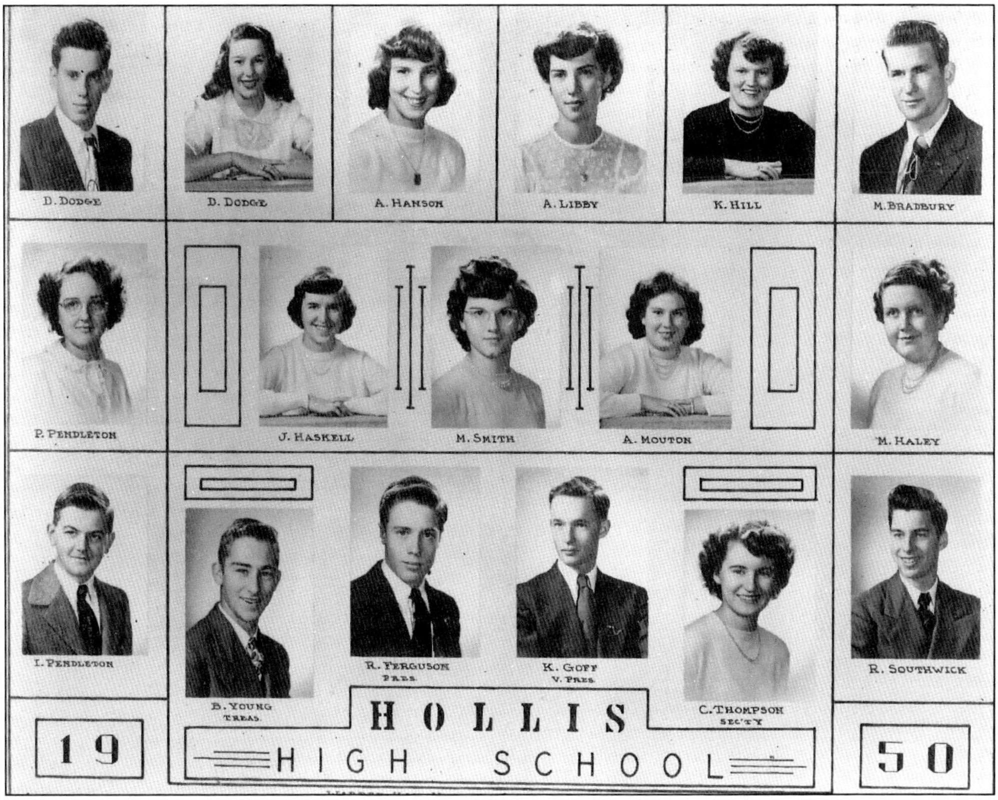

Hollis High School, Class of 1950. From left to right are: (bottom row) I. Pendleton, B. Young (treasurer), R. Ferguson (president), K. Goff (vice president), C. Thompson (secretary), and R. Southwick; (middle row) P. Pendleton, J. Haskell, M. Smith, A. Mouton, and M. Haley; (top row) D. Dodge (boy), D. Dodge (girl), A. Hanson, A. Libby, K. Hill, and M. Bradbury.

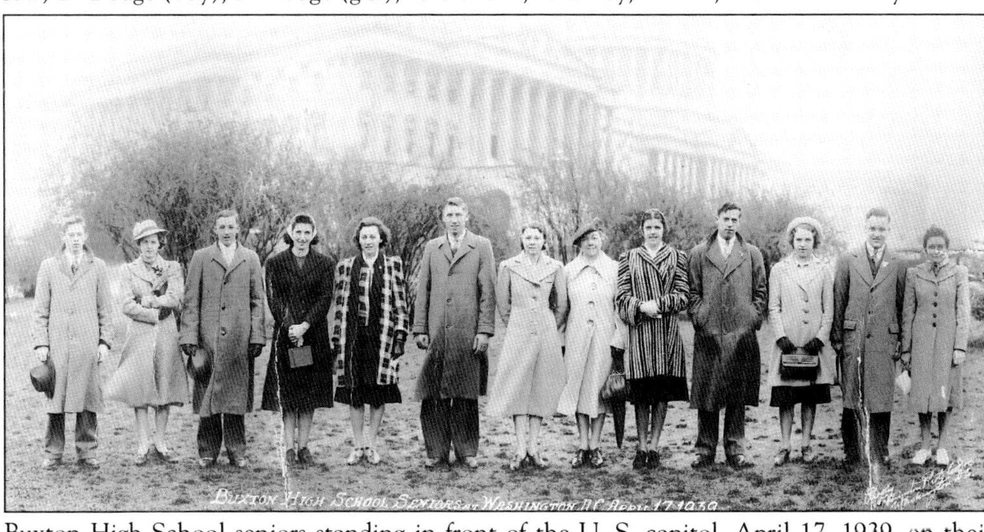

Buxton High School seniors standing in front of the U. S. capitol, April 17, 1939, on their Washington trip. From left to right are: Merton Sargent, Barbara Thomas, Ralph Haley, Harriett Boulter, Vilda Newcomb, Kenneth Owen, Dora Jewett, Agnes Emery, Mary Snell, Reginald Plummer Sr., Doris Cousins, Ernest Stevens, and Jean Jewett.

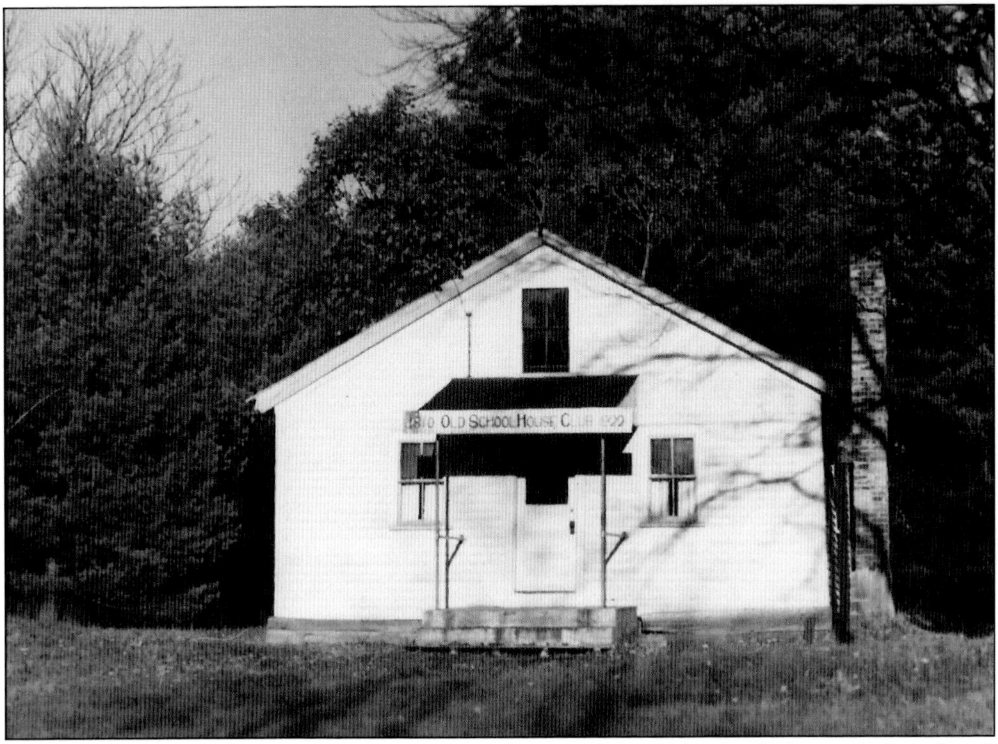

A former school house in Hollis, *c.* 1930s, later the site of the Old School House Club and, still later, the Sunshine Club. It was a school from 1810 to 1922 and burned in the 1947 forest fires.

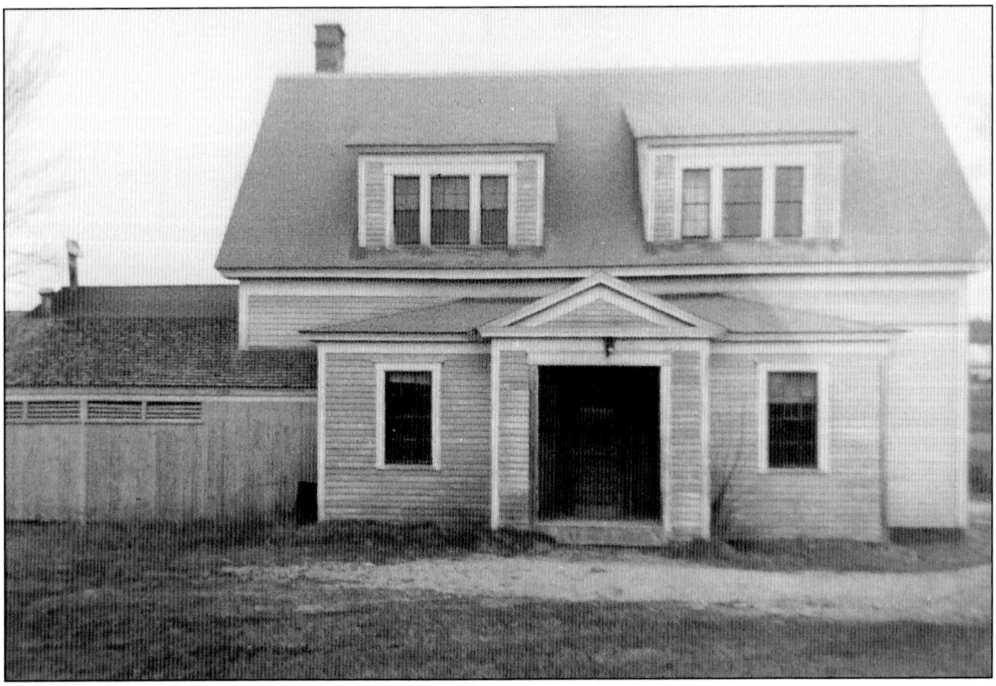

Hollis High School in 1943, the year after it was abandoned. Students from the area now go to Bonny Eagle High School in Buxton.

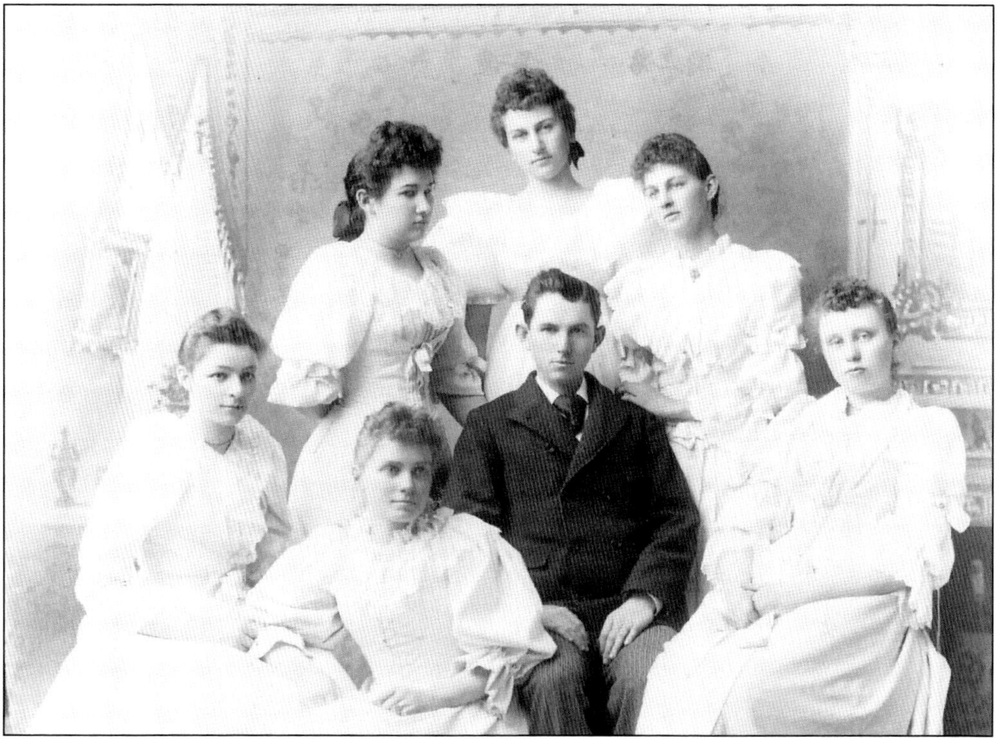

At left rear, Sadie (Moody) Brackett, teacher at the East Limington School about 1907. From left to right are: (first row) Philip Christie, unknown Coulard, John Harmon, Albert Roberts, Cora Black, Orville Storer, and Mellie Small; (second row) George Chick, Lizzie Storer, Esther Christie, Florence Black, Doris Chase, Mary Black, Mellie Black, and Lista Chick; (third row) Myrtle Chick, Annie Smith, Emma Storer, Mae Chase, Florence Nason, Gladys Brackett, and Phoebe Harmon.

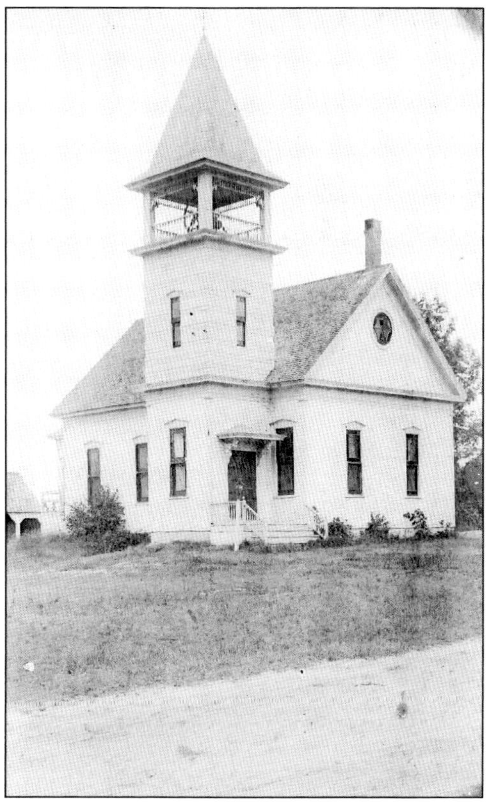

Methodist Episcopal Church at Clark's Mills, c. 1938.

Old Tory Meeting House in Buxton, c. 1920s.

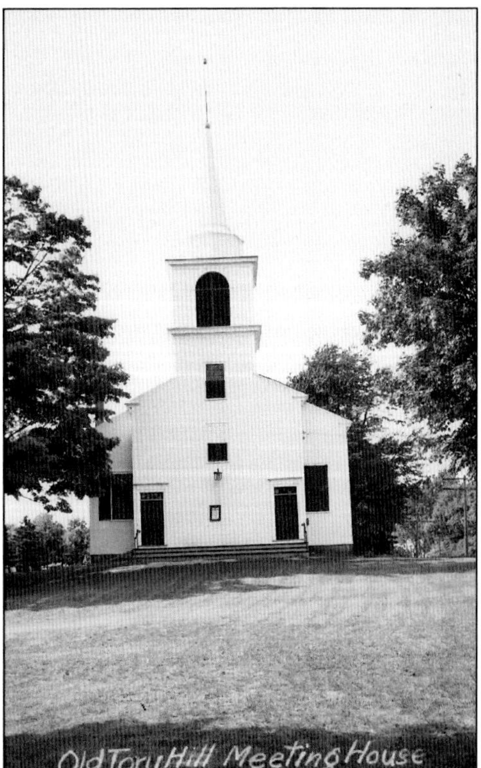

A c. 1910s view of the Old Tory Hill Meeting House in Buxton.

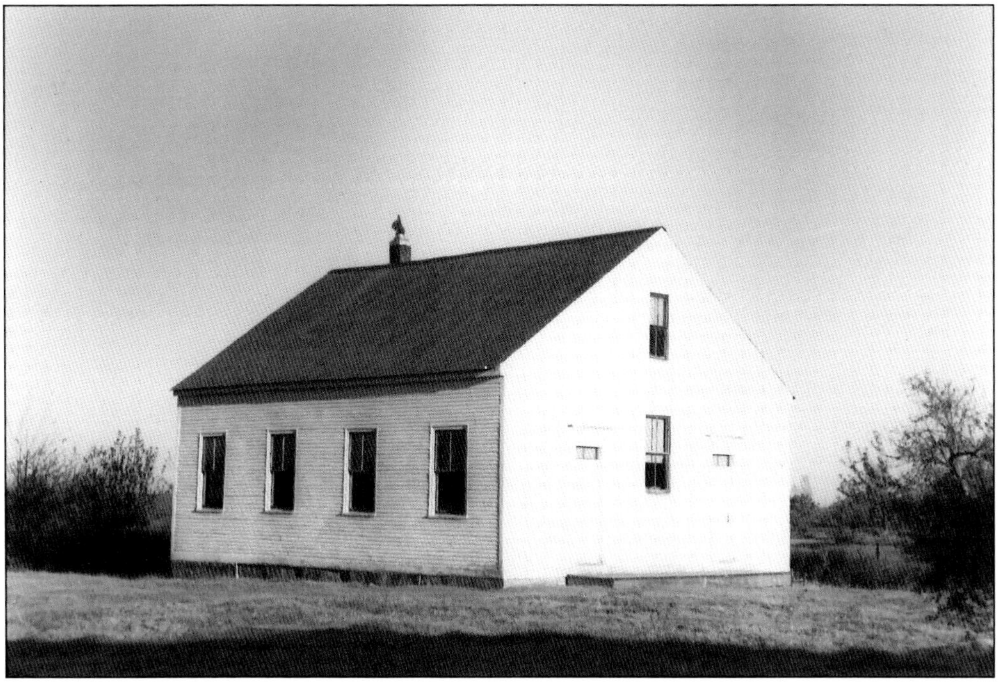

Pleasant Hill Baptist Church. Dedicated in 1840, this church burned in the 1947 forest fires.

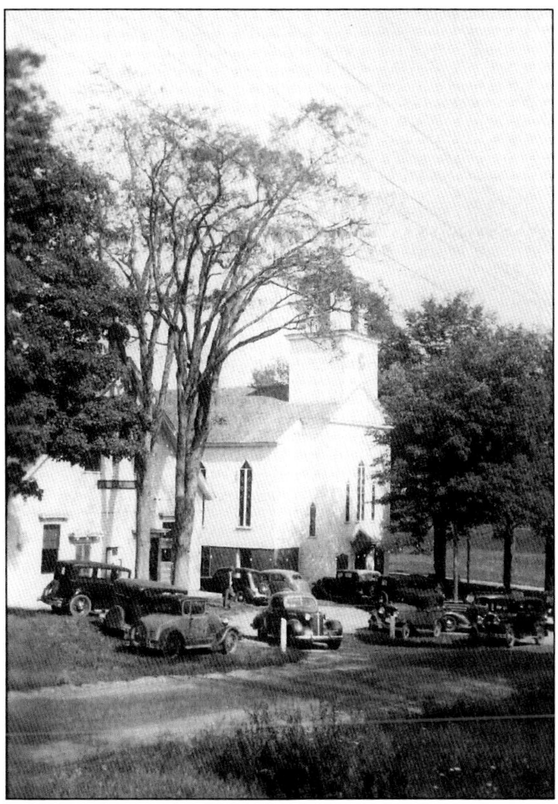

Baptist Church at Buxton Center around 1938–1943.

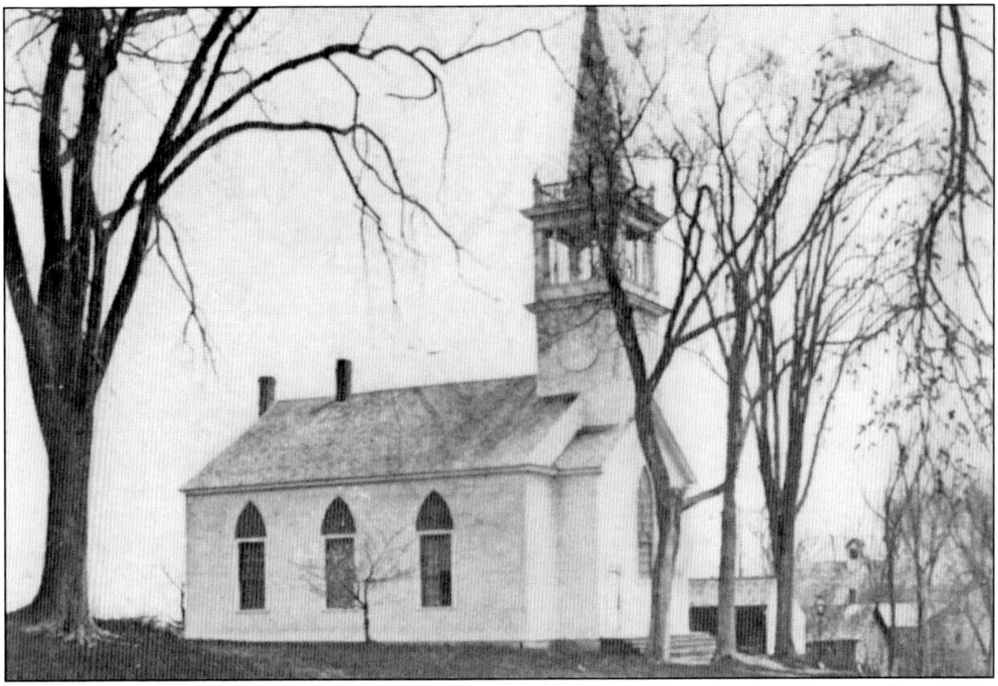

Limington Congregational Church. It was built in 1835, replacing the church erected in 1789.

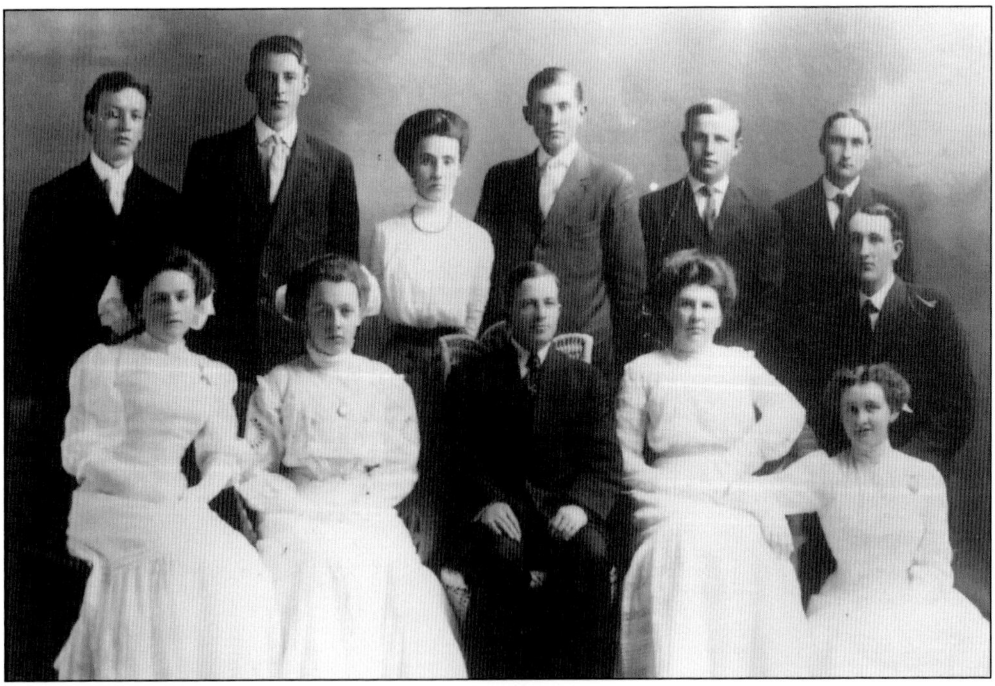

Celia Crawford's Sunday School class, East Limington, about 1905. From left to right are: (front row) Doris Chase, Philip Christie, Orville Storer (in teacher's lap), Catherine Chase, Elizabeth Storer, and Esther Christie; (back row) unknown, unknown, Myrtle Chick, Celia Crawford (teacher), unknown, and May Chase.

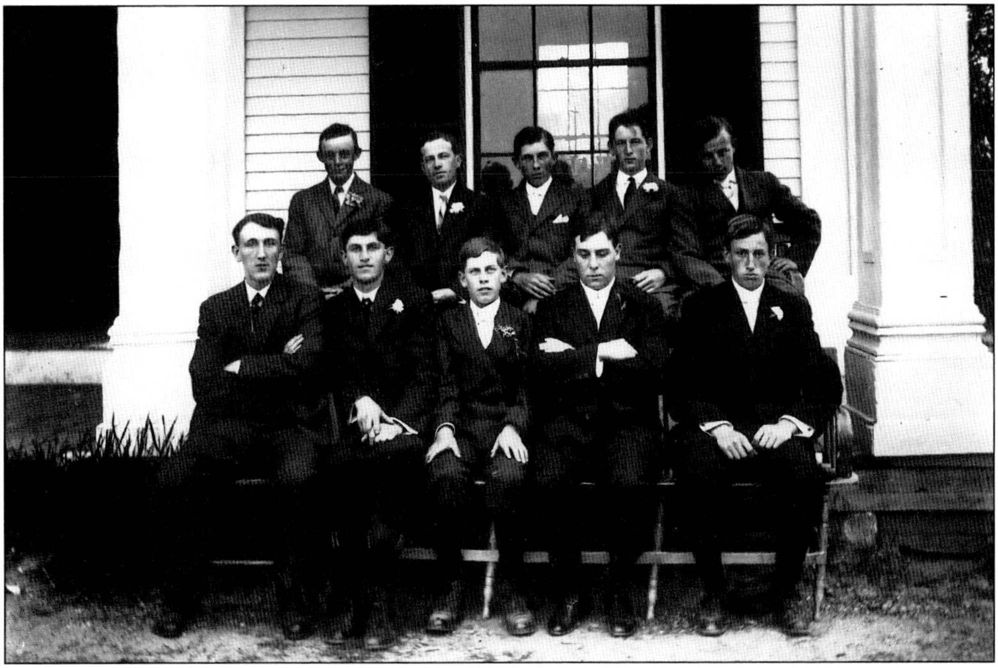

Sunday School at East Limington about 1907 or 1908. (front row) (1) Mellie Small, (2) Louise Chase, (3) Doris Chase. (4) Philip Christie, (5) Catherine Chase, (6) Esther Christie, (7) Elizabeth Storer, (8) Fannie Nason, (9) Gladys Brackett, (10) Mary Stack, and (11) Elwyn Foss; (second row) (1) George Chase, (2) Harry Chick, (3) Carrie Chick, (4) Marion Chase, (5) Ethel Foss, (6) Myrtle Chick, (7) Florence Nason, (8) Gussie Berry, (9) May Chase, (10) Gertrude Foss, and (11) Elwyn Foss; (back row) Rev. Davis and teachers Celia Crawford, Addie Christie, and Miss Millet.

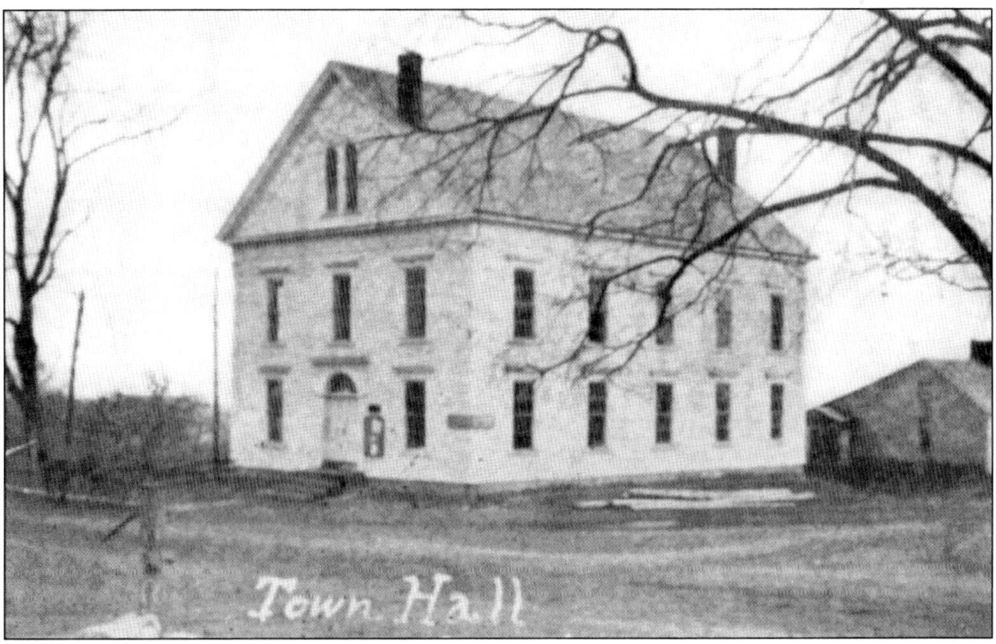

Limington Town Hall, 1900s or earlier.

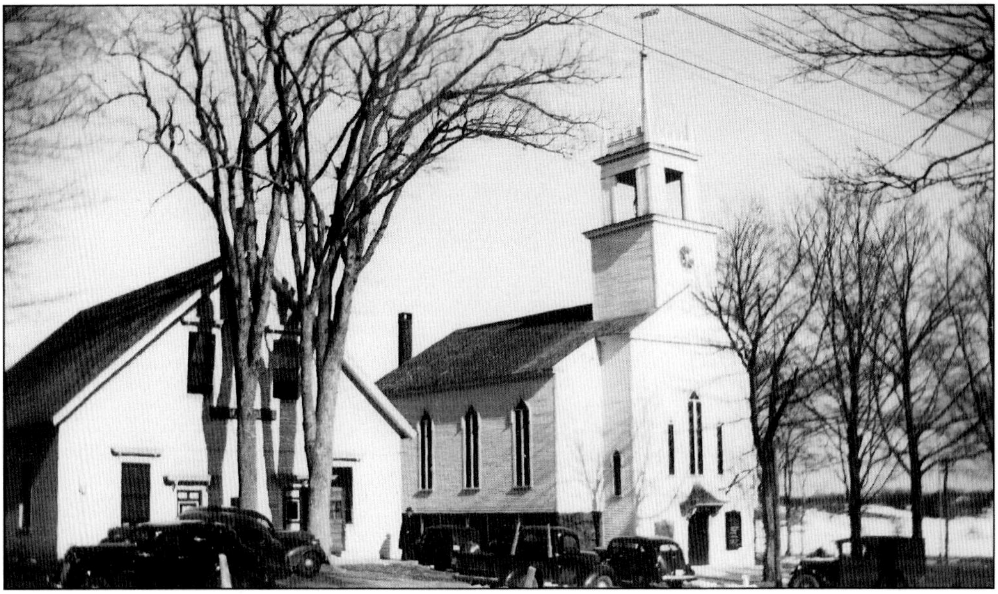

Buxton Center with the town hall on the left and the Baptist Church on the left. The church was dedicated November 8, 1820 by Rev. Loring. The town hall vault has stored the town's records since 1754 around the late 1930s or early 1940s.

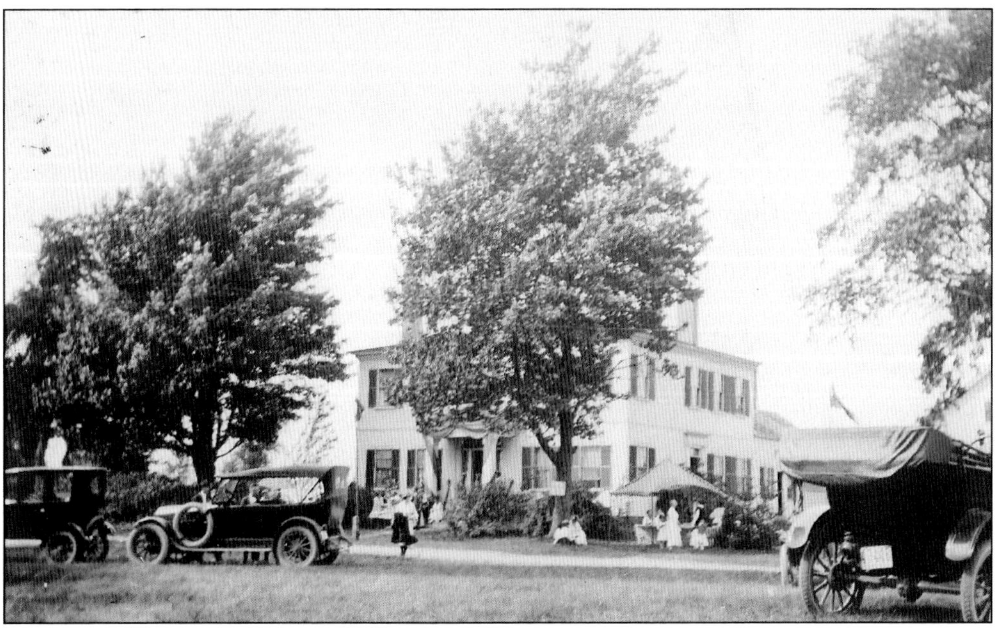

The Brewster Mansion, *c.* 1920s. The mansion is located in Buxton, somewhat east of Salmon Falls, at Tory Hill.

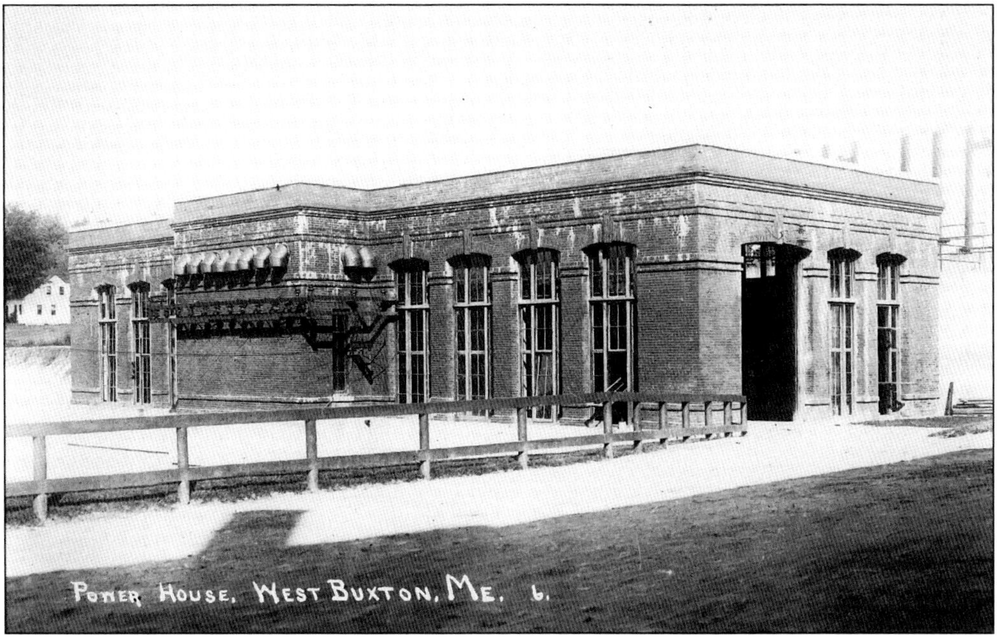

Power house at West Buxton, c. 1920s. This was then operated by Cumberland County Power & Light Company.

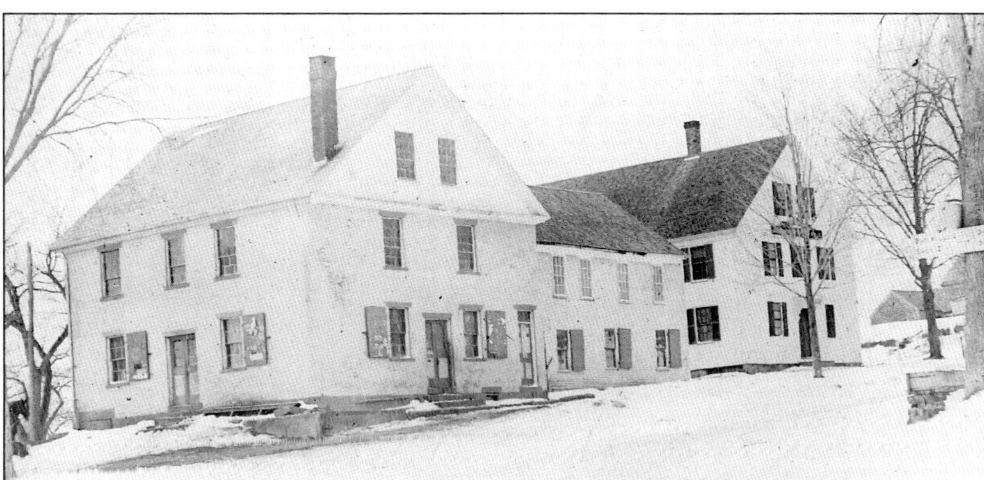
S. Hanson & Company store, coat shop, and Knights of Pythias Hall, Buxton Center, c. 1920s.

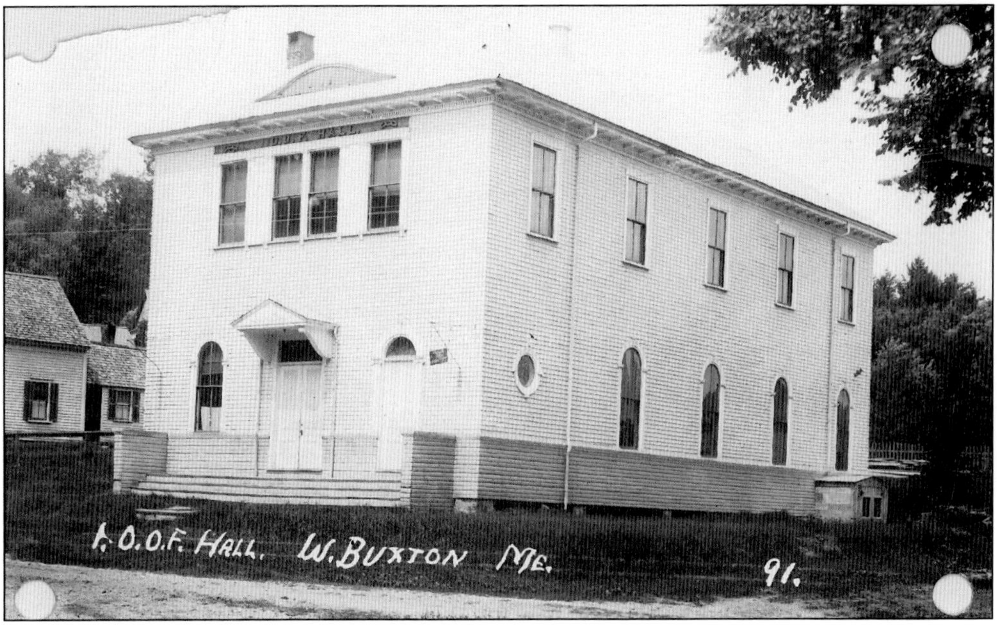

IOOF (Independent Order of Odd Fellows) Hall, West Buxton, *c.* 1920s.

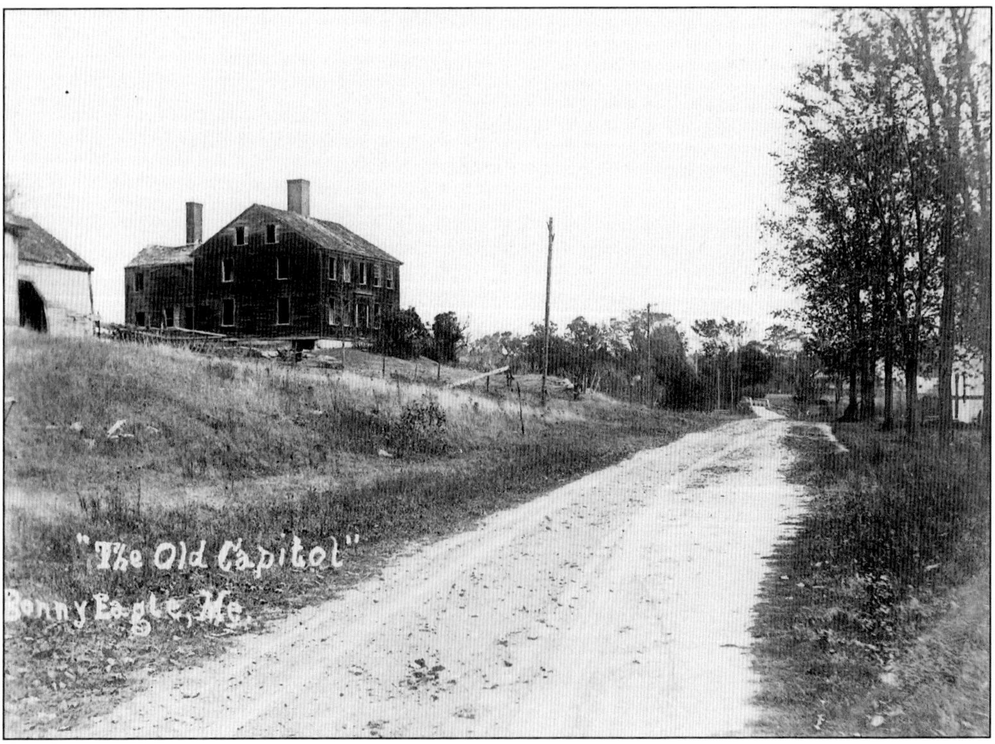

"The Old Capitol," Bonny Eagle in Buxton, *c.* 1910s. All we know is that it was the house where Aunt Cad was married July 4, 1863. That's on a postcard to Miss Georgie Anderson.

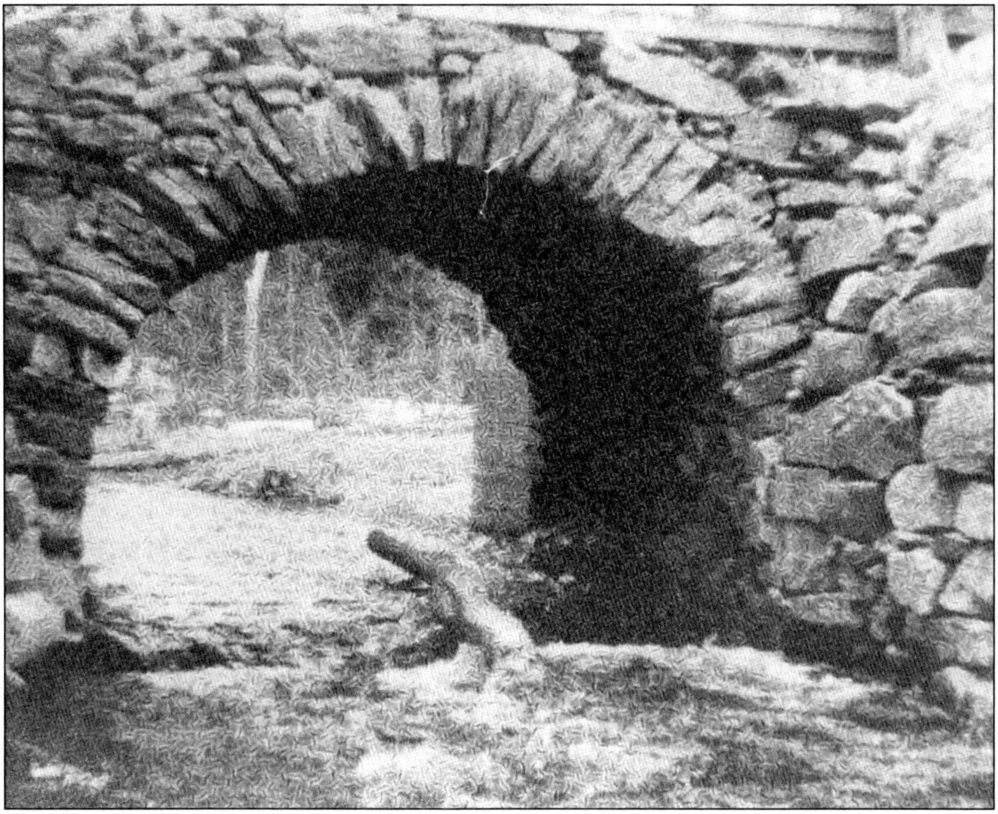

Waterman Road Bridge, West Buxton, eliminated twelve to eighteen years ago.

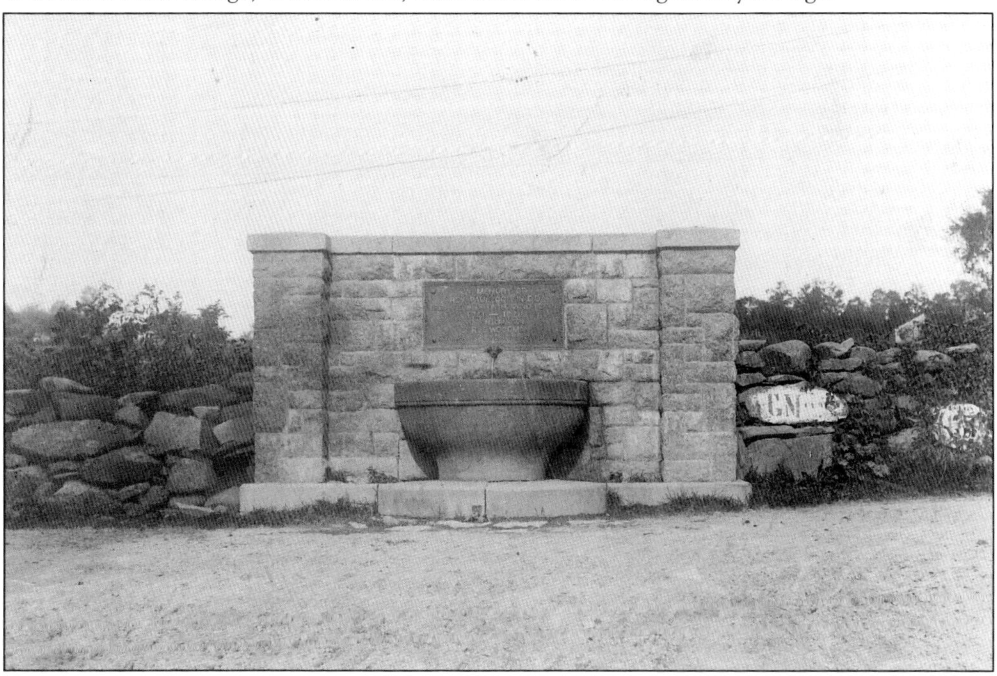

An old watering trough at Bar Mills, *c.* 1900s.

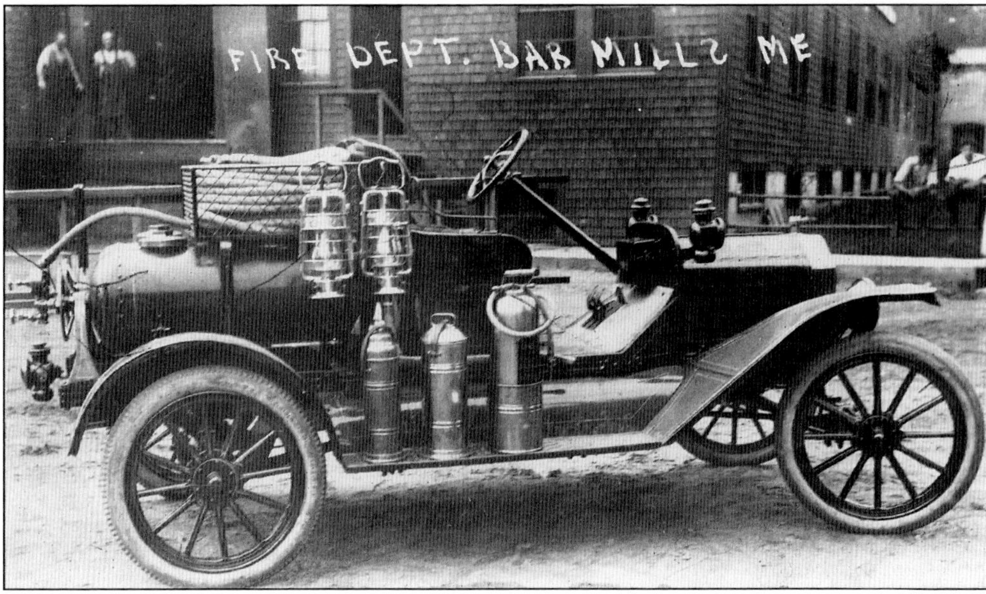

An early fire truck belonging to the Bar Mills Fire Department, *c.* 1920s.

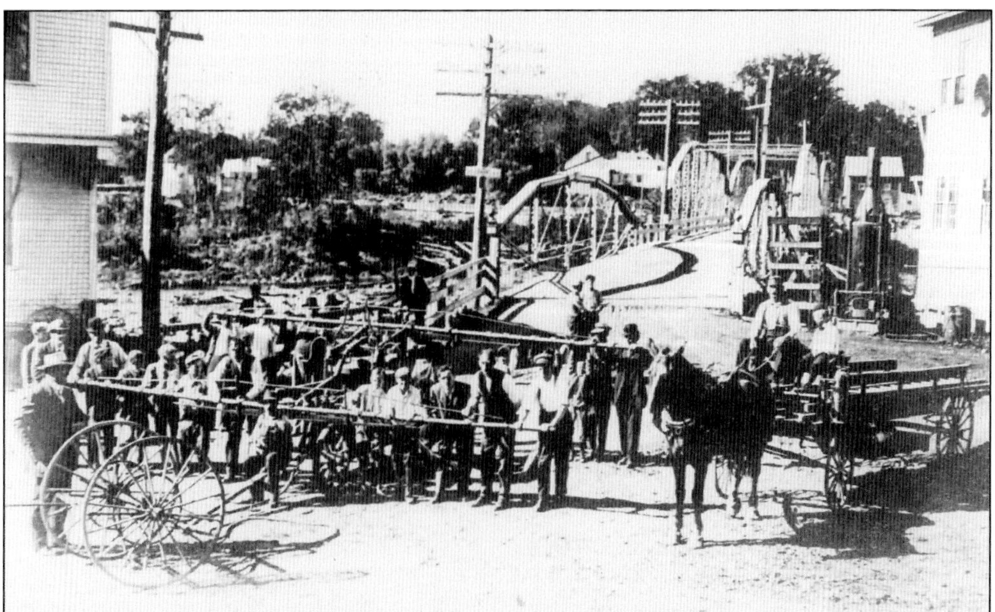

Bar Mills on the Buxton side of the Saco River with a fire department pumper, *c.* 1910s.

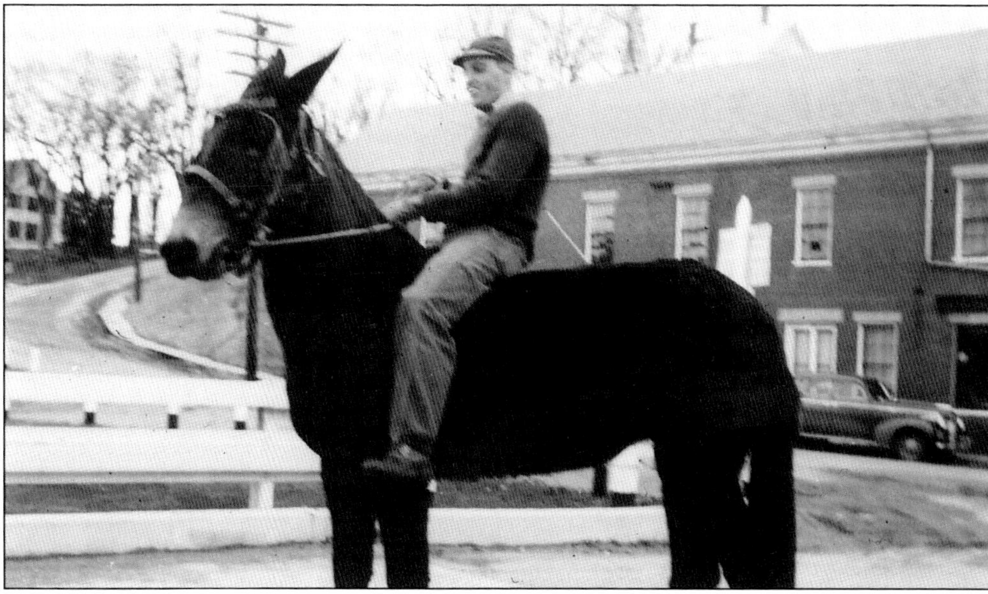

An Army mule on the West Buxton bridge in 1940, a year before the United States entered World War II. The rider is Donald Plummer.

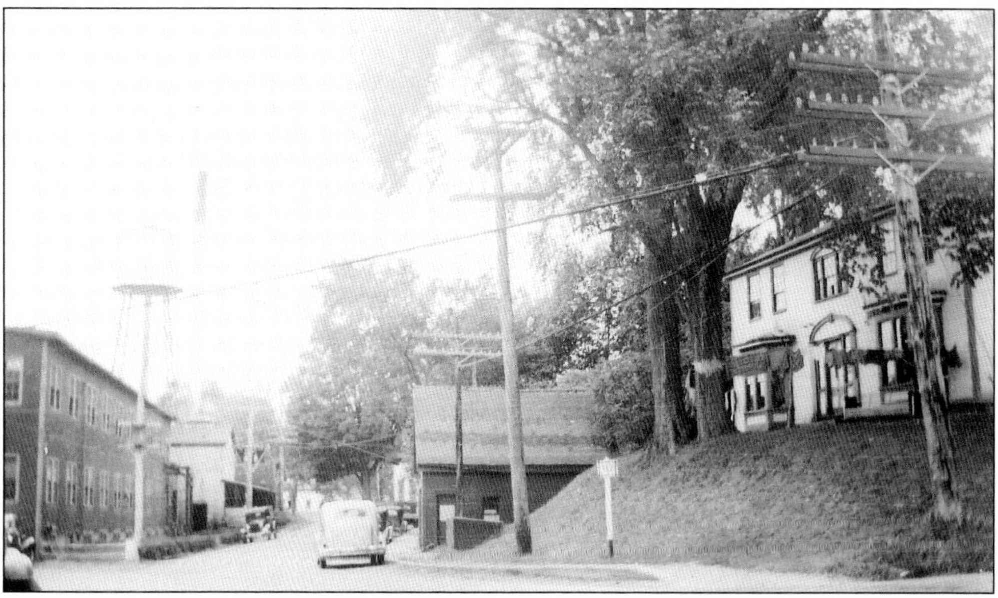

Bar Mills in August, 1940, with a mill at the left.

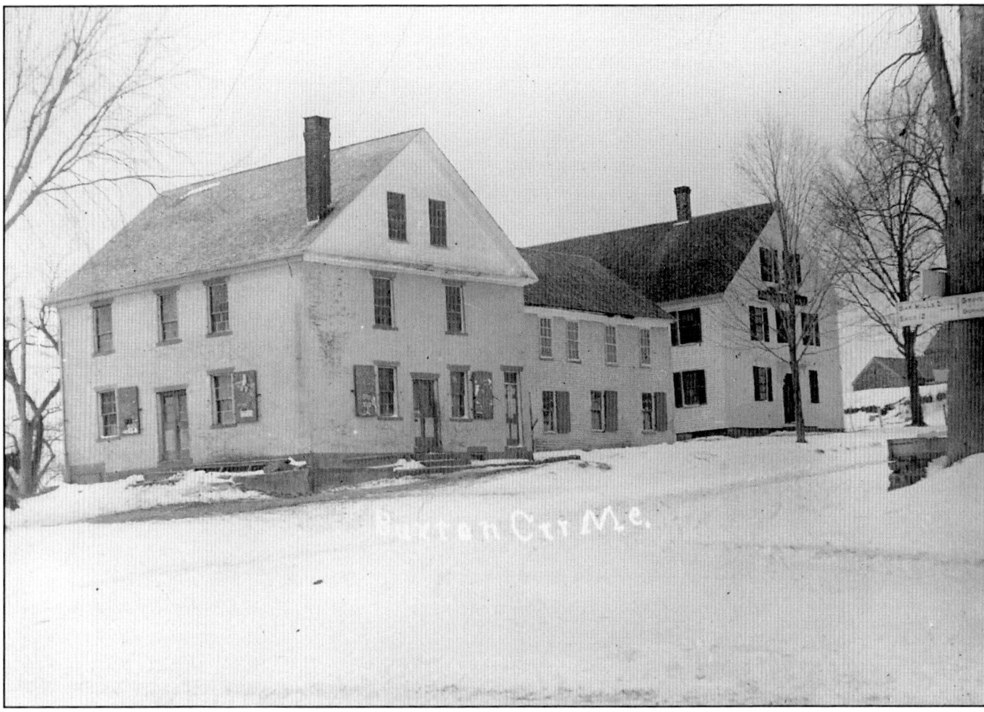

The Buxton-Hollis Historical Society building at Buxton Center. It was earlier a store, a coat manufacturing plant, and a doctor's office, *c.* 1940s.

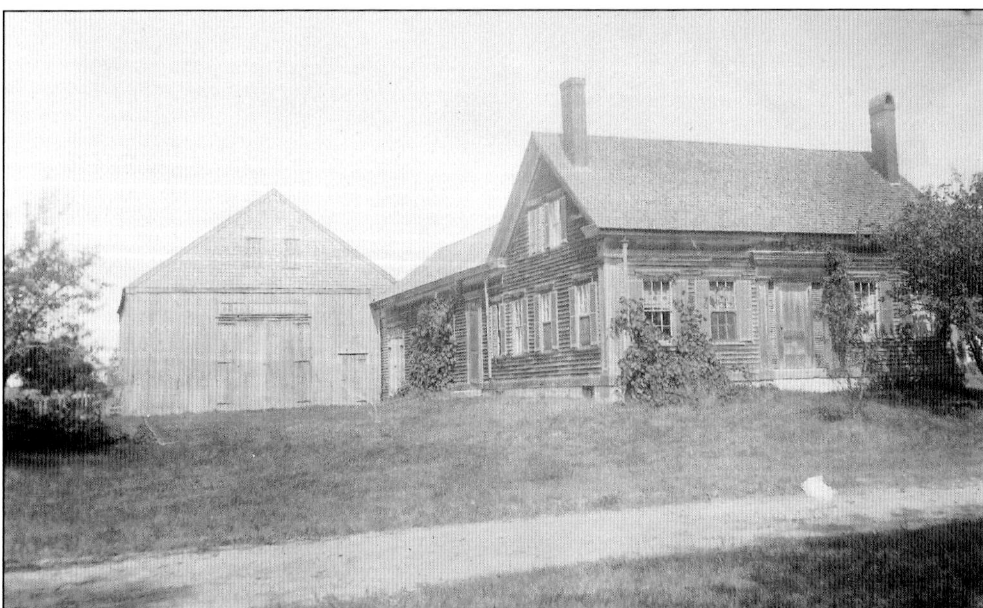

The Enoch Davis house on the Groveville Road in Buxton, *c.* 1940s. The barn is gone. Groveville is another section of Buxton.

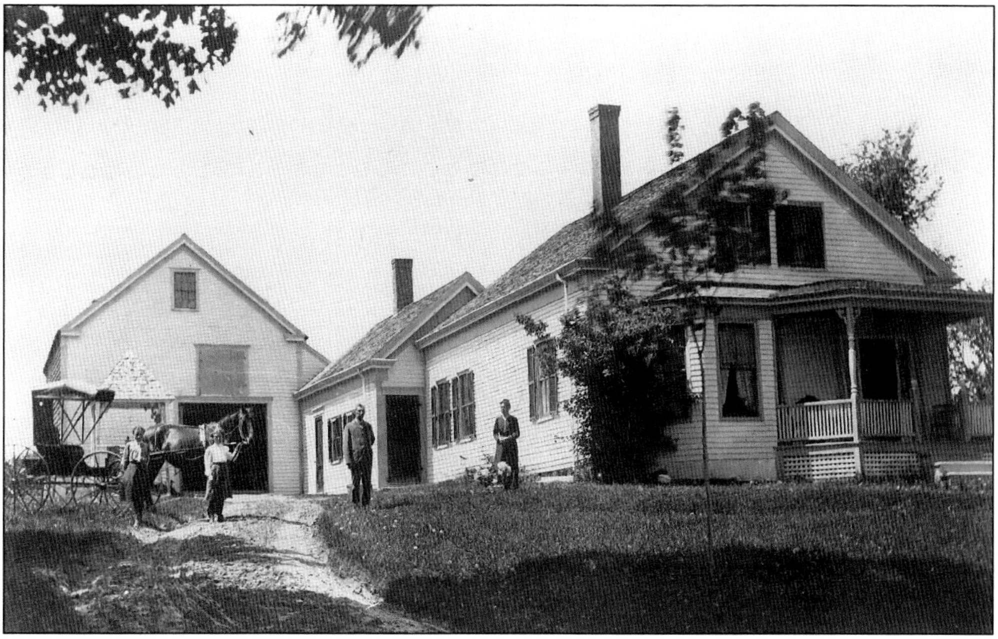

A home on the Haines Meadow Road, Buxton Center, *c.* 1900s.

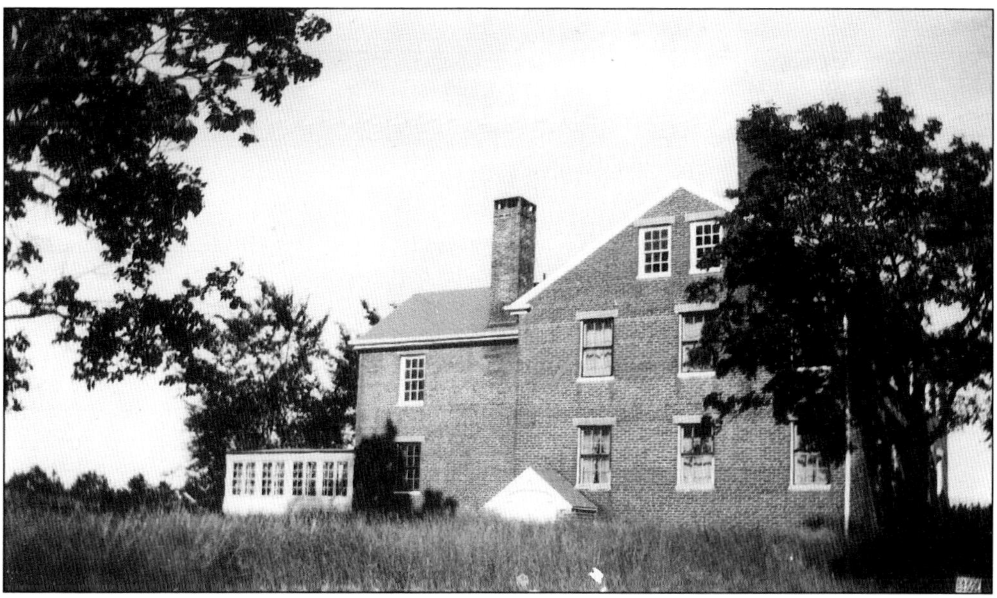

The former "Brick Tavern, located on Route 117 at the intersection of Hardscrabble Road, just beyond Killock Brooks, in July 1946. The author has never seen as many brick houses in any Maine area as in this one. Local folks say that's because there were several brickyards here.

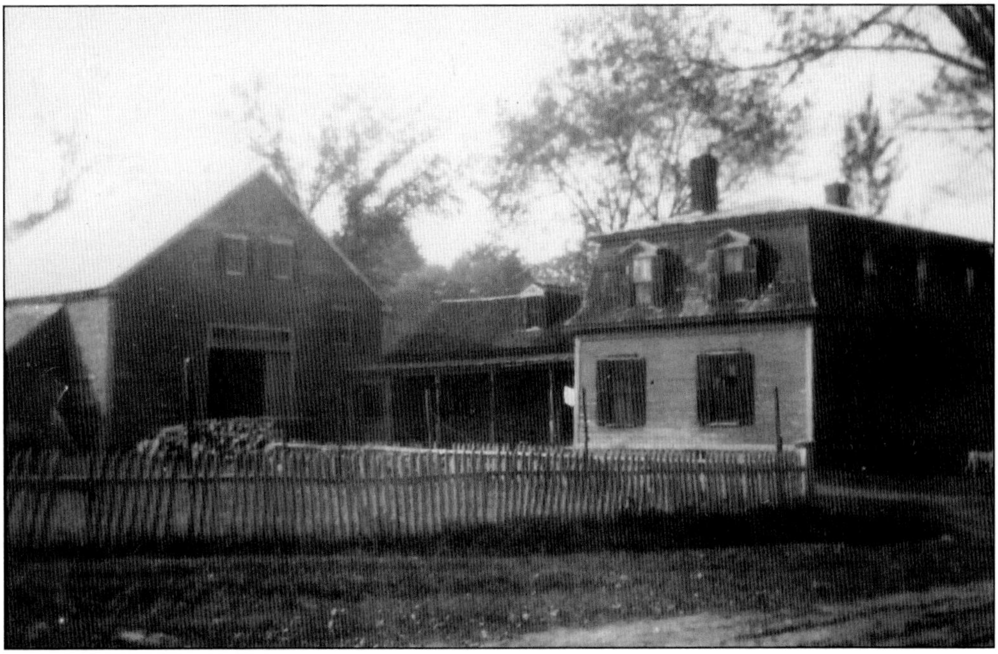

The house on the southwesterly side of Route 35 (or River Road) and High Street (or Plains Road) in Hollis. Note the stone dog at the far right, *c.* 1930s.

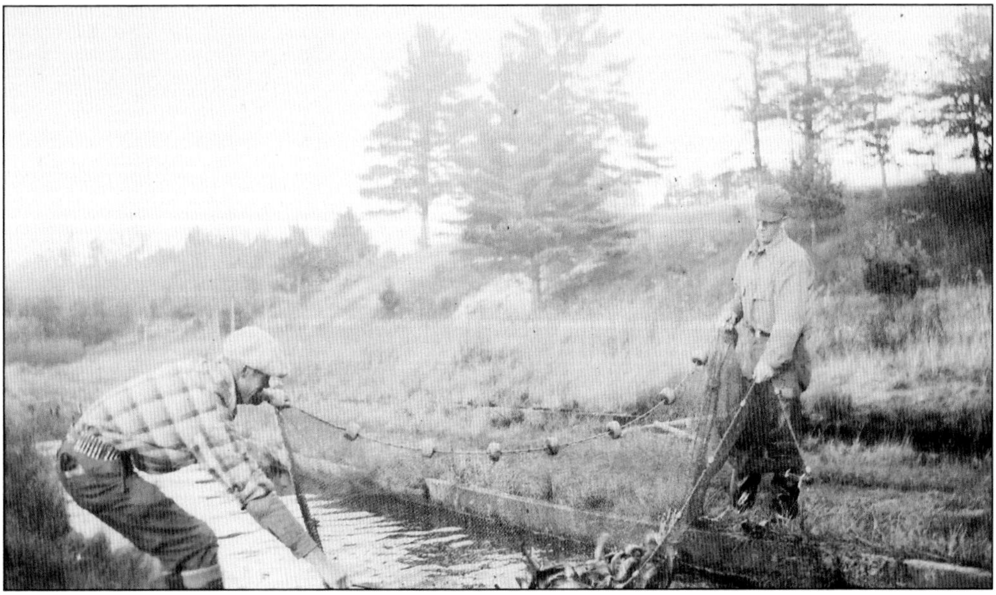

The Shy Beaver trout pond, located on the northerly side of Plains Road in Hollis, on November 13, 1931.

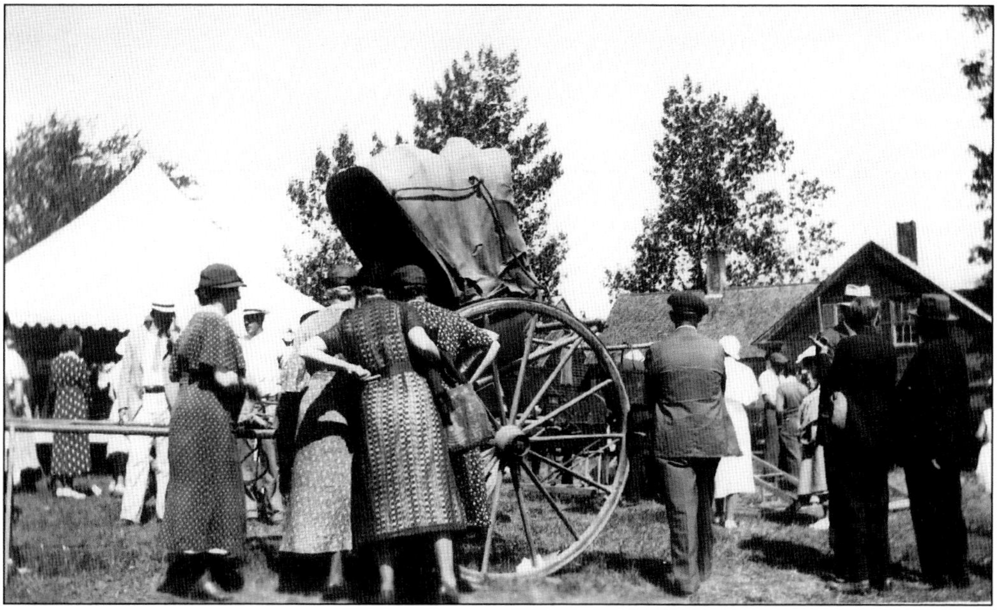

The one-horse shay which made a round trip from Buxton to Boston in 1792. It was shown at the York County Farm Bureau Field Day in Hollis, August 28, 1936.

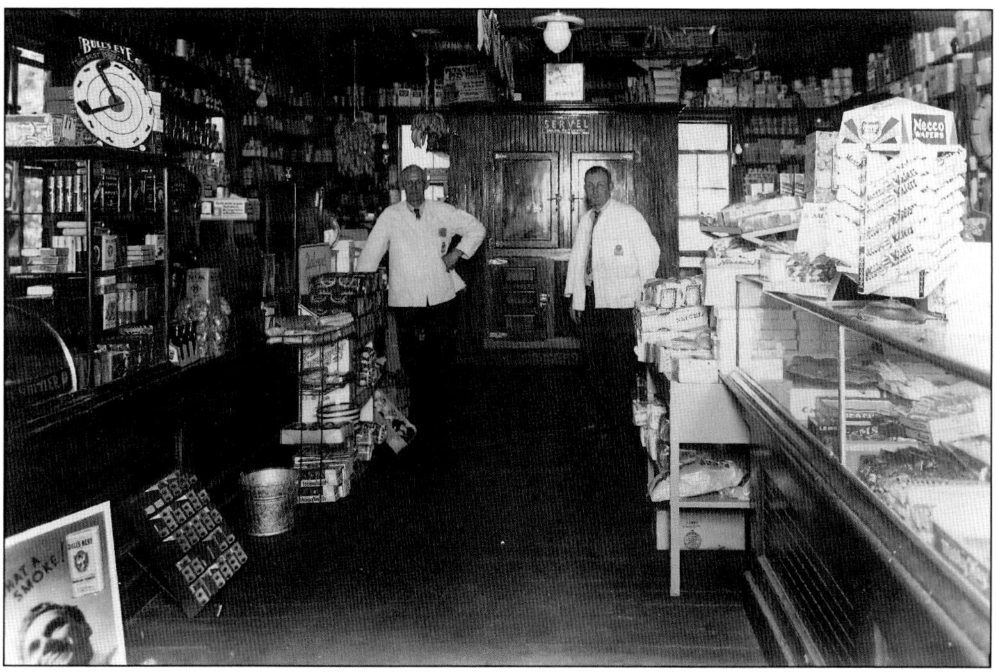

The Hall & Sands store at Bar Mills, *c.* 1920s. Guy Hall is on the left and Lester Sands is on the right. Note the Necco wafers display on the right, the Servel sign at the center rear, as well as the Dill's Best, What A Smoke! sign at the left lower front, and the Bull's Eye, the Best Pipe Made advertisement at the left upper front.

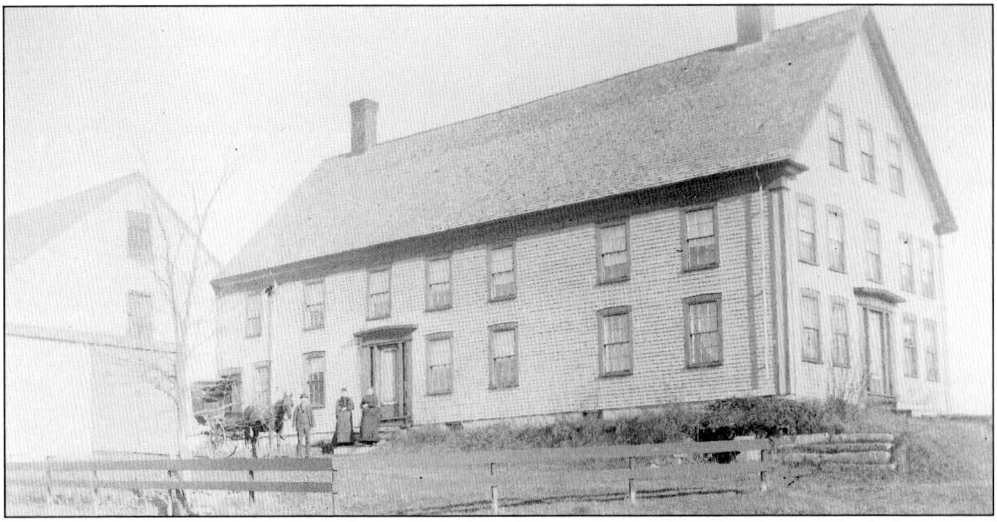

The tavern where the stage coaches stopped and river drivers boarded. It was built by Daniel Darrah against his mother's old one-story building on Saco Hill, Buxton, *c.* 1890s.

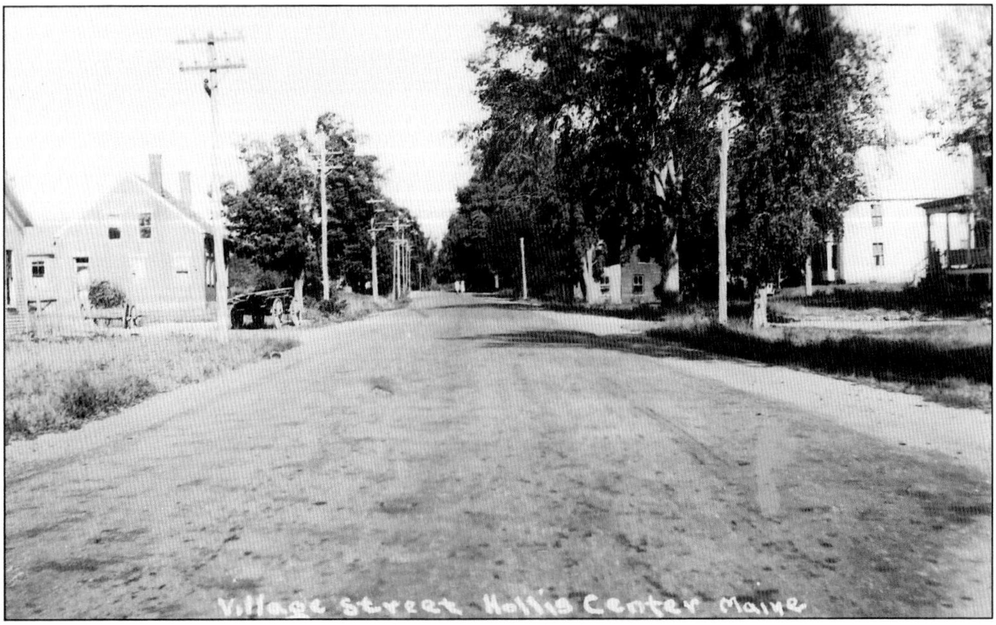

U.S. Route 202 leading from Hollis Center, *c.* 1920s.

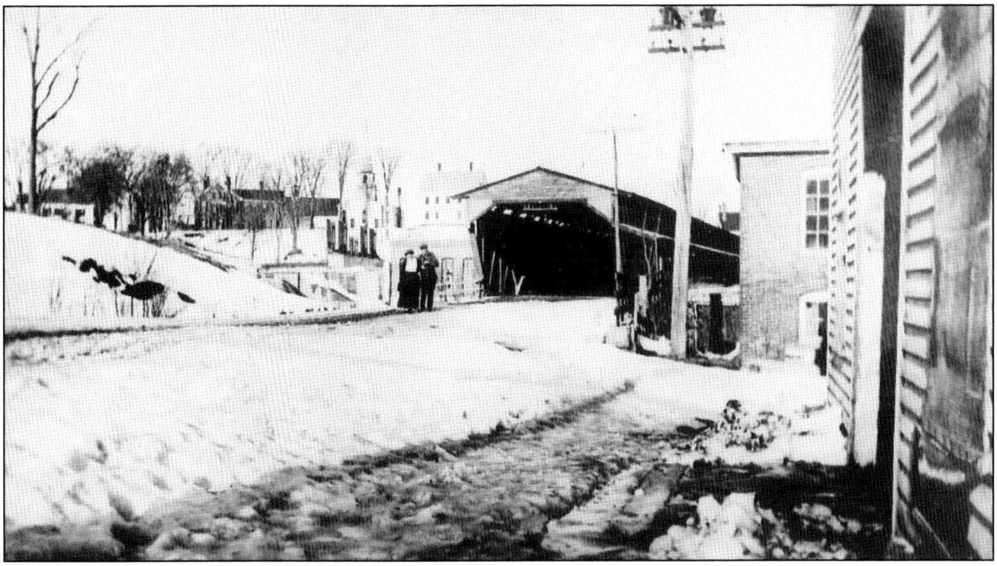

The Hollis side of the covered bridge to West Buxton. The building in the foreground is Ed Brown's store while the brick building was part of Hargrave's Mill, c. 1920s.

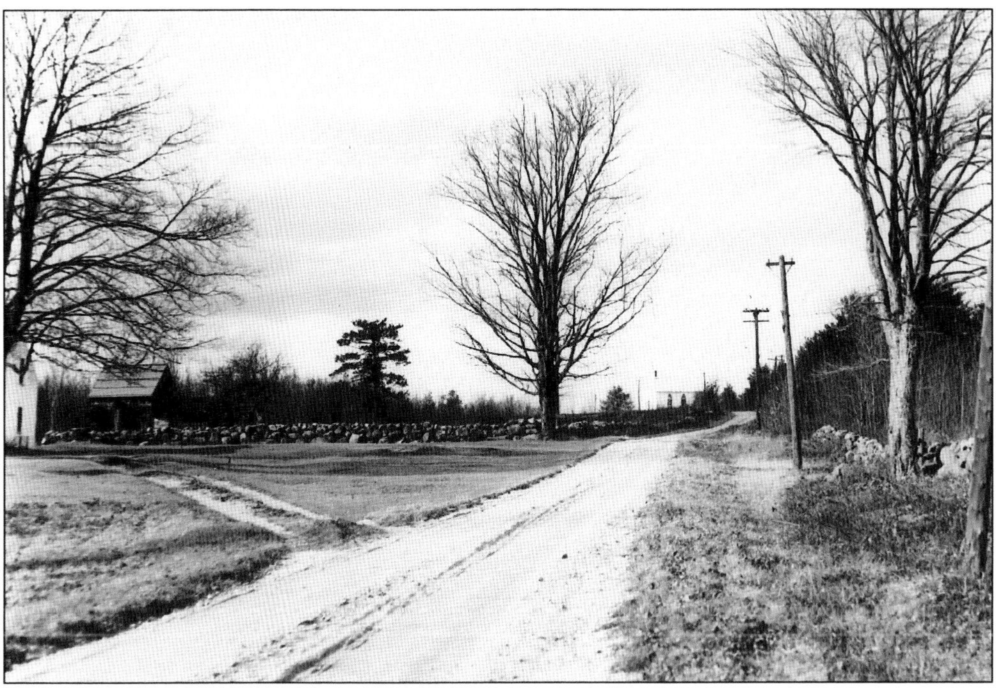

Bear Hill in 1945.

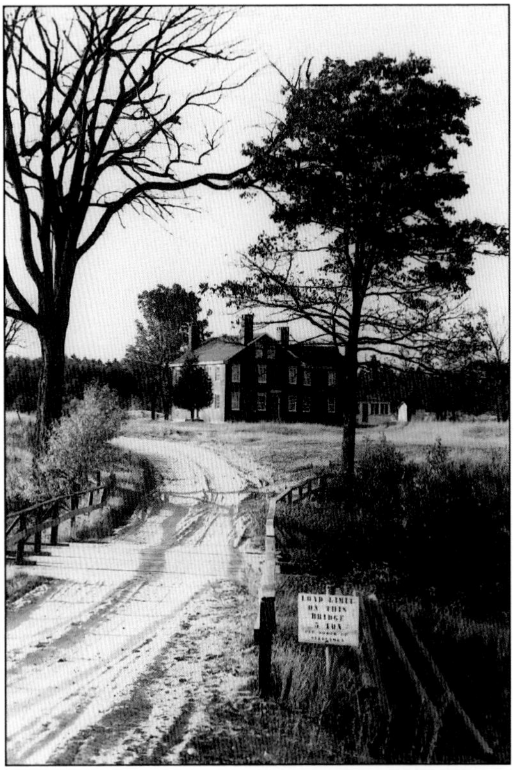

The former "Brick Tavern, located on Route 117 at the intersection of Hardscrabble Road, in 1945 (see p. 49).

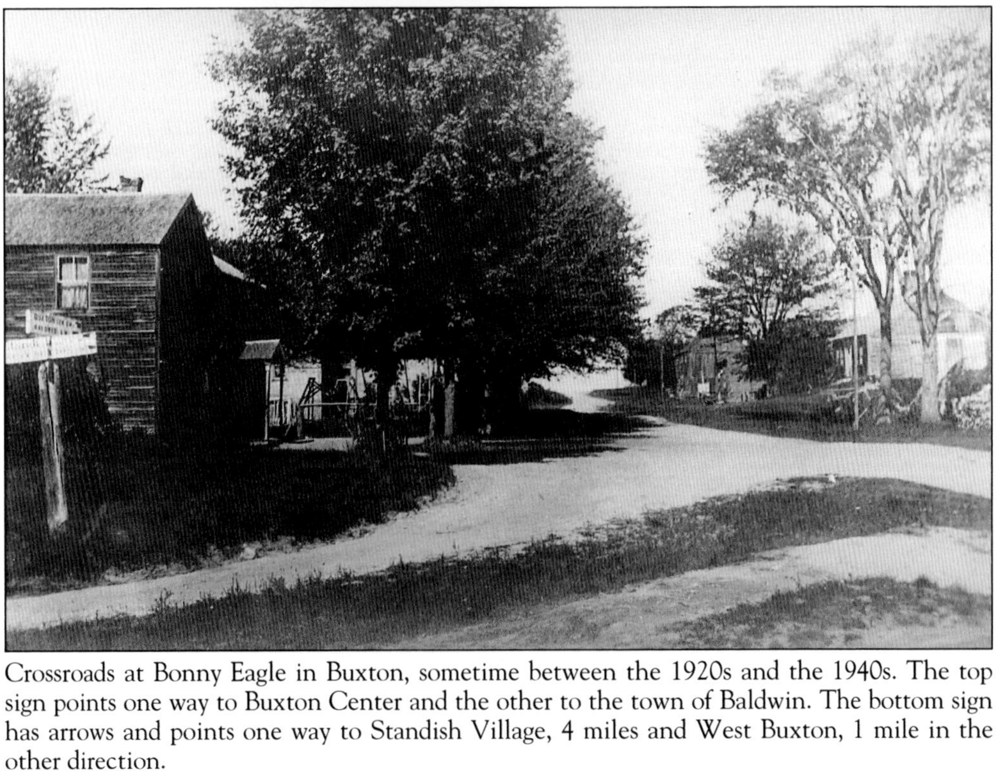

Crossroads at Bonny Eagle in Buxton, sometime between the 1920s and the 1940s. The top sign points one way to Buxton Center and the other to the town of Baldwin. The bottom sign has arrows and points one way to Standish Village, 4 miles and West Buxton, 1 mile in the other direction.

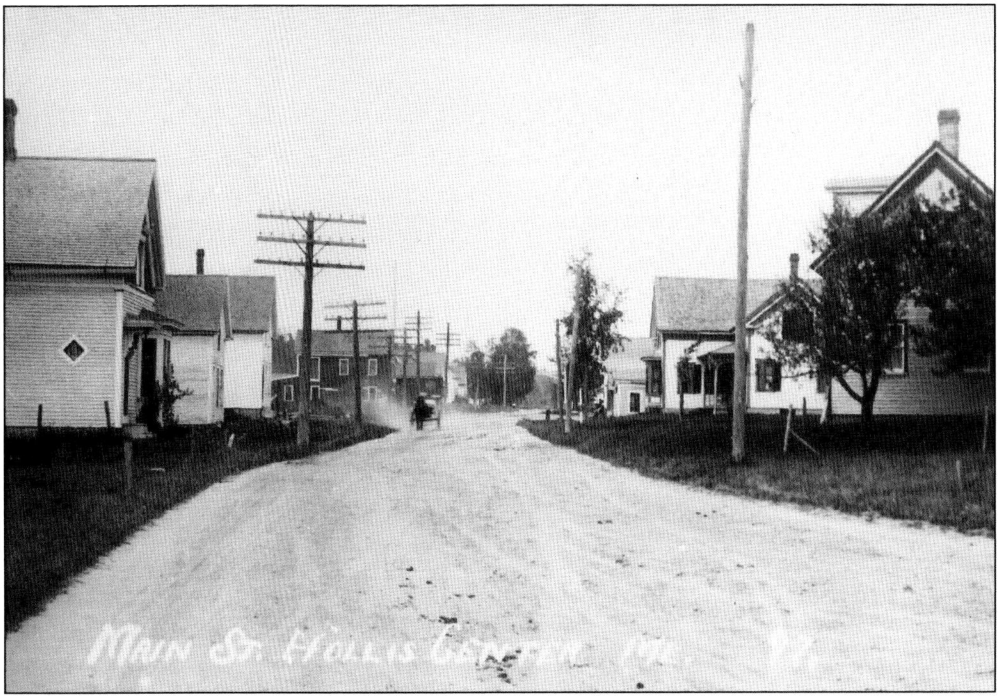

Main Street in Hollis Center, *c.* 1910s. The first house on the left was torn down and a church erected on its site in 1927, much to the irritation of Lon Jellerson, who lived across the street (later Norris Haskell's home). Lon said he was going to plant trees in his yard so he wouldn't be able to see the church.

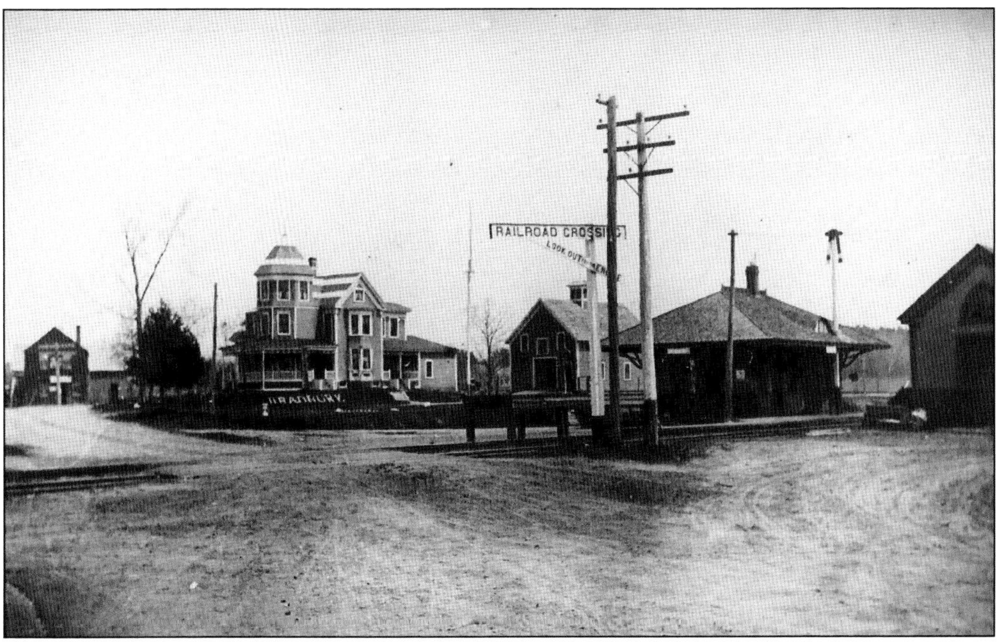

The building at the far left, background, was Orrington Berry's blacksmith shop. It was a store operated later by Albert Hanson, then by Lester "Doc" Dennett, and finally by Ruby Smith. The Bradbury home and Bradbury railroad station are on the center and right, *c.* 1920s.

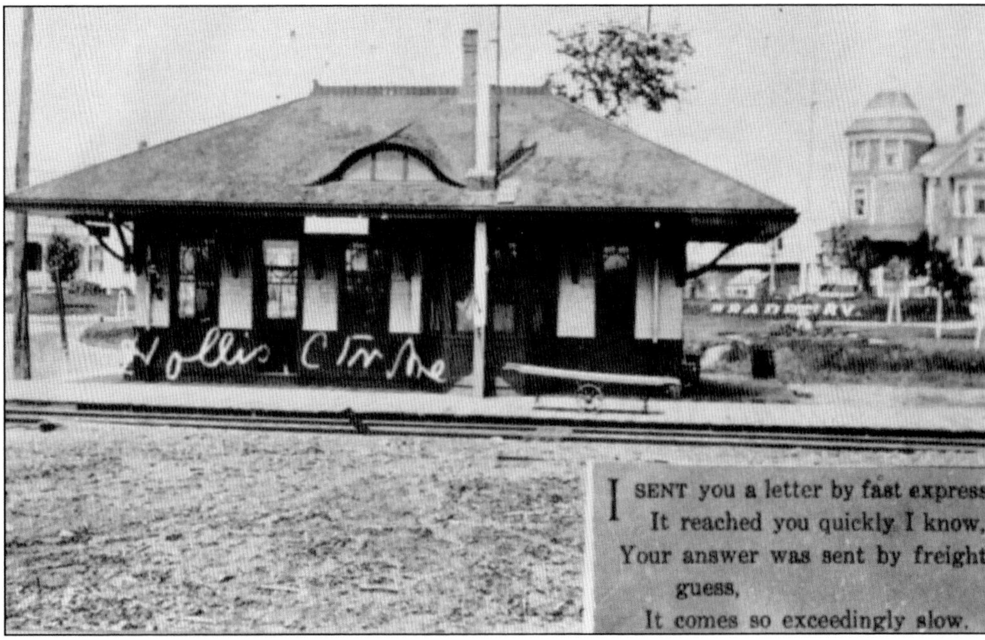

The Hollis Center railroad station. It says on the postcard: "I sent you a letter by fast express. It reached you quickly, I know. Your answer was sent by freight, I guess. It comes so exceedingly slow," c. 1920s.

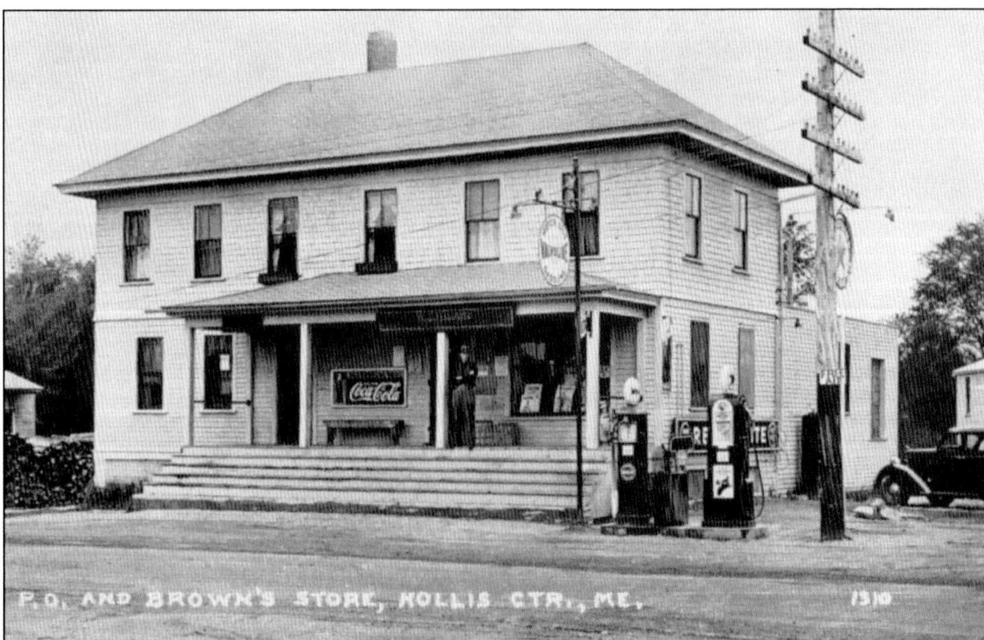

Post Office and Brown's Store, Hollis Center, c. 1940s. Wilbur "Jib" Brown stands on the porch where he emitted a constant stream of tobacco juice, usually in the general direction of a large carton behind the store counter but with only so-so aim.

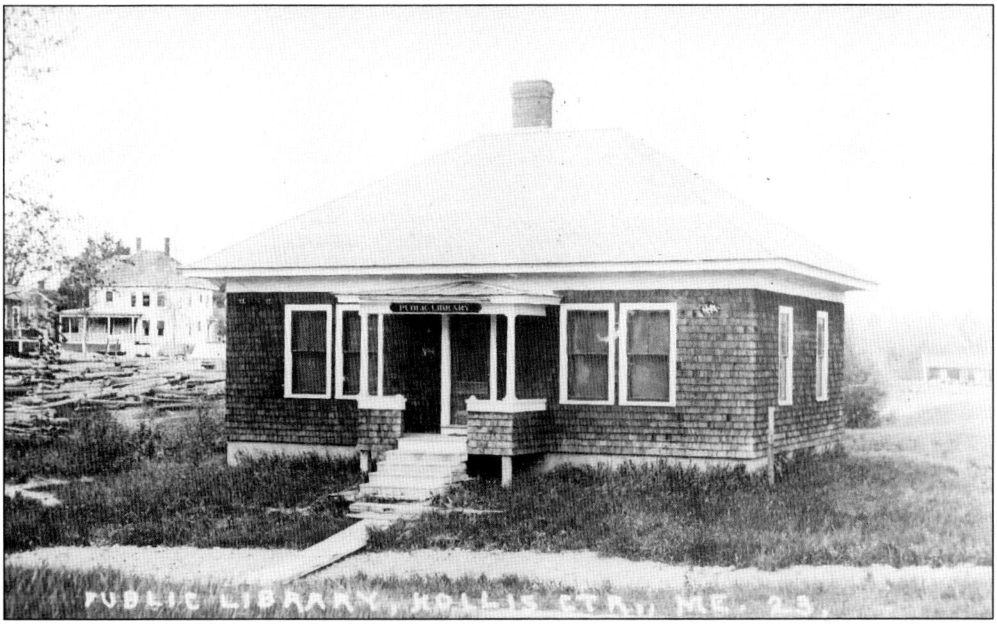

The Hollis Center Public Library, *c.*1930s. Note the logs on the bank of the brook; the building to the right of the library was a sawmill.

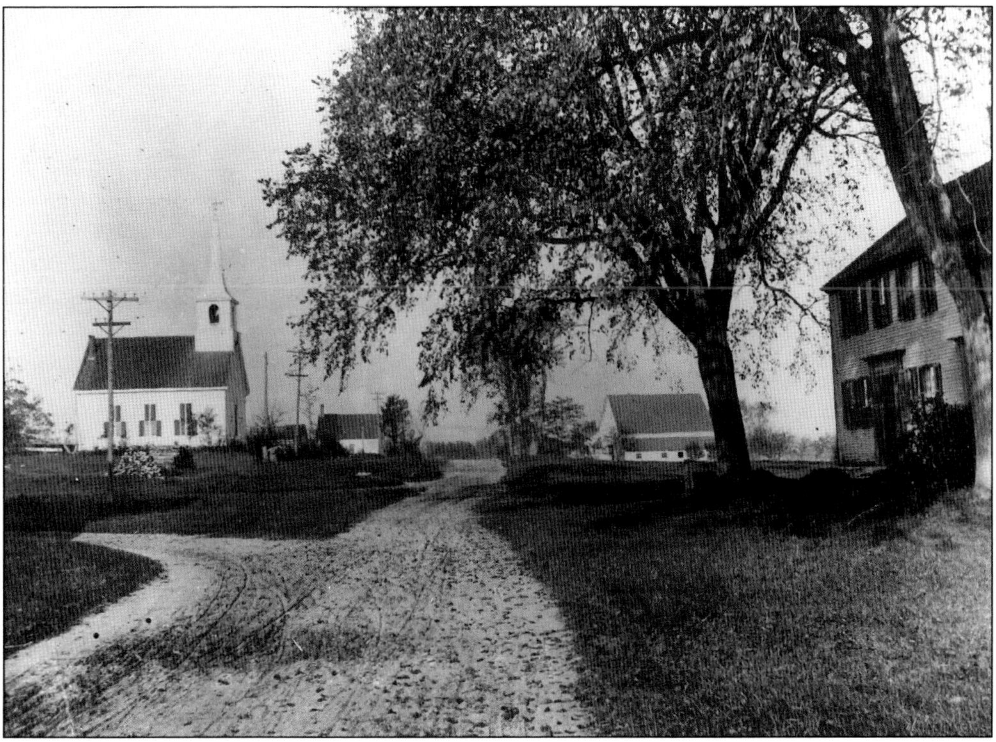

Route 25 in Limington, *c.* 1910. Route 25 is now the major route in the area and runs straight ahead. The road going to the left was better traveled because it led to two sawmills. The inn at right foreground, last owned by Lillian Small, had an ell at the rear. Rum was two cents a glass in the store part of the inn and three cents a glass in the ell.

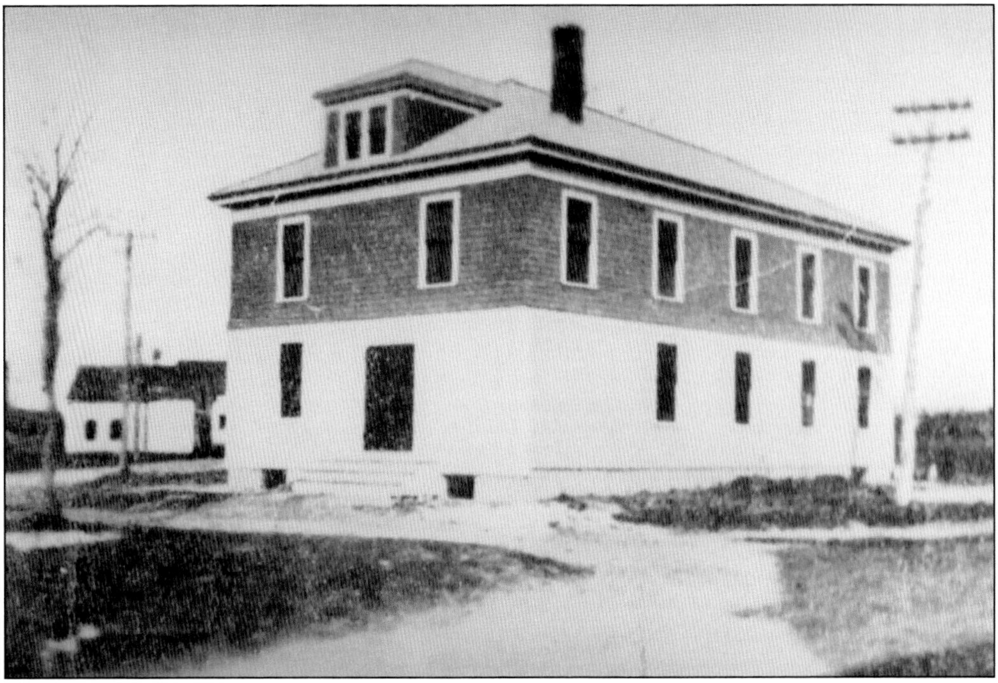

The "new" Grange Hall, *c.* early 1900s. The porch was added later

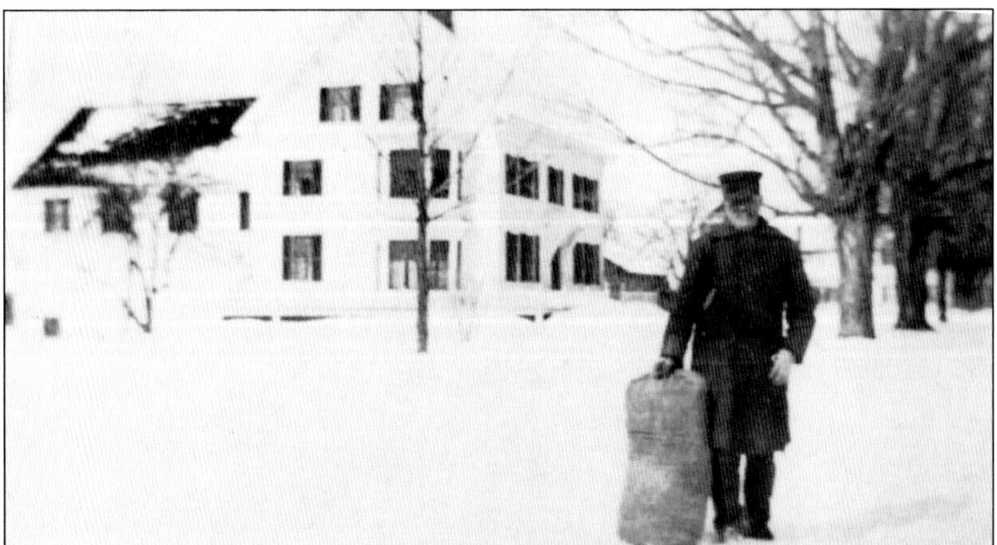

An unknown man standing in front of the Mason House, Bar Mills, *c.* 1920s. Co-owner Alice Mason didn't want the man in the picture, but he exercised his right to stay put. This was once Colonel Berry's Tavern.

Four

Farms

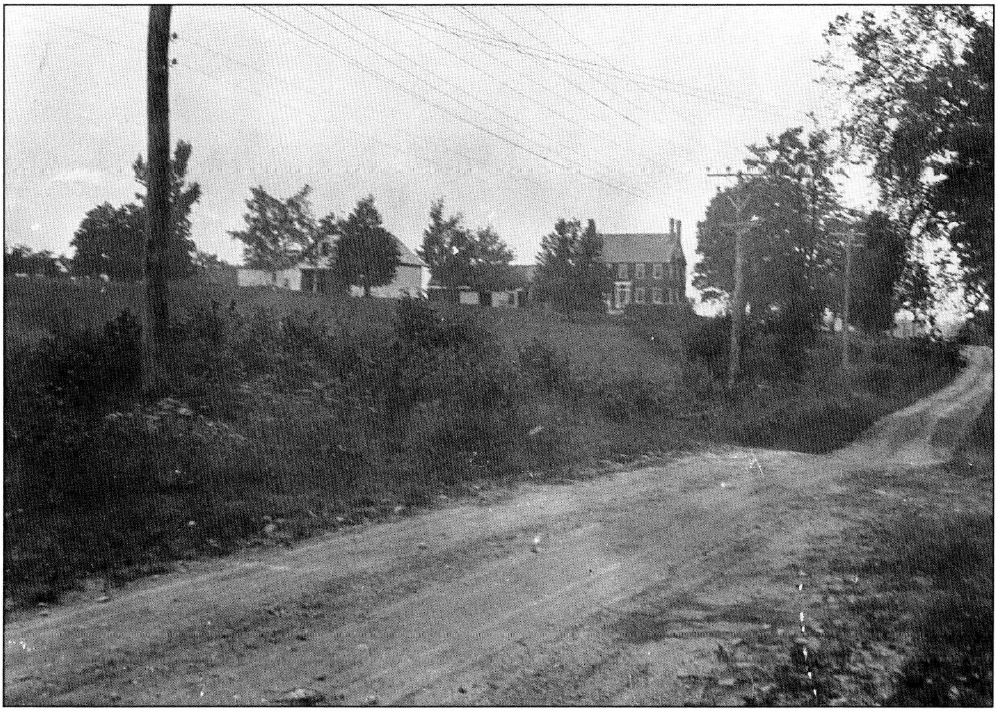

William Soule's farm in Buxton, August 29, 1930.

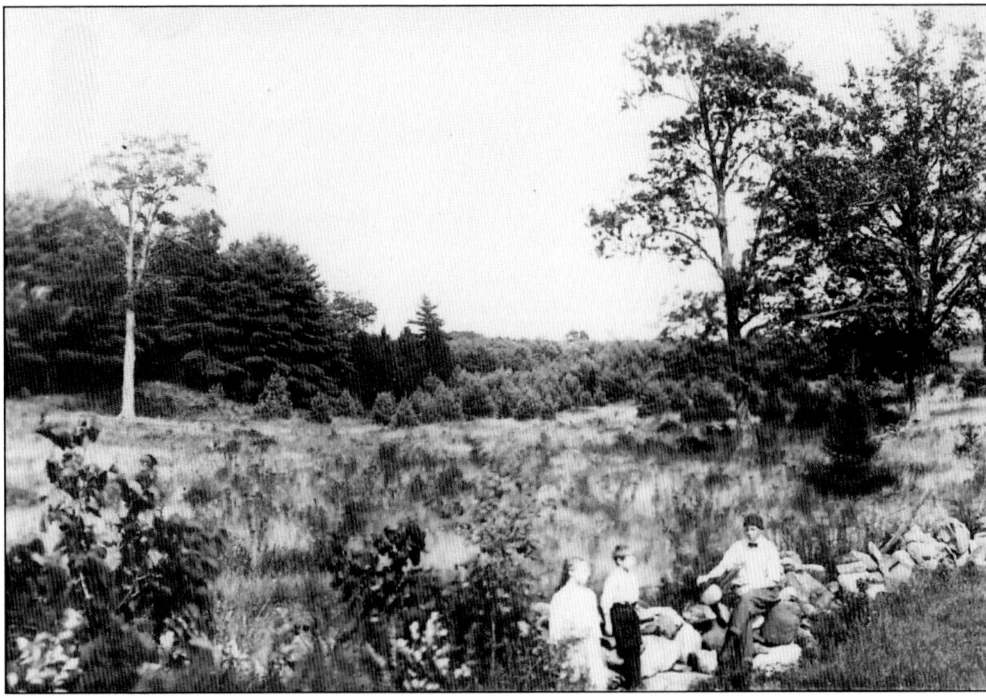

The "Little Pines" at Maplecroft Farm, Buxton, with old sugar maples in front, August 28, 1912. Muriel and Harman Harmon with Leonard, who was visiting them, are in the scene.

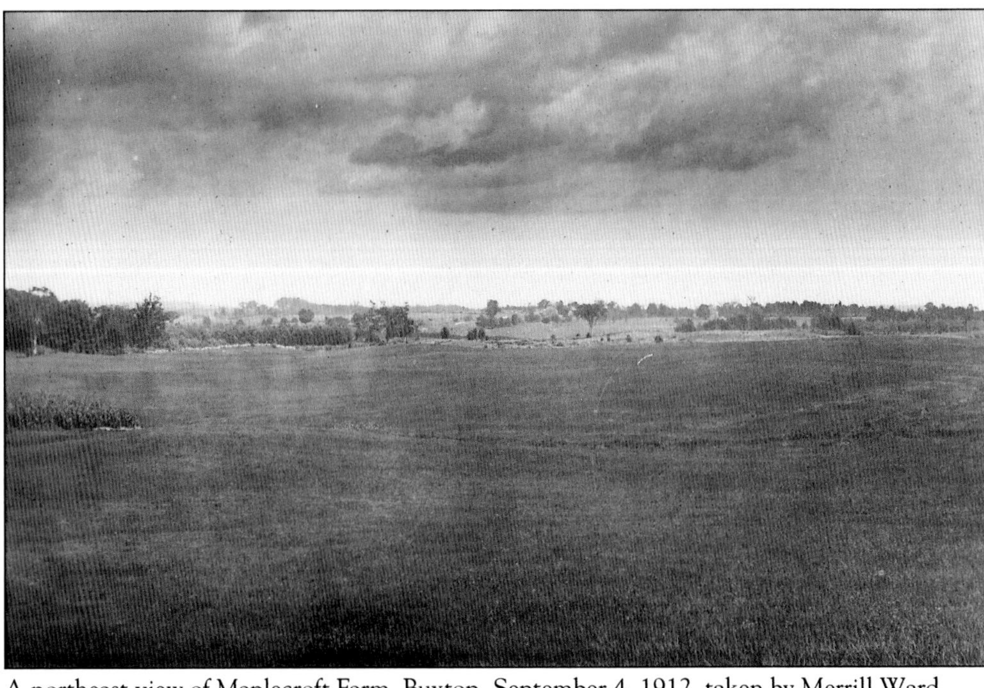

A northeast view of Maplecroft Farm, Buxton, September 4, 1912, taken by Merrill Ward.

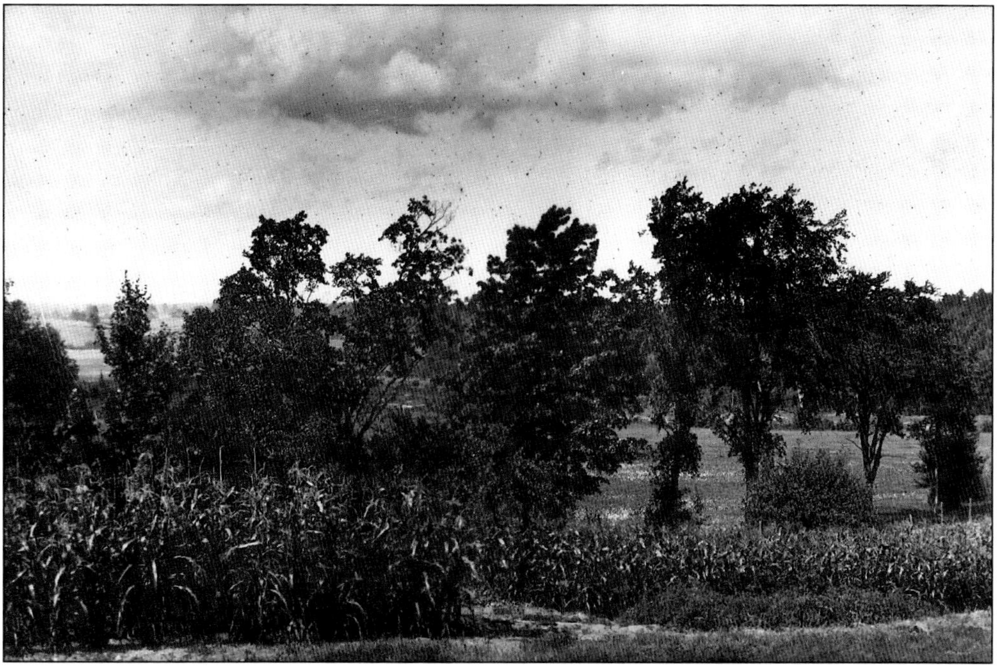

A northwest view of John H. Harmon's Maplecroft Farm, September 4, 1912, about noon. This photograph, taken two years before Harmon's death, captured the view from the hill next to the road (opposite the William Soule house) at the west corner of Maplecroft Farm. It's one of four views from the same spot taken in different directions.

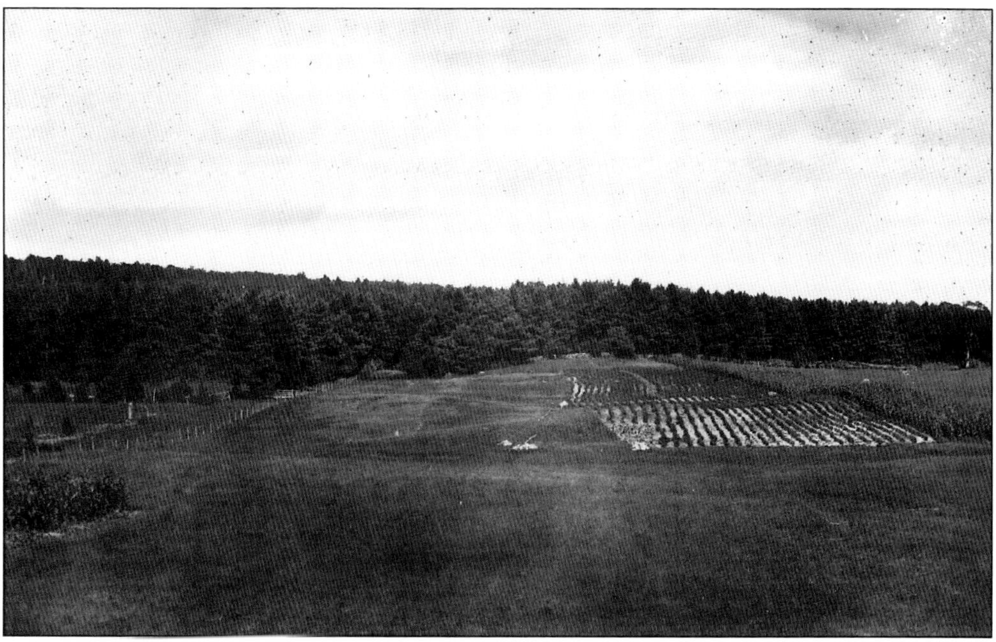

A northern view of Maplecroft Farm showing a meadow, a field potatoes and corn, and pine woods. The atmosphere had been hazy all summer, unfavorable to taking pictures with the available camera. This day, September 4, 1912, was better than most.

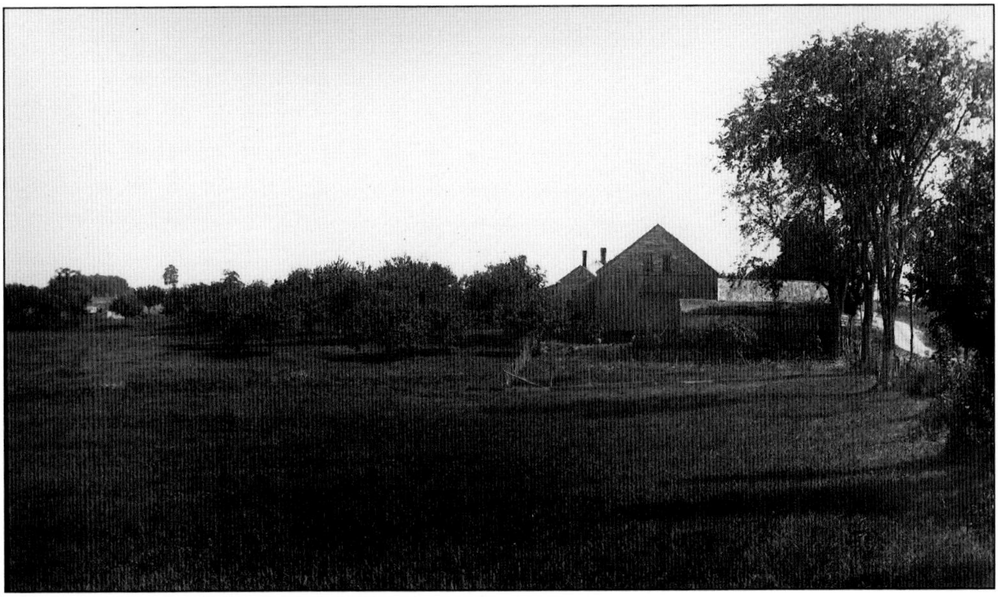

An eastern view of the orchard and farm at Maplecroft Farm.

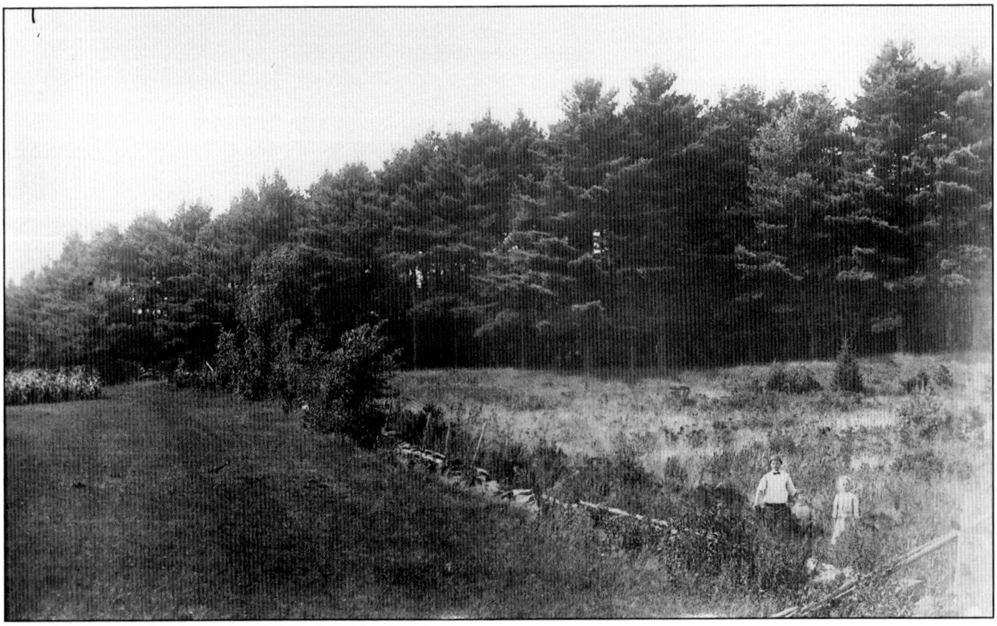

A northwest view of the pine woods in the pasture at Maplecroft Farm, August 28, 1912. These woods were greatly loved and admired by their owner, John Harmon, his children, and his grandchildren. Muriel and Harman are in this scene, as is Leonard, a divinity student who preached at South Buxton in the summer of 1912.

An old corn crib with sloping sides in Hollis, August 1932. This was in the Deerwander neighborhood.

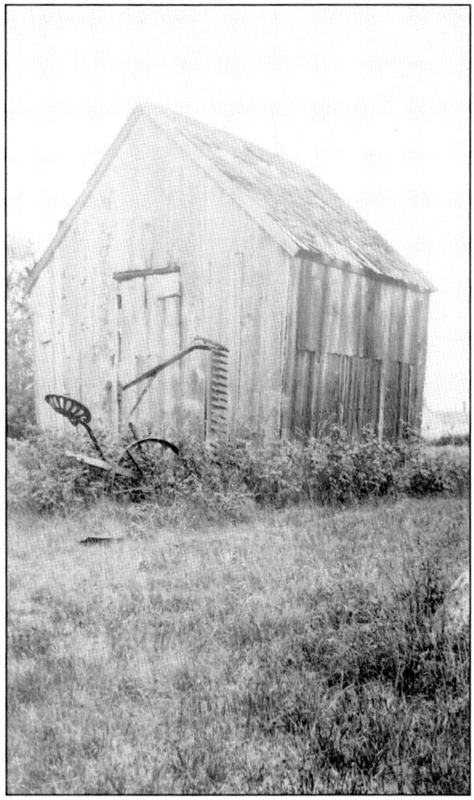

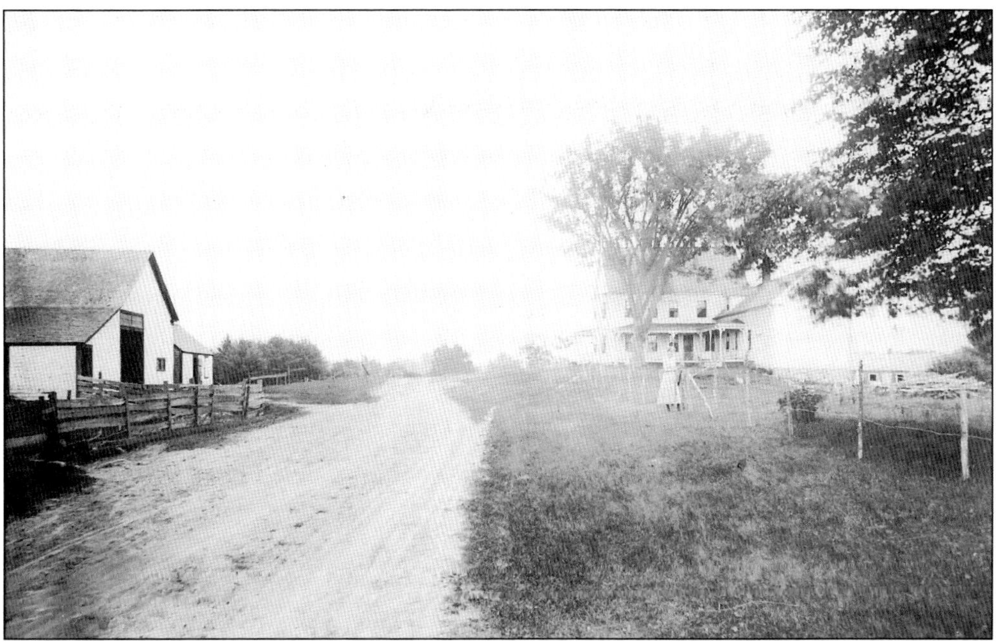

The Tyler Farm at Tyler's Corner on Route 35, Hollis, *c.* 1945.

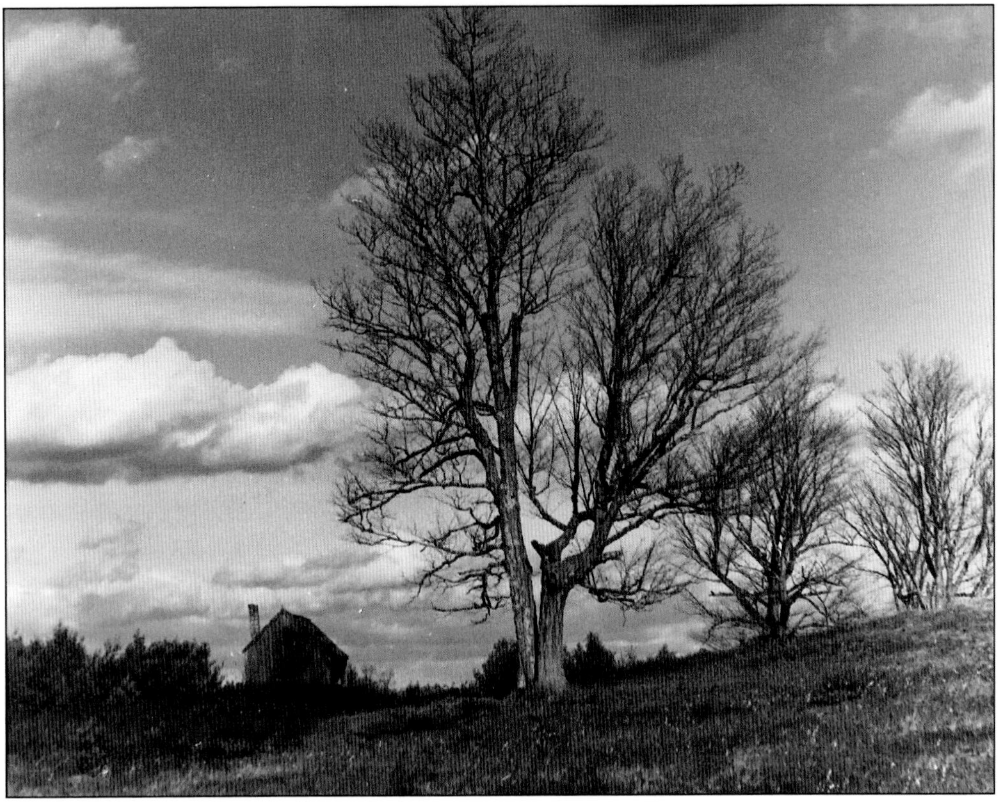

An old sap house at Bear Hill, *c.* 1945.

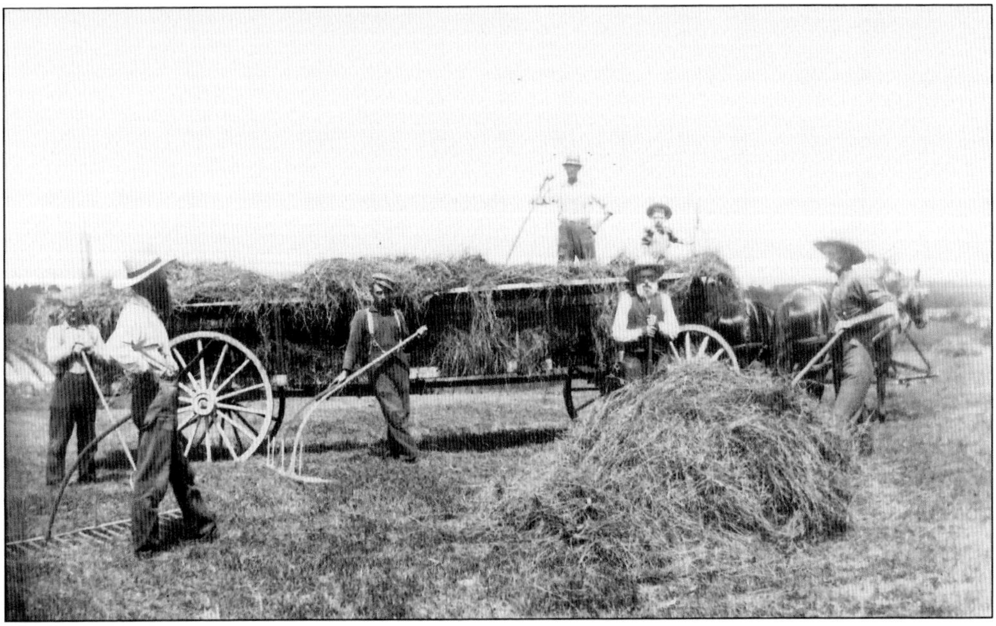

A hayfield scene at the Moulton Farm in the early 1900s. From left to right are an unidentified man, Orin Hanson, Will Hanson, William Moulton, Frank Moulton, Ray Moulton, and Cecil Berry (on the load).

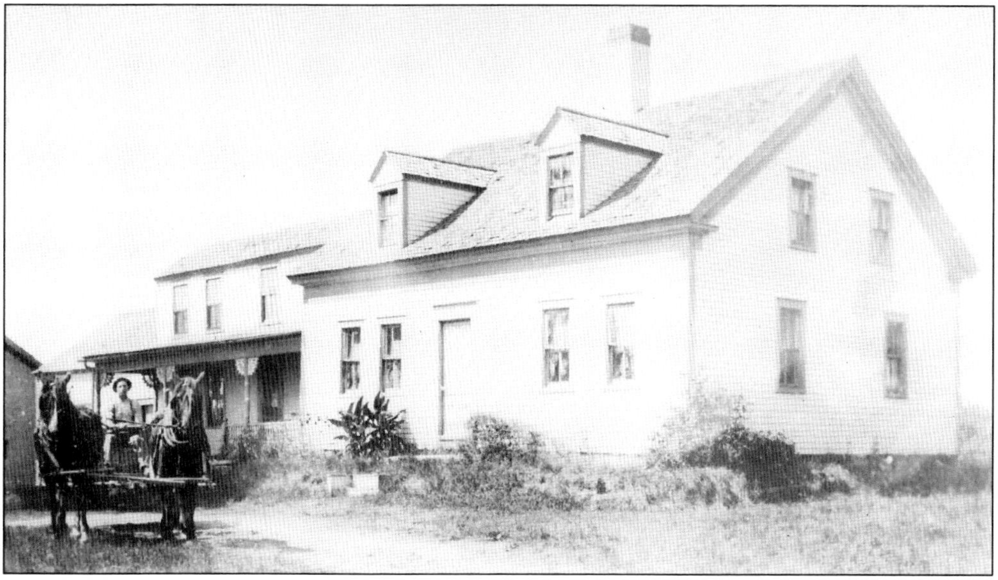

Roy Moulton, William Swett Moulton's son, at his father's farm on The Cape Road, *c*.1910s.

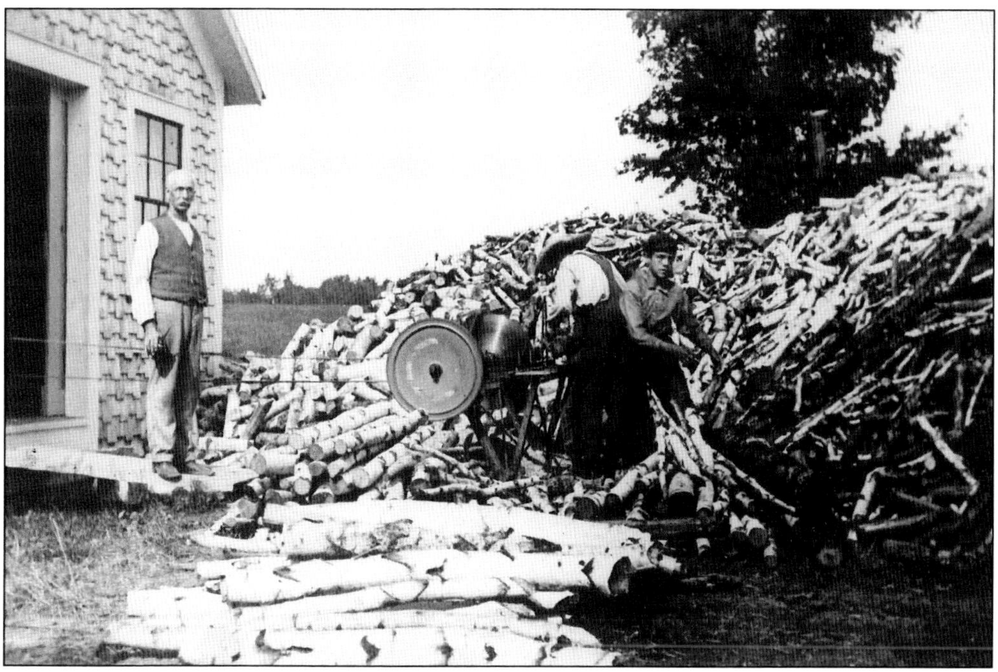

Sumner Haley, Henry Kimball, and Alvah Kimball sawing wood at Haley's farm. This photograph was taken by Flora Palmer, Haley's housekeeper, in the 1900s.

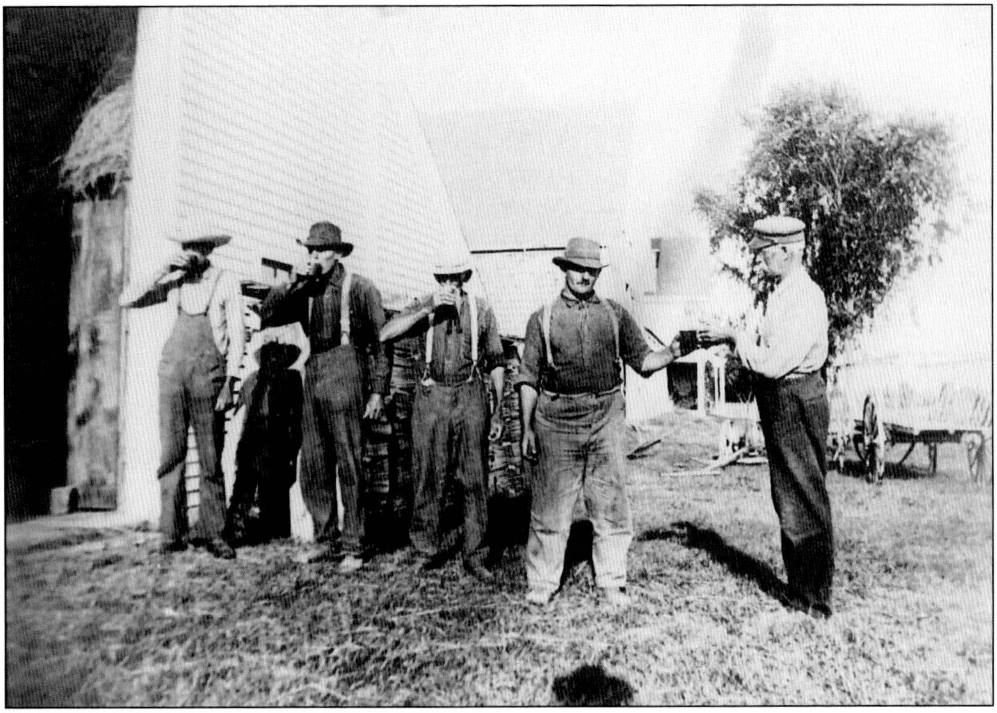

Getting a drink while haying at Sumner Haley's farm. From left to right are Henry Kimball, Ike Woodman, Asa Palmer (the husband of Haley's housekeeper), John Woodman, and Haley in the early 1900s.

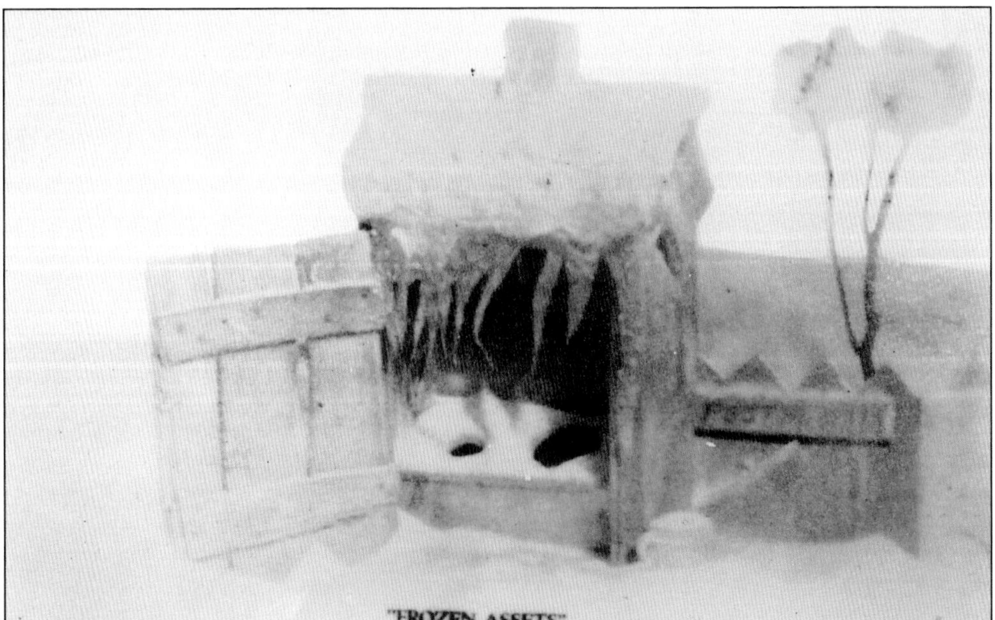

How's things on the farm? These are frozen assets on a two-hole backhouse. It was real cool, c. almost any winter until quite recently.

Five

Oxen

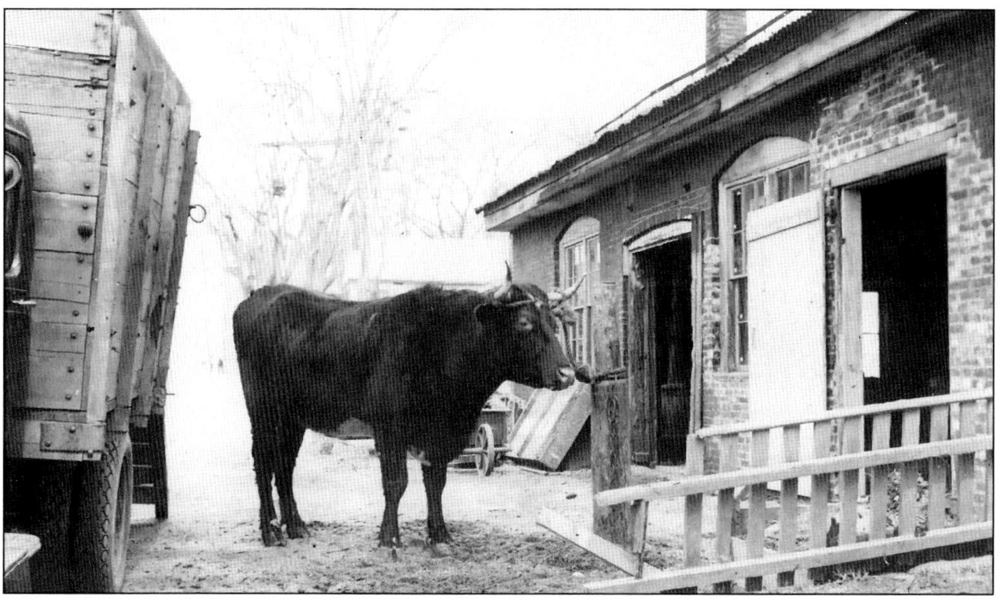

An ox standing between the truck that brought it in and the one-hundred-year-old blacksmith shop in West Buxton where it was to be shod, *c.* 1930s. His name was Zine and his mate was Star, and both were at the Sands blacksmith shop. At the time the photograph was taken Star was being shod in the two-hundred-year-old ox sling inside the shop. The sling was in constant use until the Sands smithy (located north of the present West Buxton Public Library) closed.

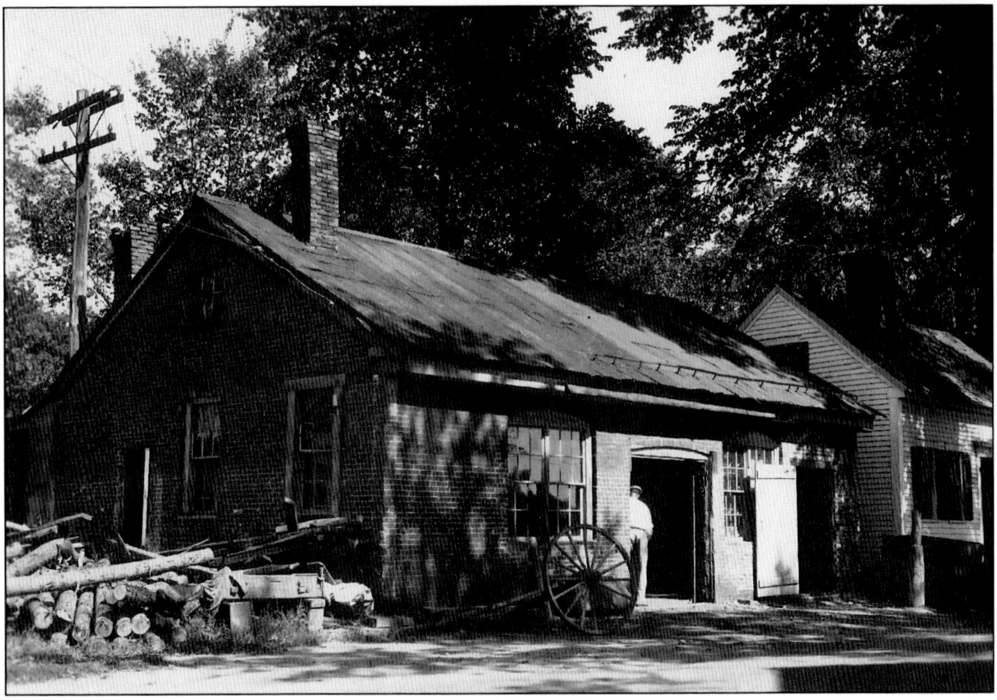

The Joseph F. Sands blacksmith shop in West Buxton on the Saco River. Note that it's under trees. "Under the spreading chestnut tree, the village smithy stands," Longfellow wrote.

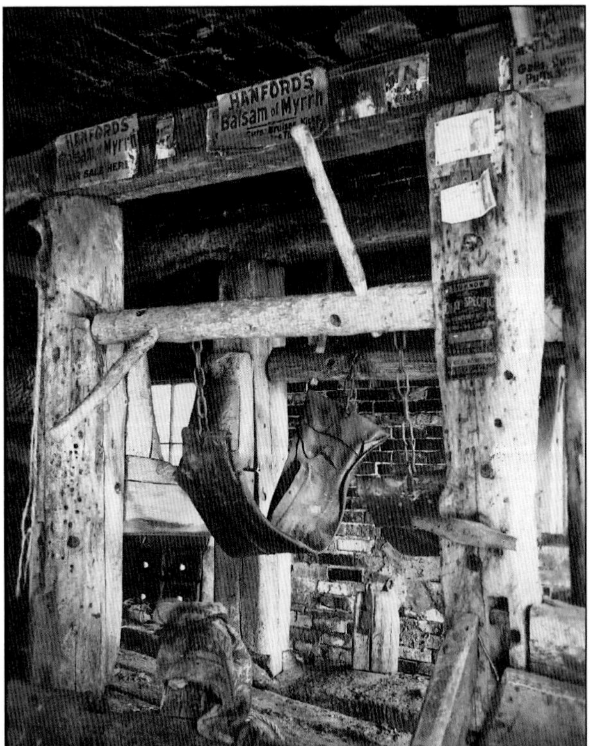

The two-hundred-year-old ox sling in Joseph Sands' blacksmith shop around 1939.

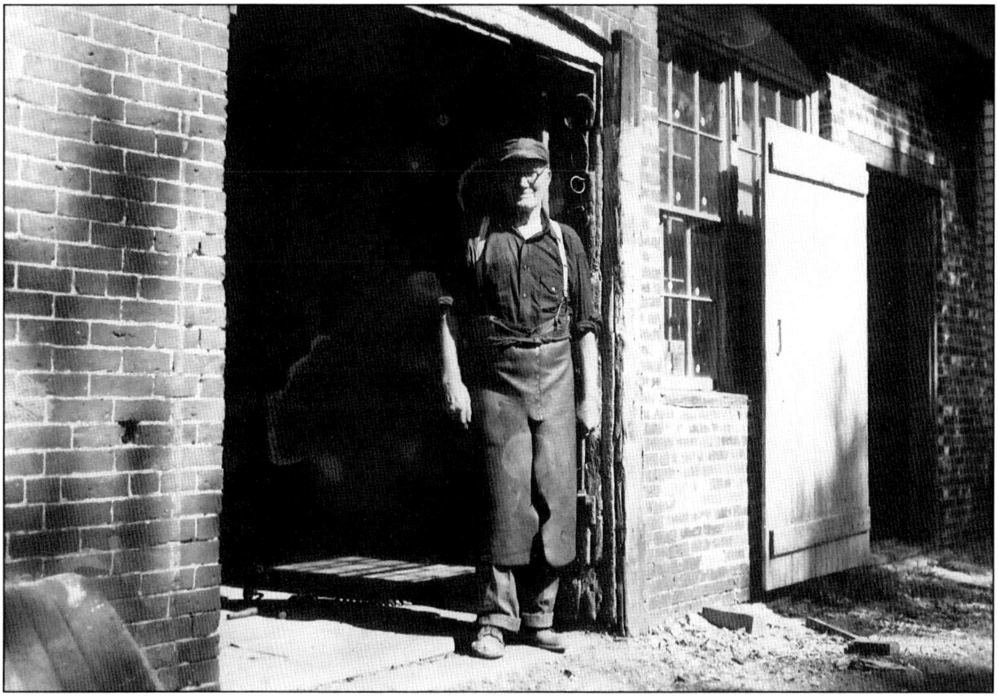

Joseph F. Sands, who blacksmithed more than fifty years in West Buxton. He's wearing his leather apron in this 1939 photograph.

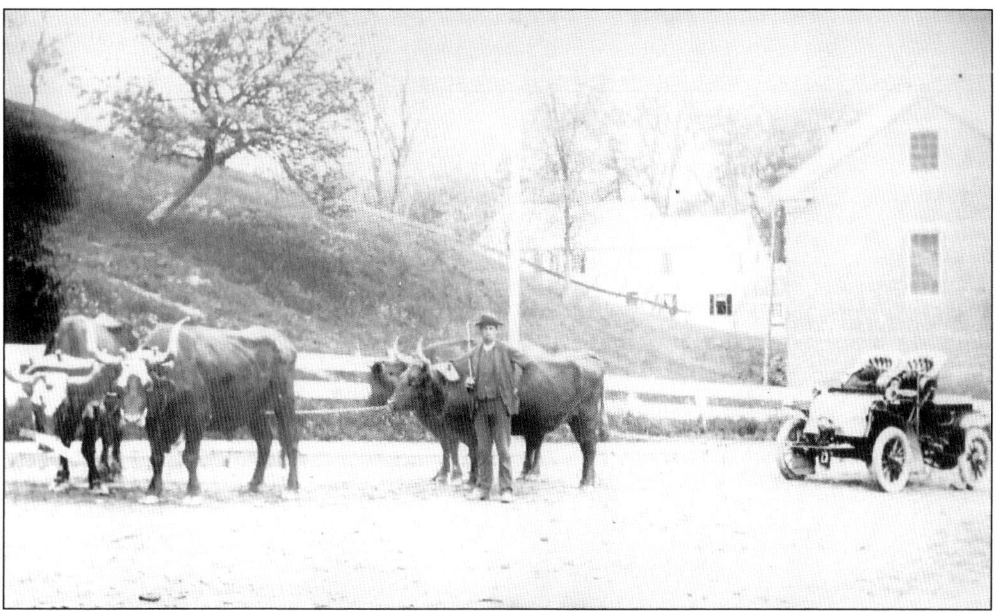

Getting an ox tow for an automobile up Powerhouse Hill in Buxton, *c.* 1920s.

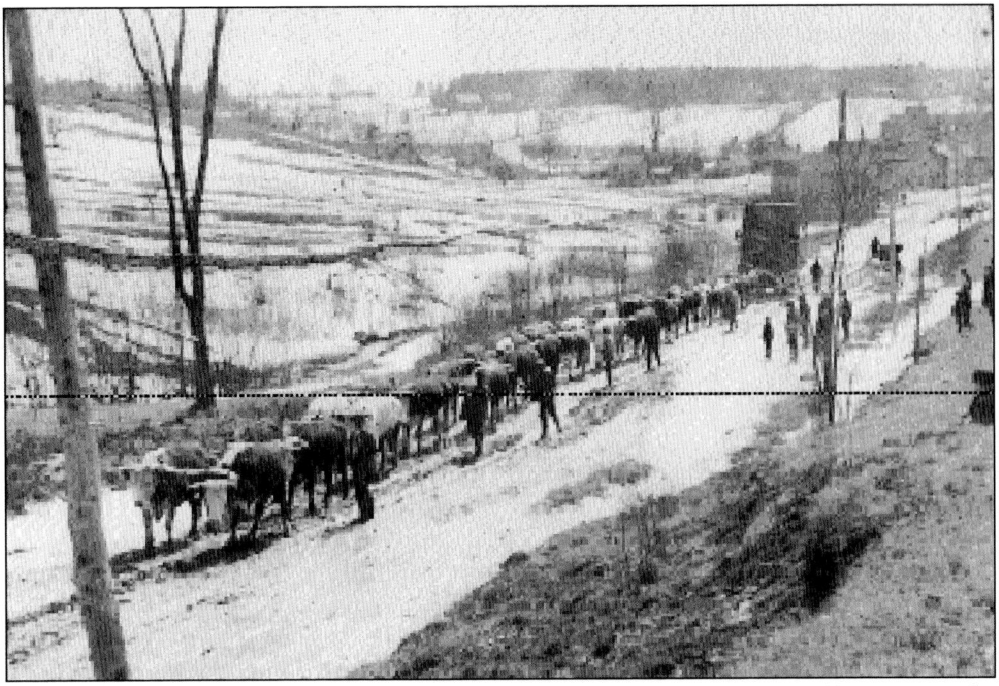

A view from Christian Row in West Buxton, looking toward West Buxton Village, 1912. The old woolen mill in West Buxton, which burned in 1940, can be seen to the upper right in the photograph.

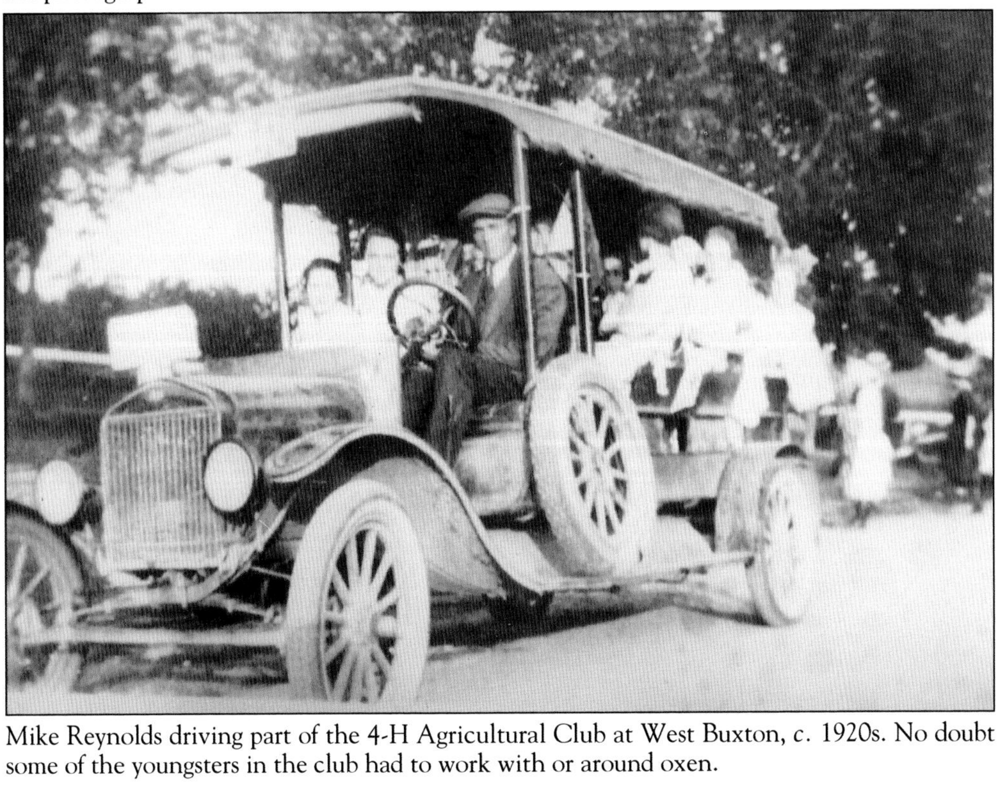

Mike Reynolds driving part of the 4-H Agricultural Club at West Buxton, *c.* 1920s. No doubt some of the youngsters in the club had to work with or around oxen.

Six

Leisure Time and Recreation

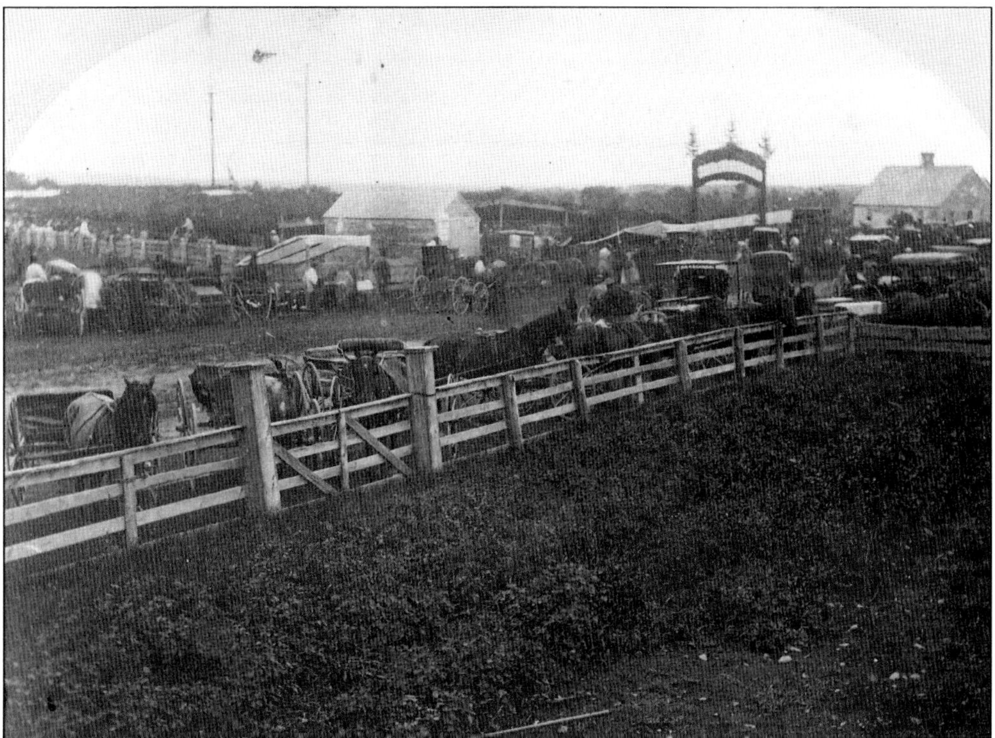

Buggies and horses along the rail at the Buxton Centennial Celebration, August 14, 1872. About 8,500 people attended from all over the country. Invitations were sent to all those (who could be found) who had ever lived in Buxton.

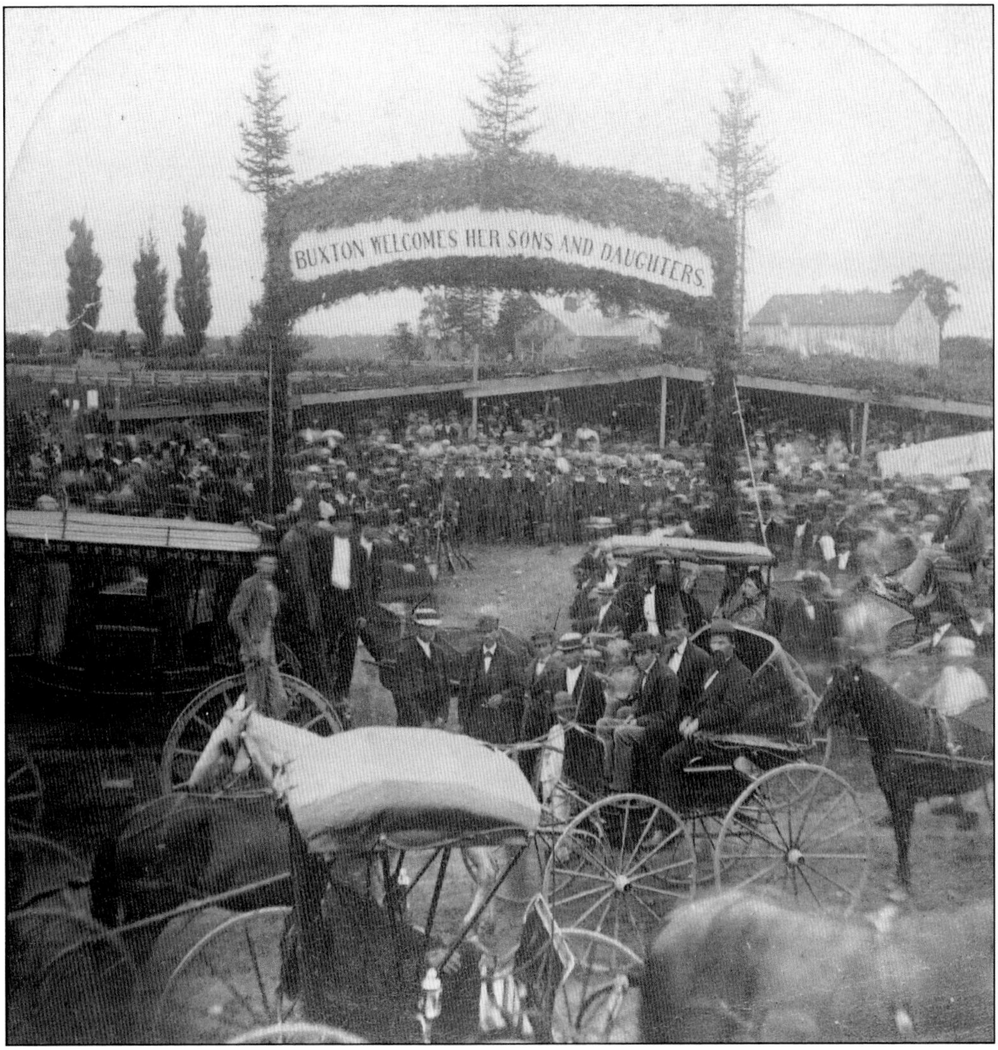

A front view of the 100-by-220-foot "Coliseum" at the Buxton Centennial Celebration. Speeches from the event were collected in a book and published. It was a tremendous success. It was apparent that many of those who had left Buxton were eager to return there, if only for a day or so. Many of those giving speeches were people who had moved away. The desire to travel and resettle elsewhere was strong at this time, and it didn't slow until the turn of the century.

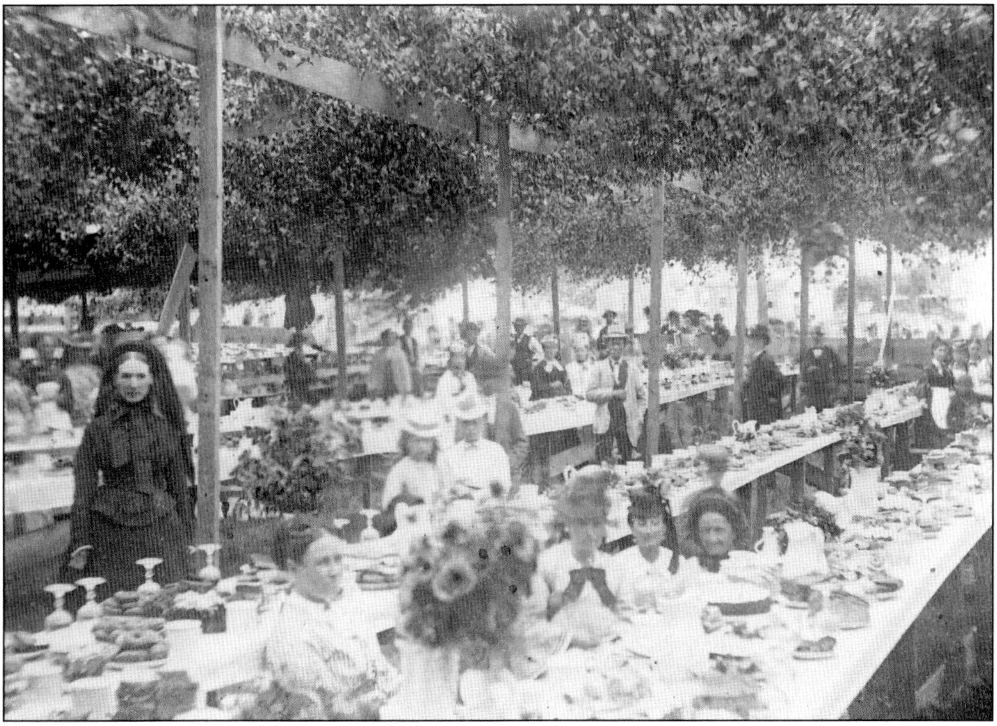

The tables before dinner at the Buxton Centennial Celebration, August 14, 1872. Each table was 1,200 feet long.

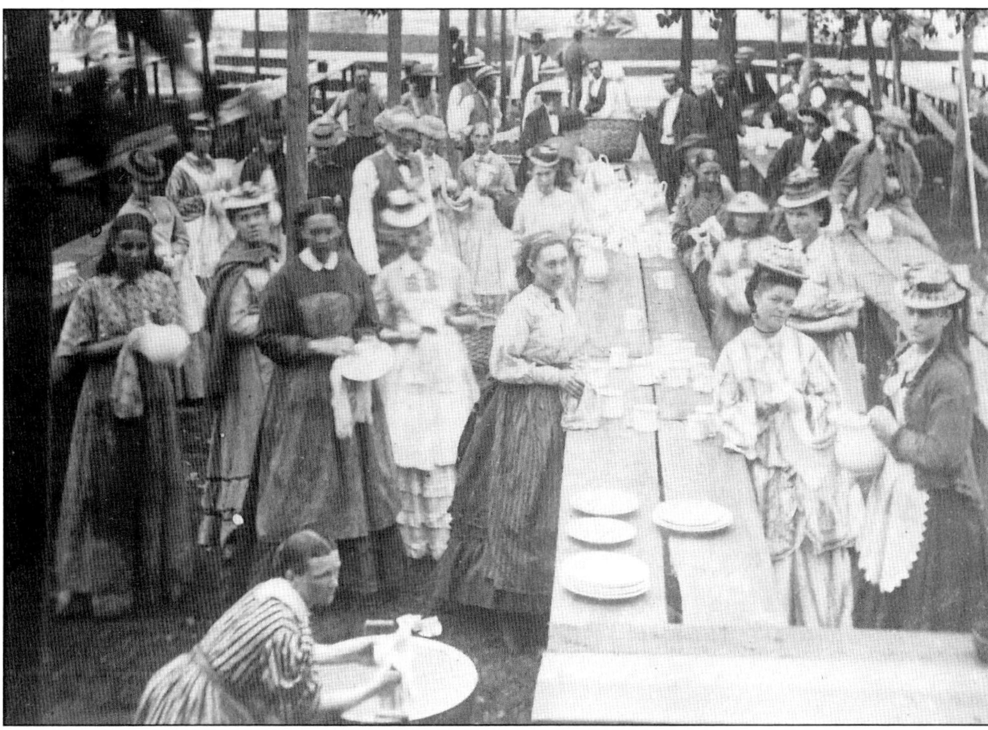

Clearing the tables with the Committee of Arrangements ladies at work.

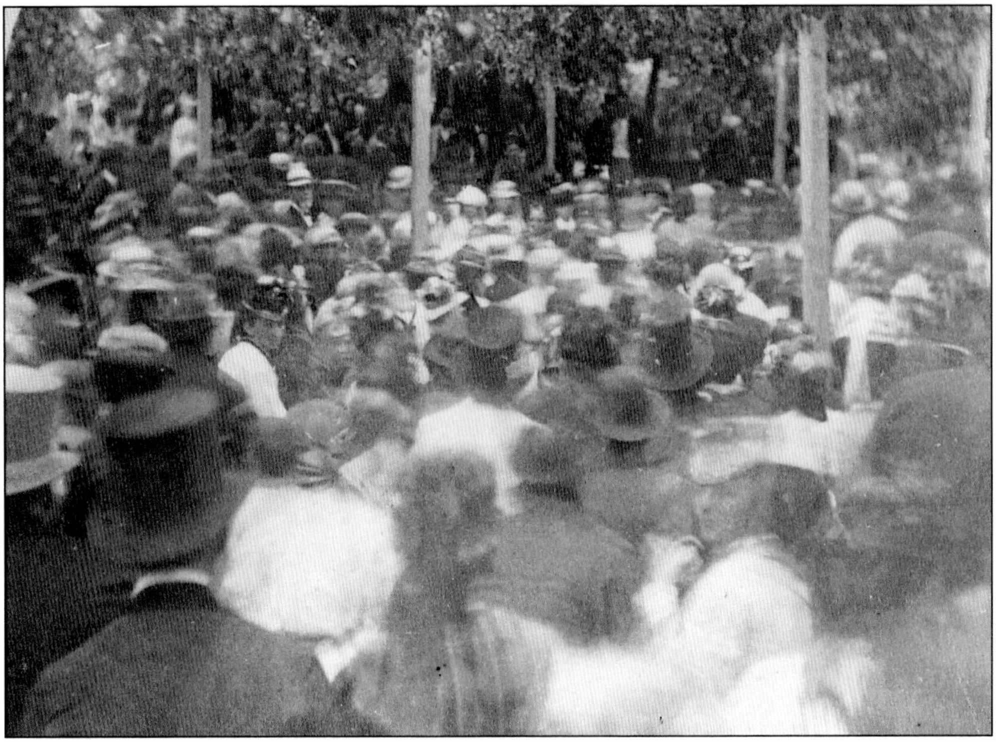

Images of the crowds at the Buxton Centennial Celebration.

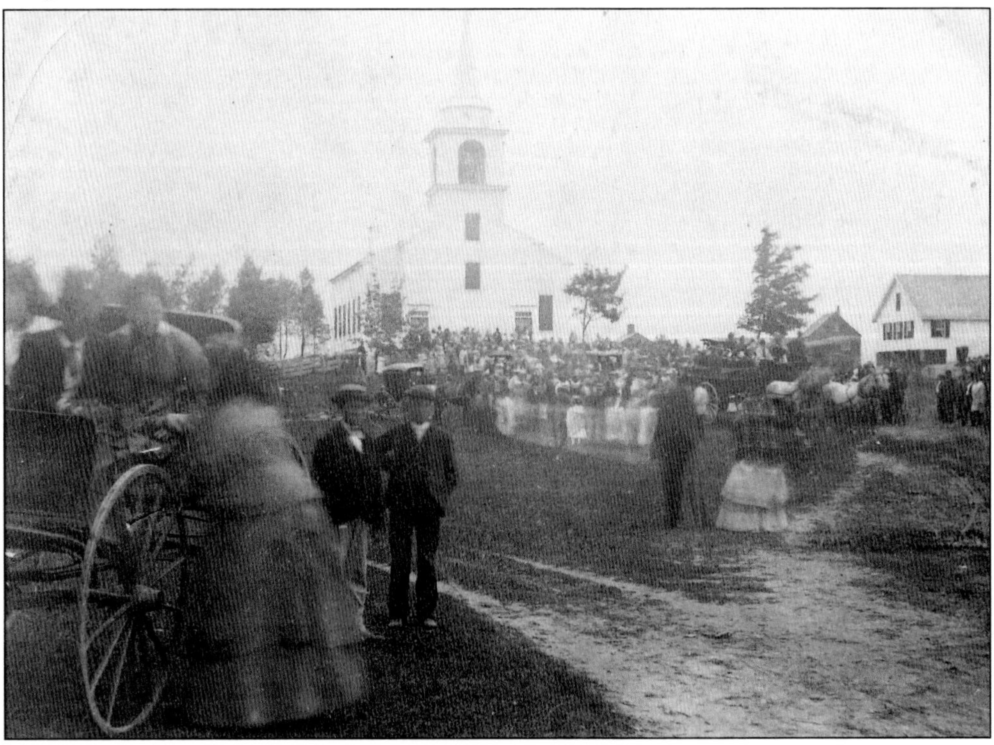

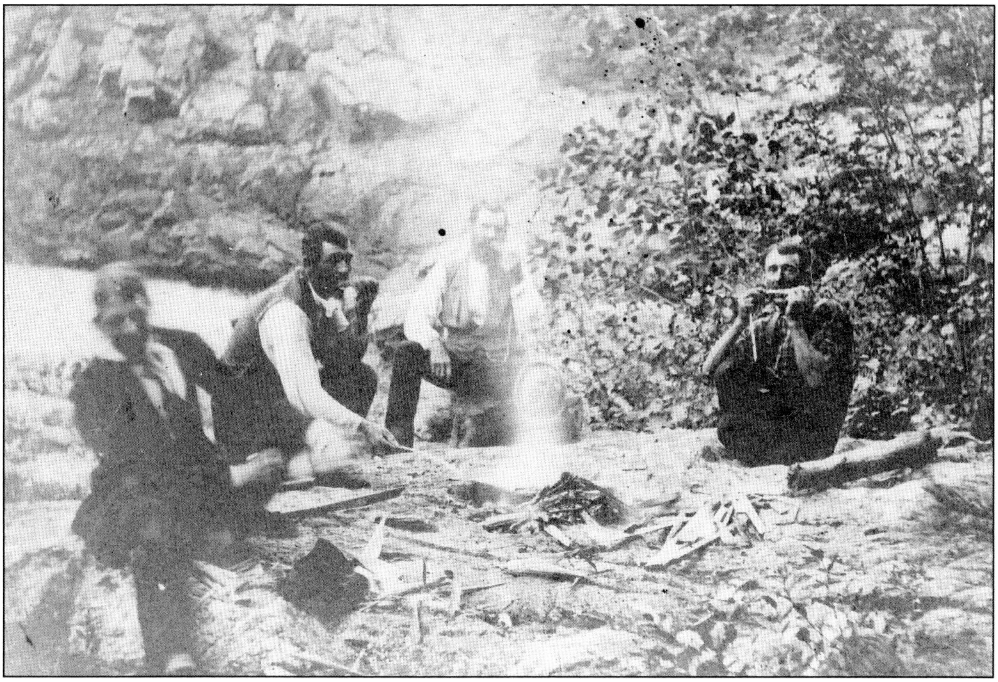

A scene on the Saco River in Buxton and Hollis with four men cooking a meal, *c.* 1870s.

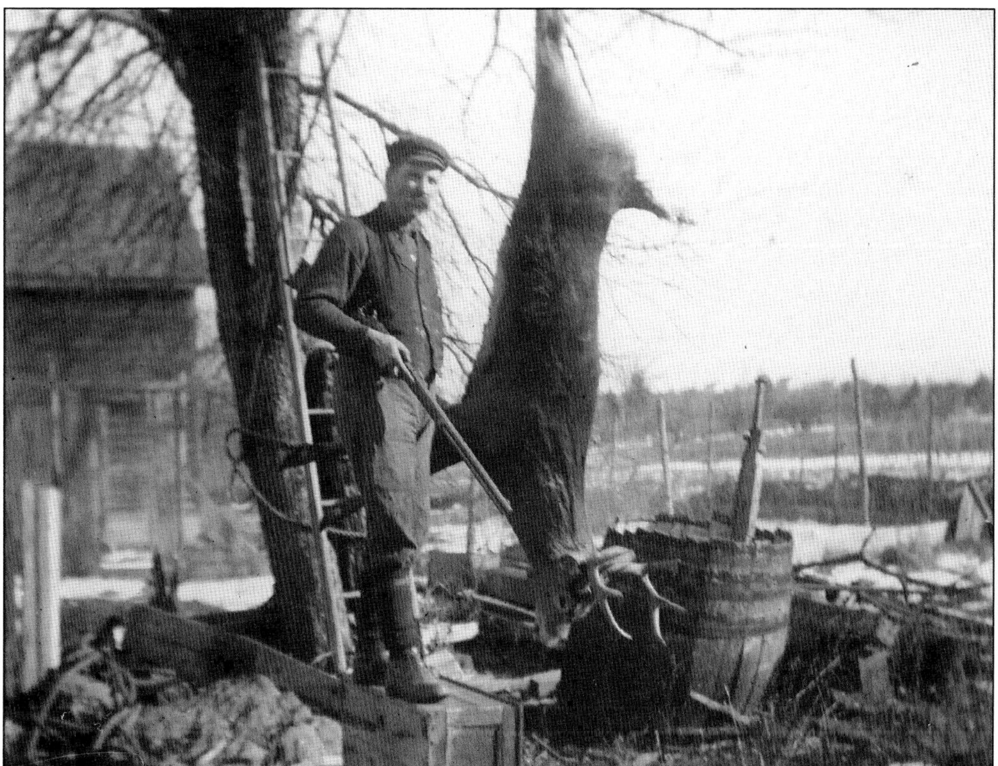

Jack Smith with a good buck in the early 1900s.

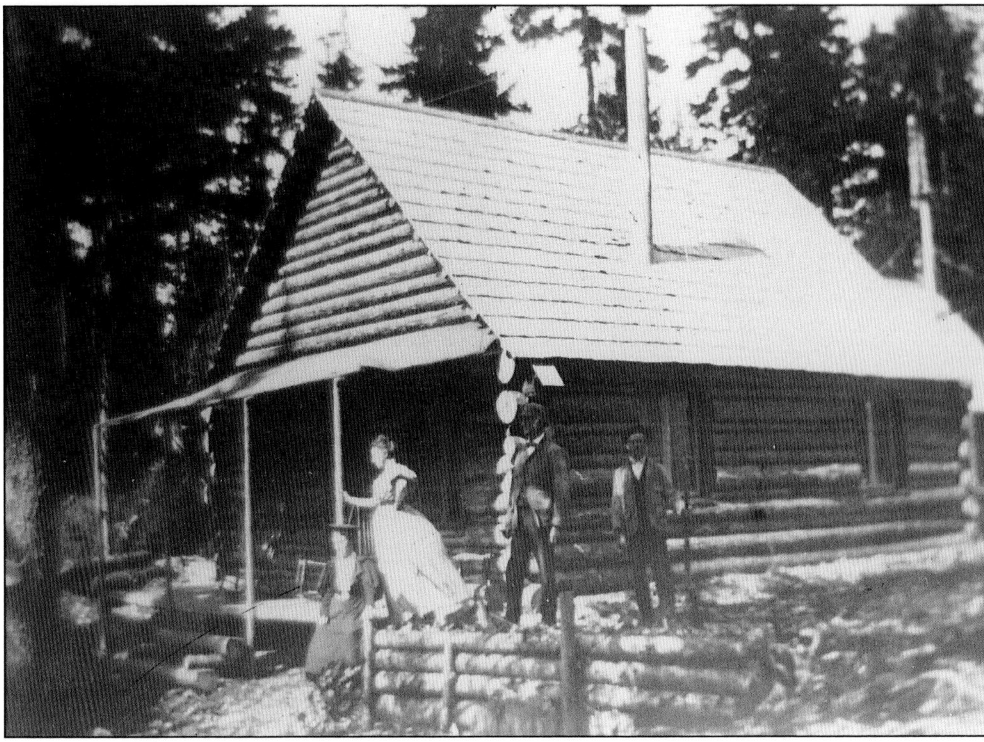

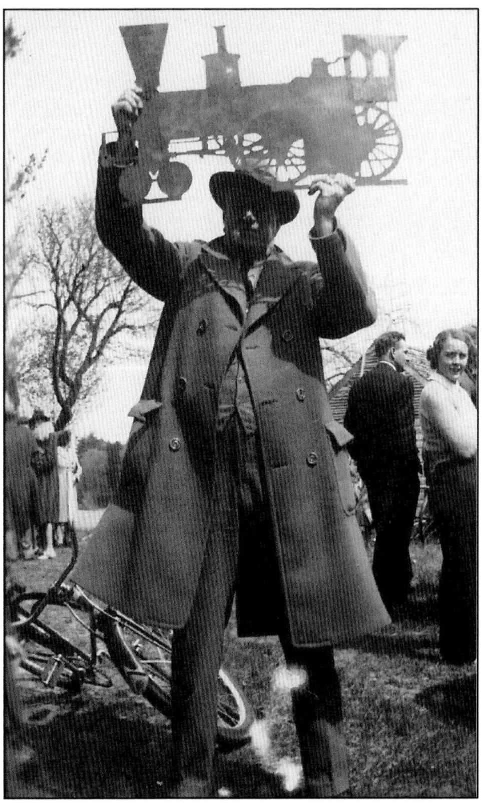

Charles Perry's camp, *c.* 1890s. With the rivers and lakes close at hand, few area residents needed to build camps, but some did exist.

A wood-burning locomotive weather vane (*c.* 1850) bought by Herman E. Roberts at Dunnell's auction, May 9, 1942.

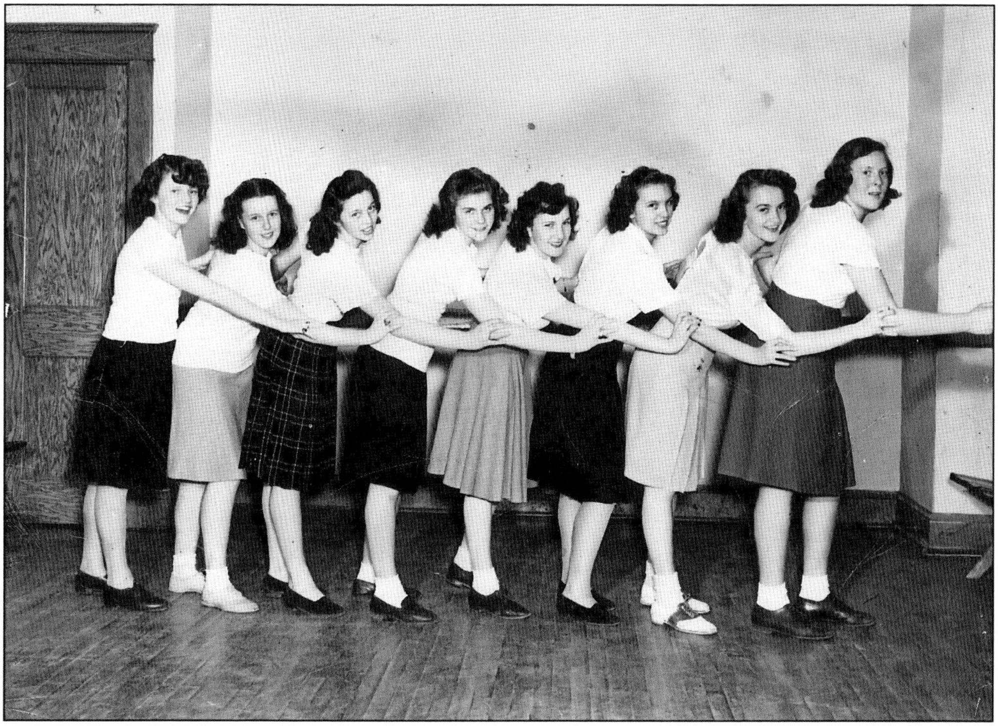

Cheerleaders at Buxton High School, 1946–47.

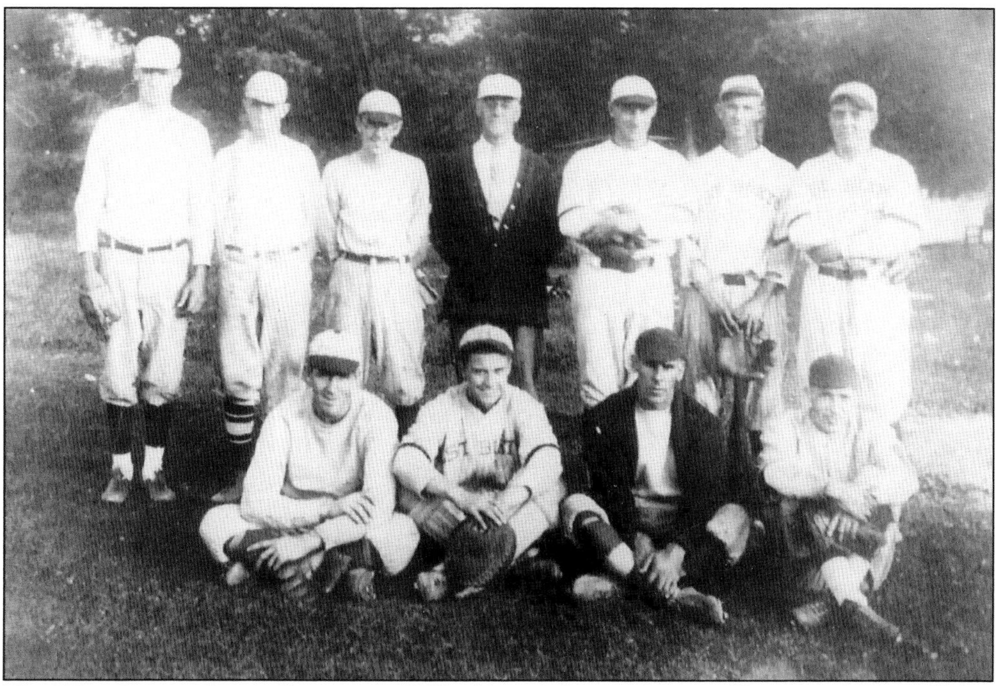

The West Buxton baseball team, c. 1920s. From left to right are: (front row) Elmer Kelso, Joseph Warren, unknown, and Calvin Day; (back row) Roy Smith, Cecil Waterman, Arthur McNerny, Whittaker, Gordon Graffam, Fred Davis, and possibly an Ingalls.

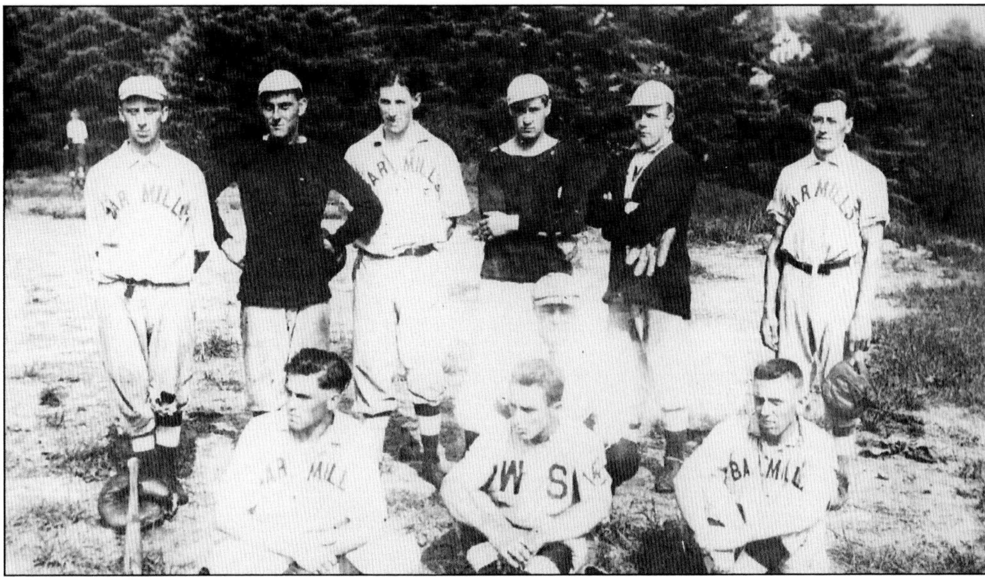

A Bar Mills baseball team, *c.* 1920s. From left to right are: (front row) Urban Hackett, Laurence Sawyer, and Bill Whittaker; (back row) Perley McLellan, Chet Dennett, Gordon Graffam, Ralph Leavitt, Arthur Whittaker, and Arthur McNerny. Bill Whittaker, the manager, is in the soft hat.

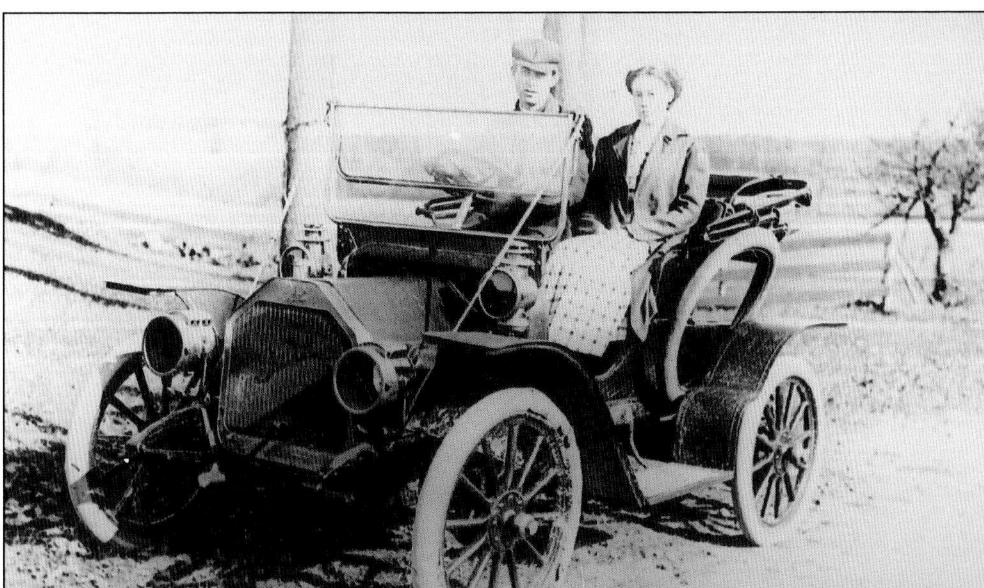

Fanny Libby Waterhouse with her brother (?), *c.* 1920s.

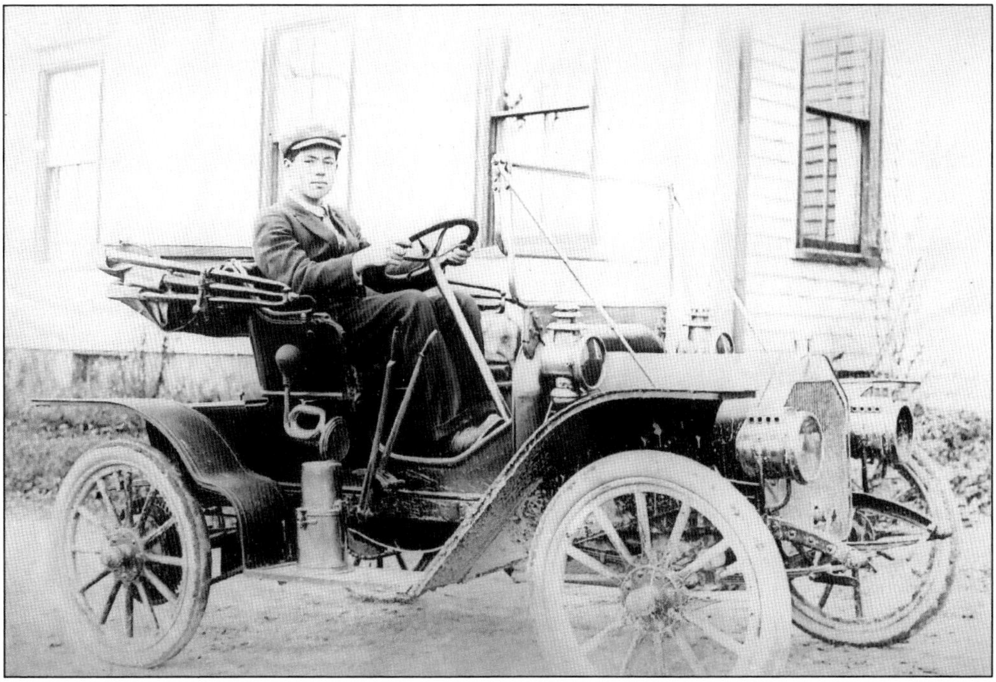

Cecil Berry in Walter Ingraham's car. Ingraham was a photographer and boarded with Harry and Louise Bradbury, *c.* 1920s.

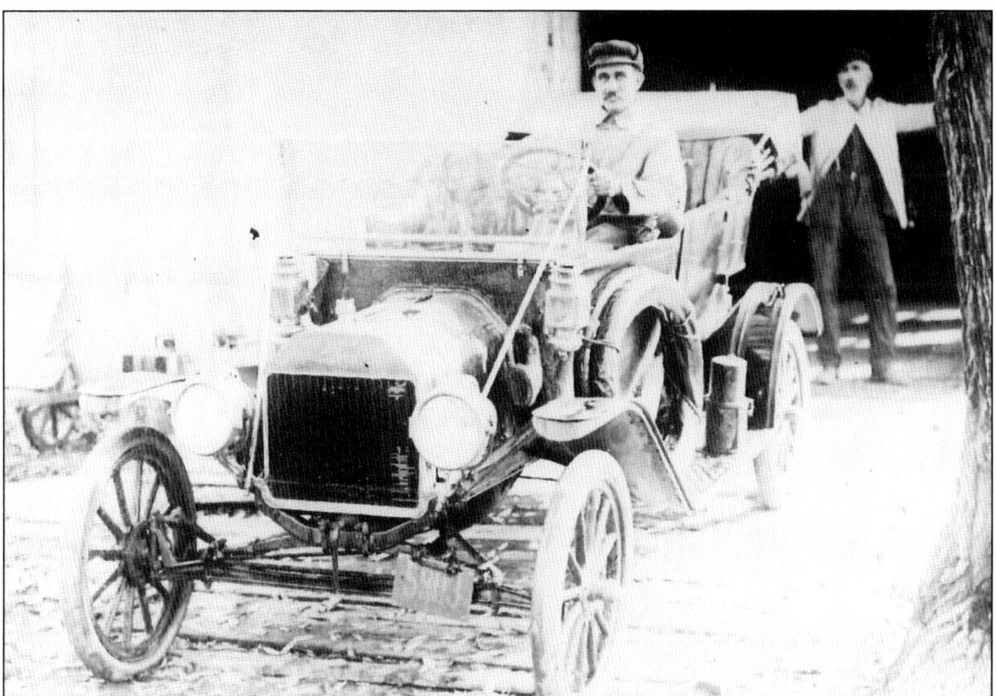

Walter Edgerly in a Ford with Maine license plate 5903, sometime between 1915 and 1925.

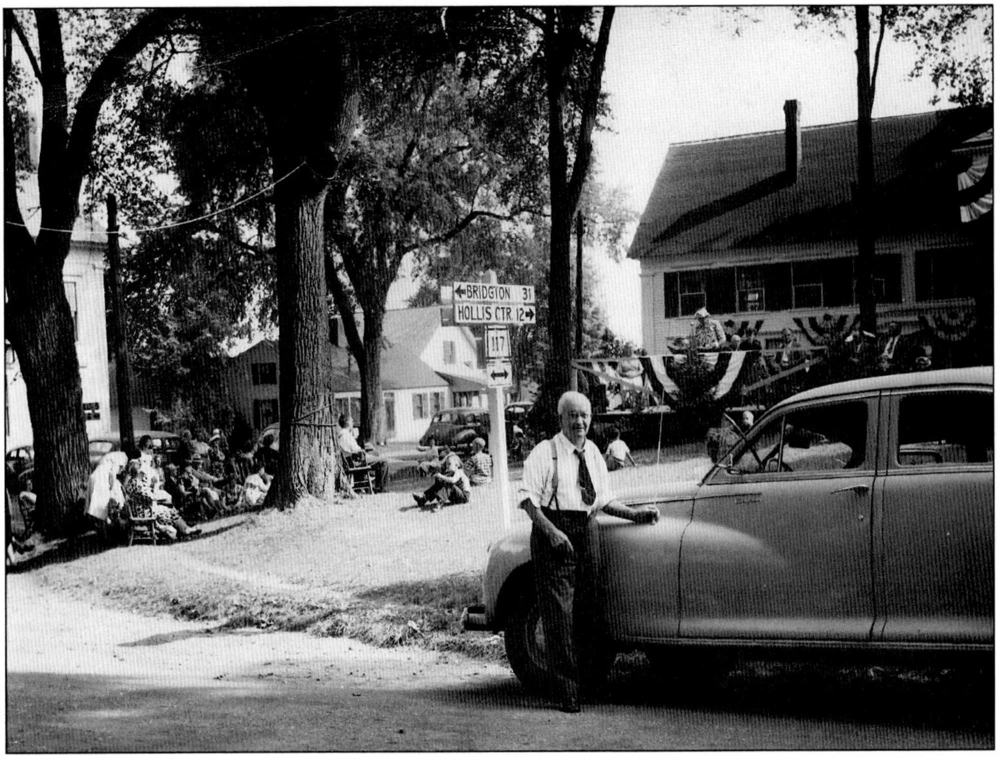

Ed Peter Chick standing by his Packard during Limington's 1948 Sesquicentennial Celebration. Note the Route 117 sign, with Bridgton 31 miles in one direction and Hollis Center 12 miles in the other.

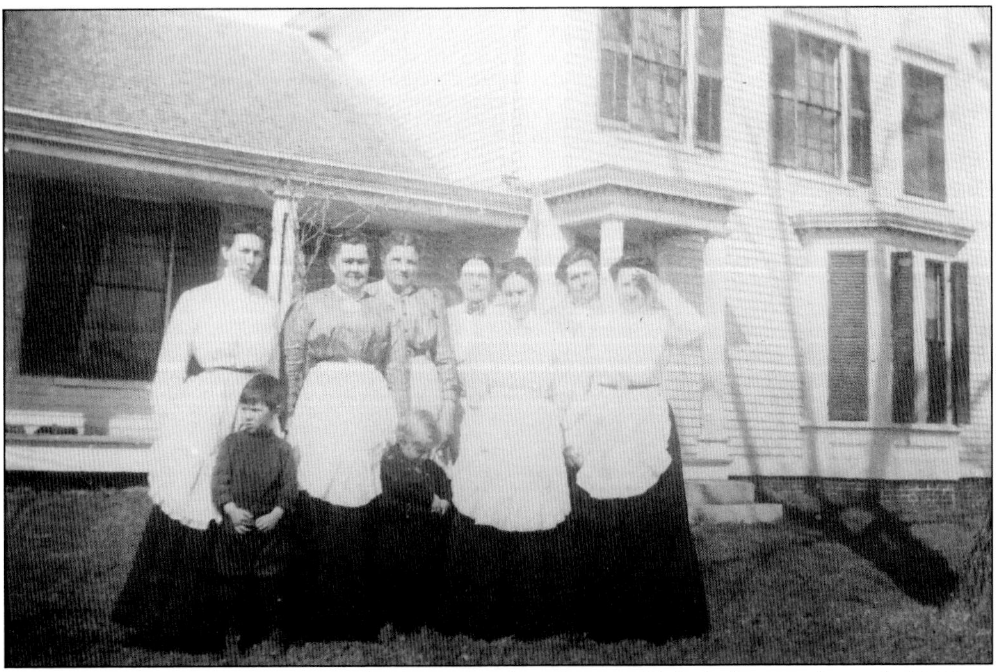

The King's Daughters Sewing Circle, River Road, at Sumner Haley's farm in the early 1900s.

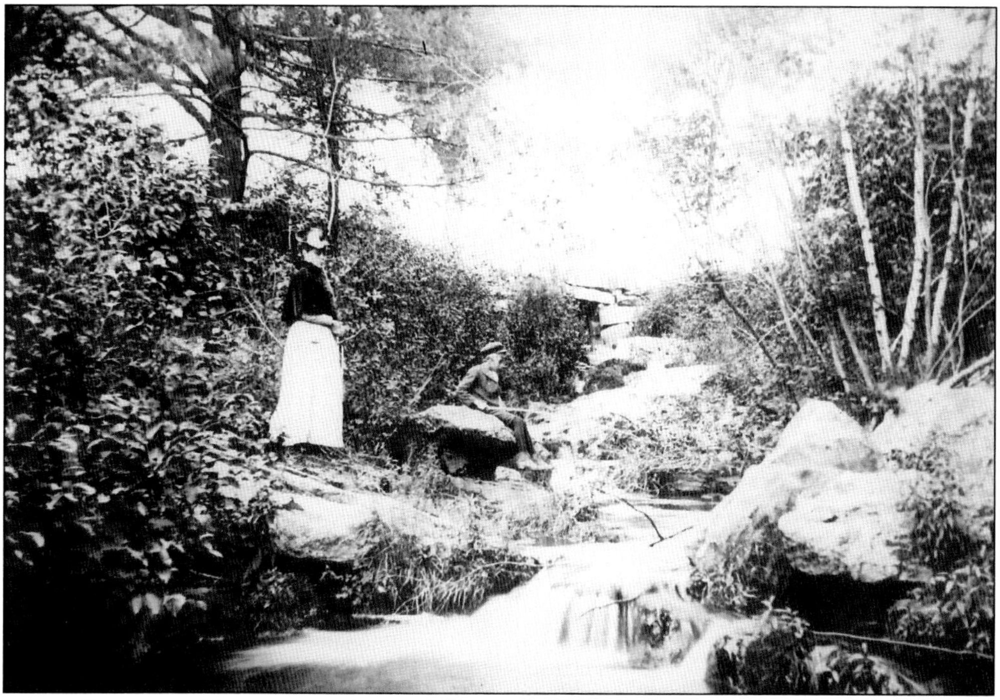

Albert Hanson and his mother, Anne, fishing at Palmer Falls, Haley Brook, around 1896. His father was Eben Hanson.

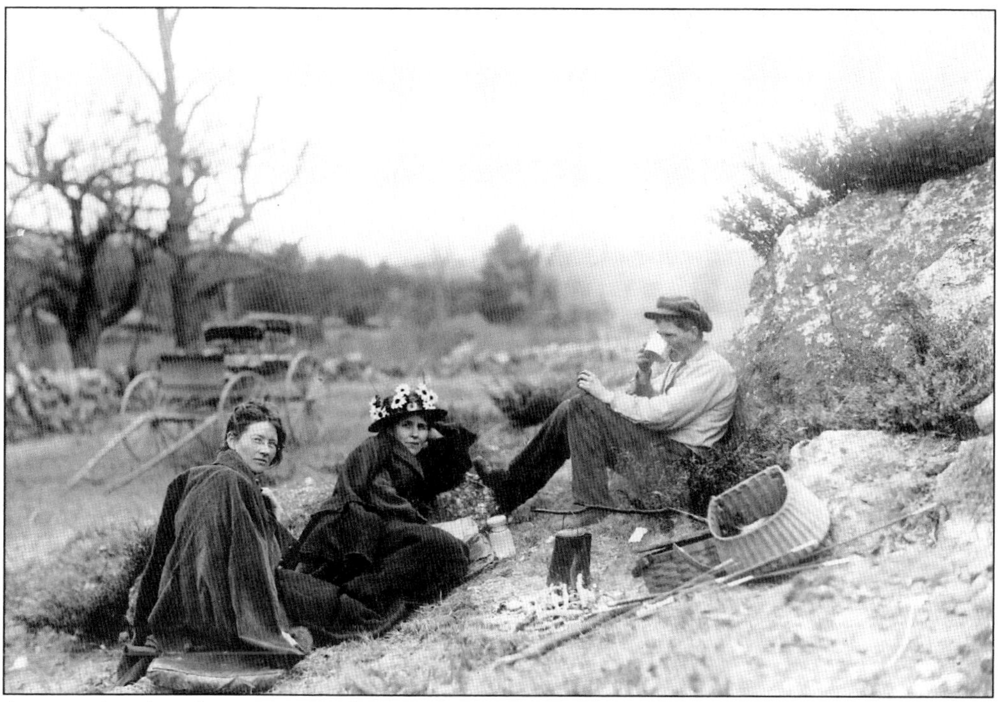

A picnic lunch in Limington in the 1900s.

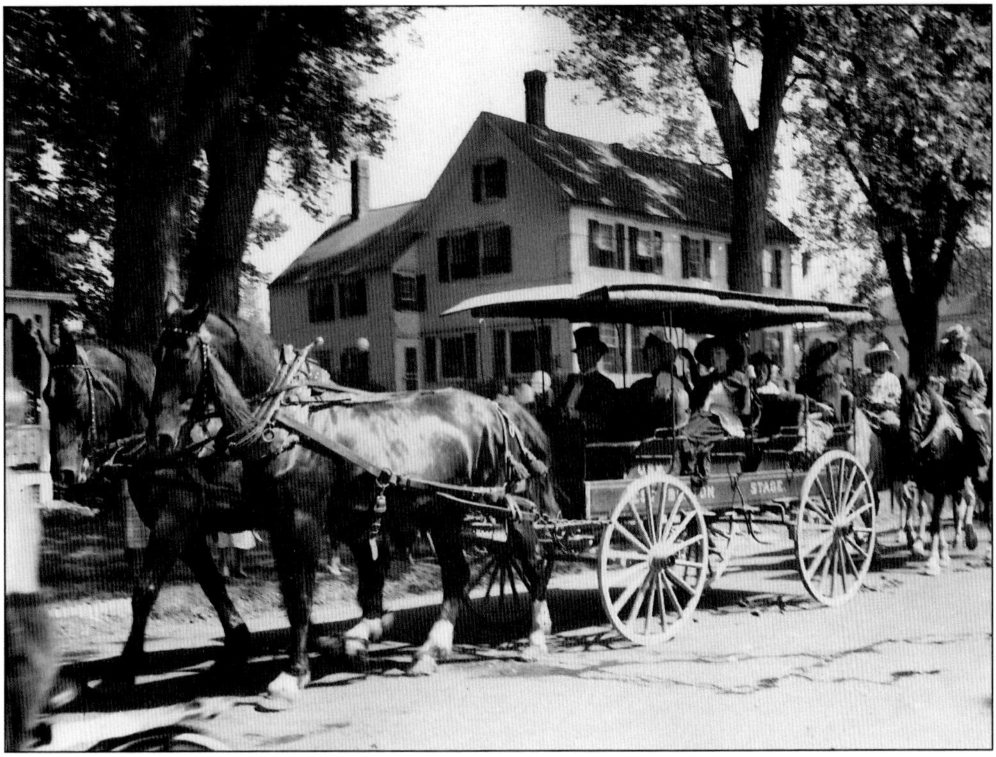

The West Buxton Stage display at the 1948 Limington Sesquicentennial Parade. Millard Gammon is the driver with Marion Chick (bonnet on her head) next to him. Ella Clark has the big hat while in the rear are Frances Pulsifer (left) and Eleanor Lear. On the horses are Verne Blake and Violet Hoyt.

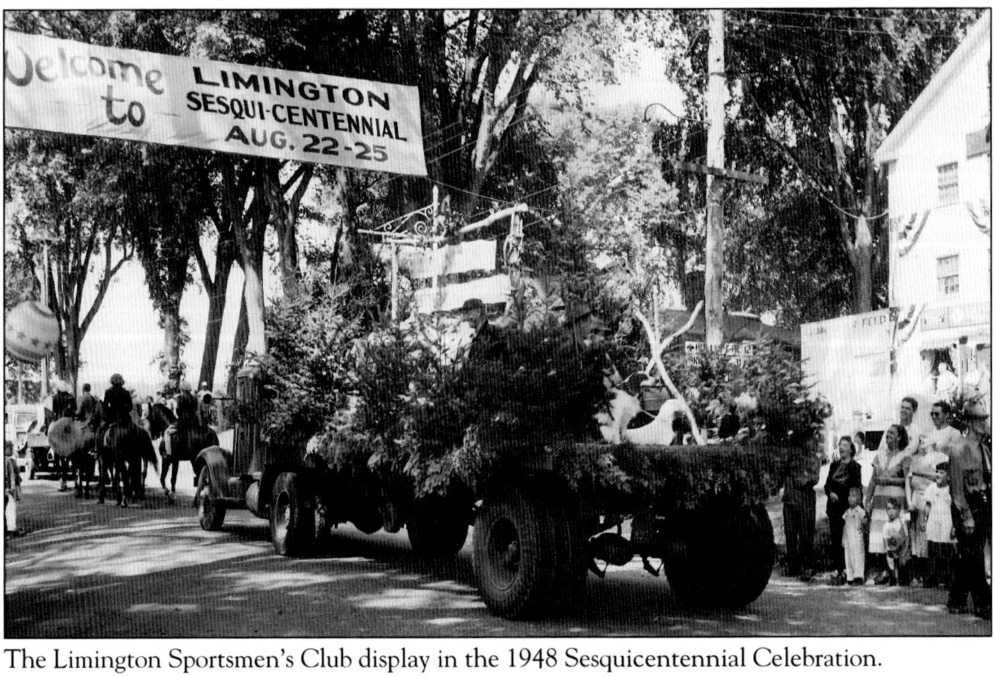

The Limington Sportsmen's Club display in the 1948 Sesquicentennial Celebration.

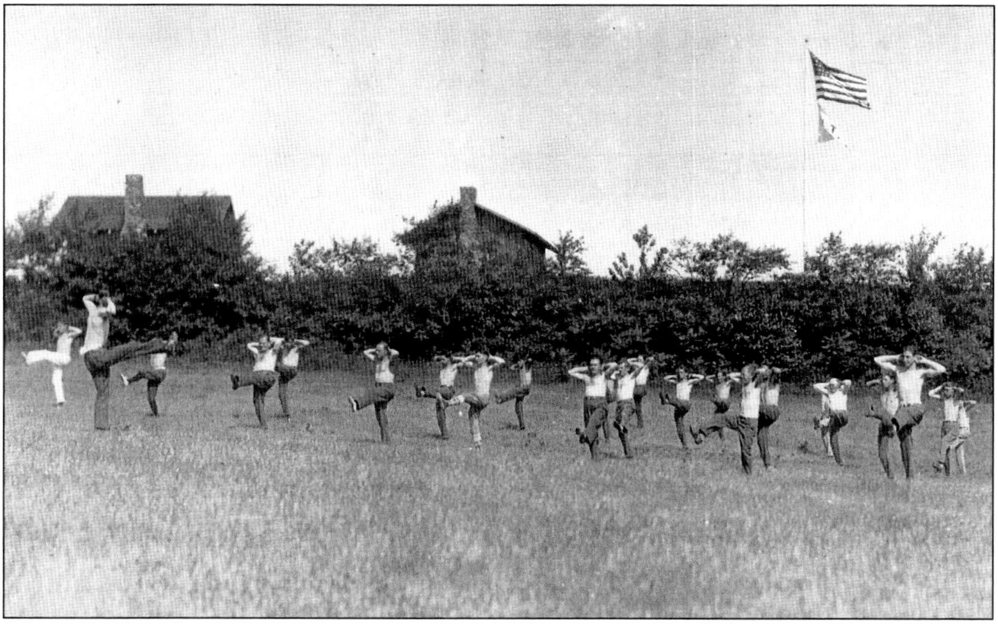

Businessmen exercising at the Vacation Training Camp in the 1920s or 1930s in Limington. This spot is now a religious retreat. Was this an early aerobics workout?

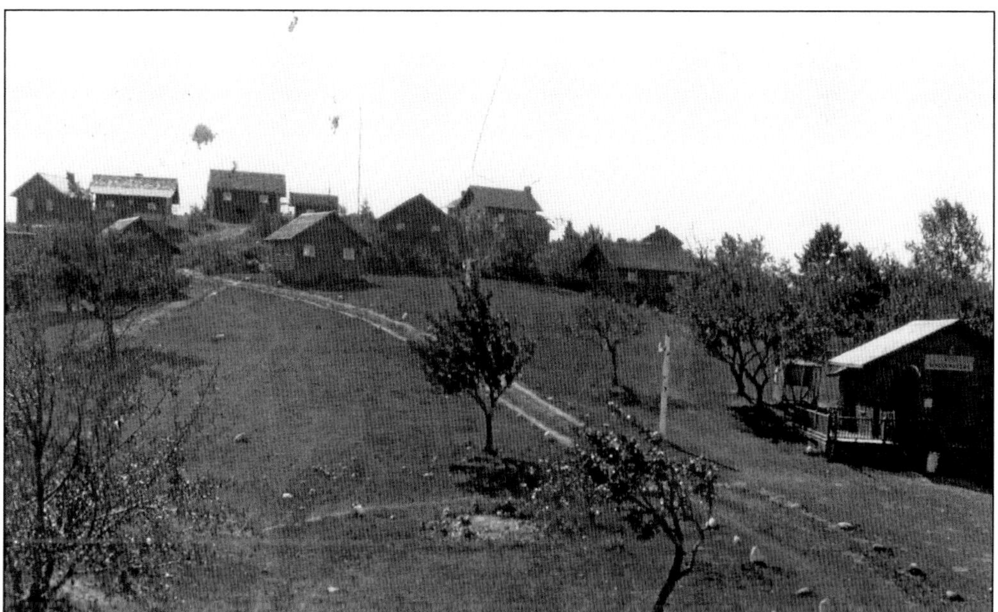

The Vacation Training Camp in Limington near the Standish town line. Its land extended down to Pequawket Lake (Horn Pond).

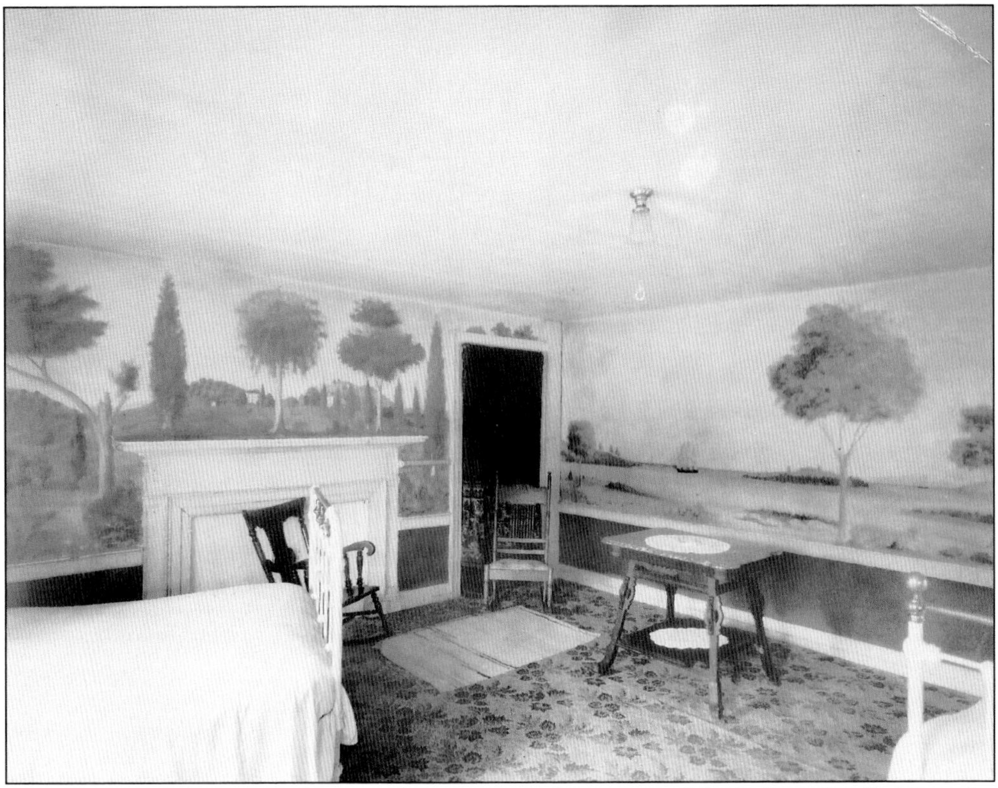

The interior of the inn on Route 25, Limington, last operated by Lillian Small. Note the paintings on the wall.

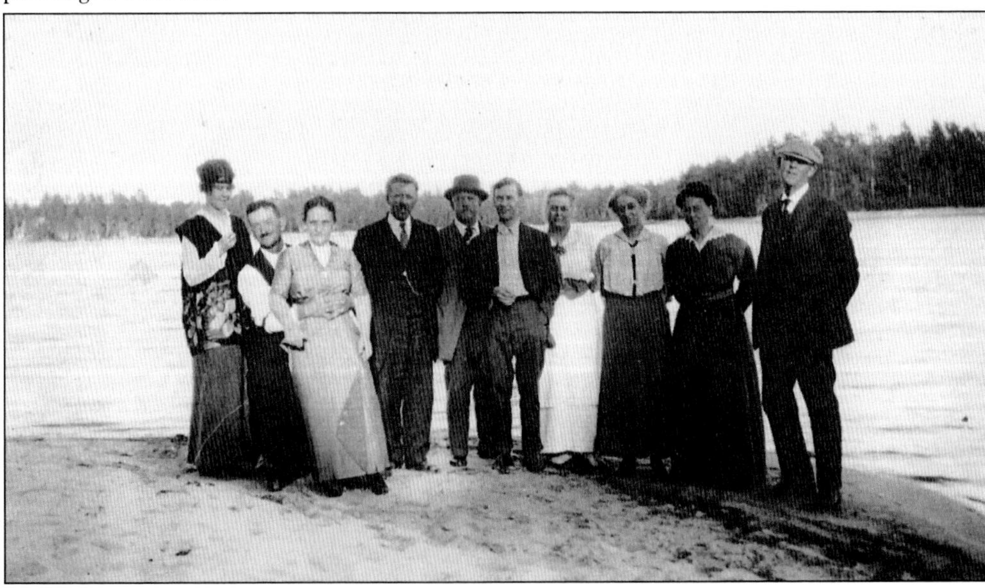

A Pequawket Lake outing in Limington, *c.* 1924. From left to right are Eleanor Baker Sturdevent (daughter of Mitch and Mae Chase Baker), Ed Peter Chick, Annie Elizabeth Prescott Chick, Charles Chase, J.F. Chase, Charles Edwin Alley, Evelyn Small Roberts Chase, Fanny Chase, Laura Larrabee Chase, and Amos Howard Chase.

Seven

The Celebrity

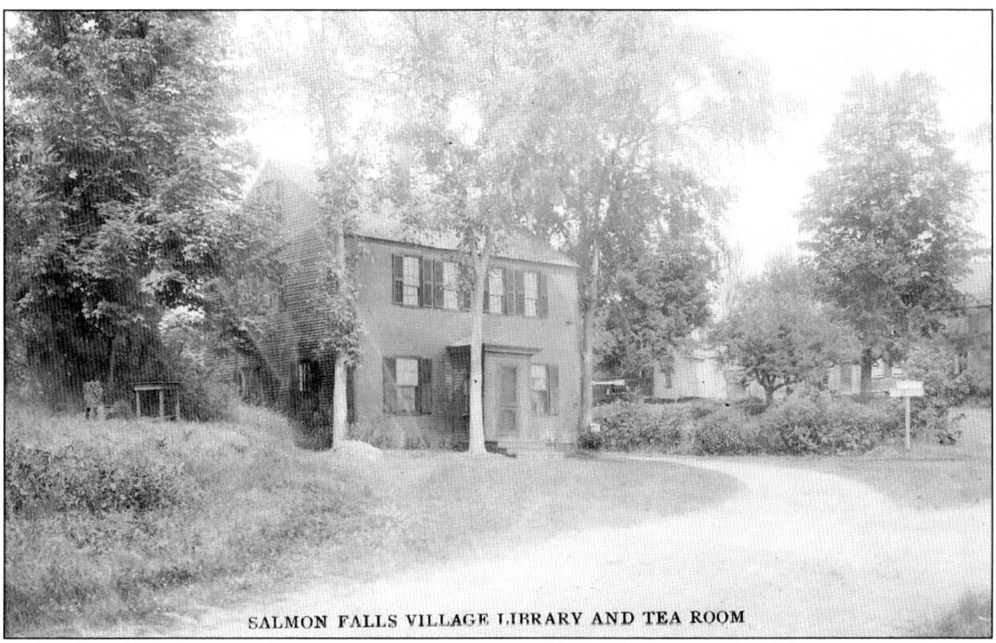

The Salmon Falls Library and Tea Room in Hollis, *c.* 1920s. Famed author Kate Douglas Wiggin (Mrs. George S. Riggs) and her sister, Nora A. Smith, were instrumental in the founding and early operation of both this library and the tea room.

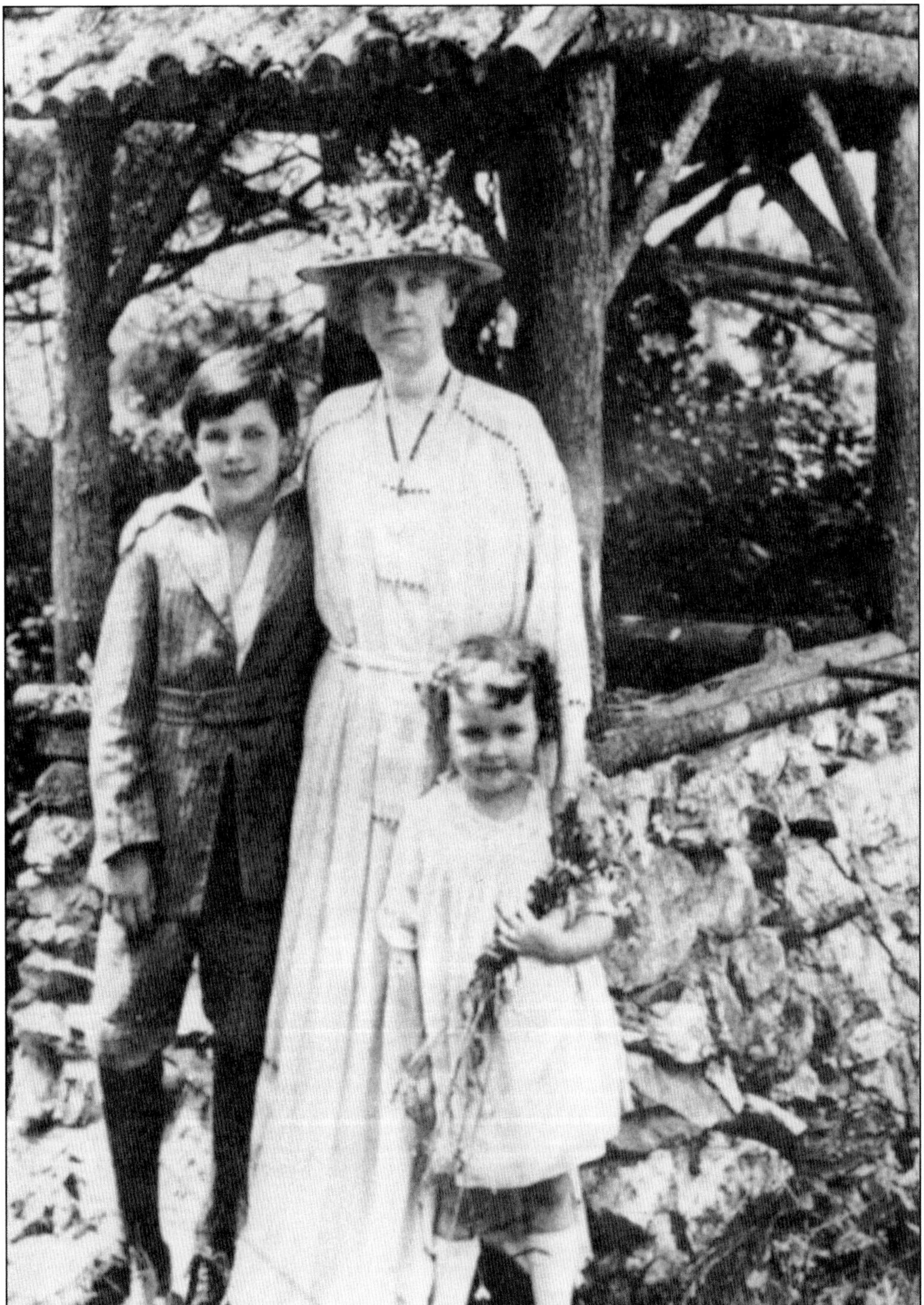

Kate Douglas Wiggin in front of a well house at her summer home, Quillcote, in Hollis. The two children are probably members of the cast of the movie *Timothy's Quest*, made from one of her novels (if so, they are Joseph Depew, who played Timothy, and Baby Helen Roland, who was Lady Gay). Many Portland people had parts in the movie.

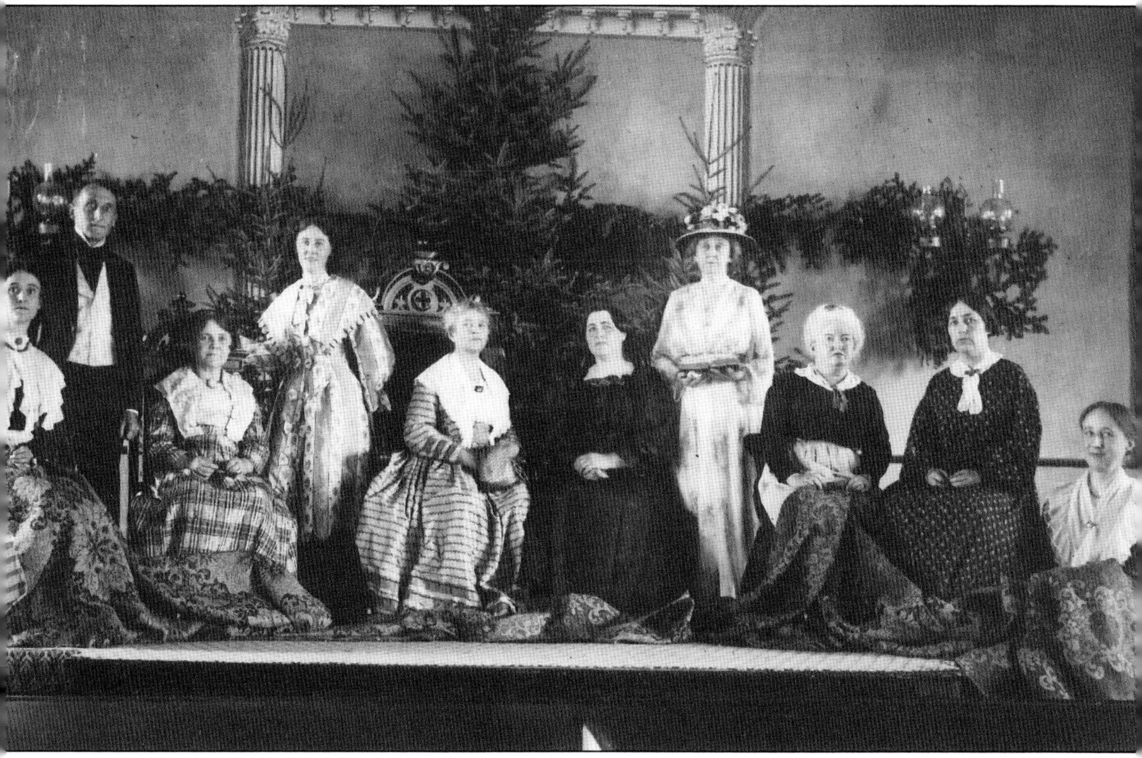

The original cast of the *Old Peabody Pew* by Kate Douglas Wiggin, which was first given at the old Tory Hill Meeting House in 1911. The story was written for performance in that church. There have been 133 performances there, originally twice a year and now once a year. The last performance was December 1, 1996.

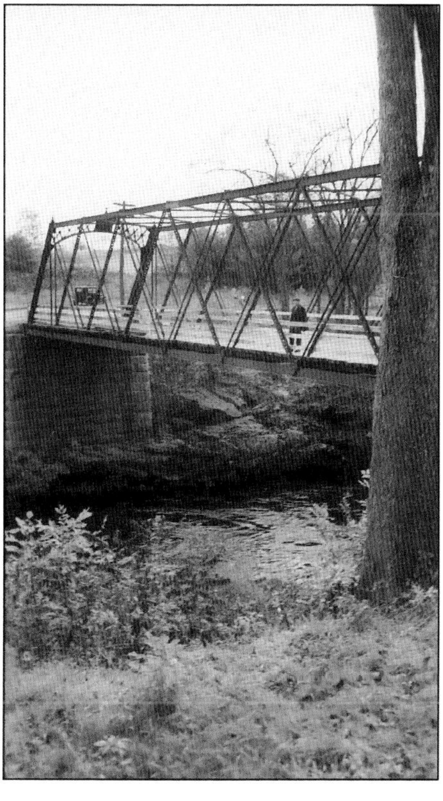

The old bridge over the Saco River at Salmon Falls, about 600 feet from Kate Douglas Wiggin's home. The vintage of the car in the image shows that Kate was probably alive when the photograph was taken. The famous writer undoubtedly swam in the Saco near Pleasant Point as she grew up.

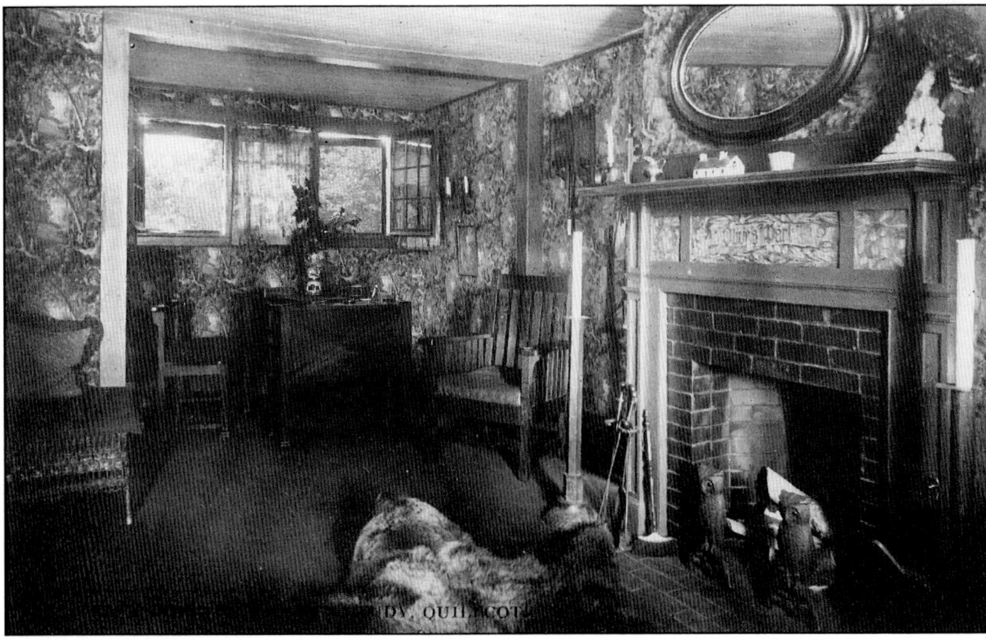

Kate Douglas Wiggin's study in Quillcote, her Hollis summer home. Her family first summered there as tenants in 1894. Kate bought the home in 1905 and made many improvements. It had been built about 1800 by Jabez Bradbury.

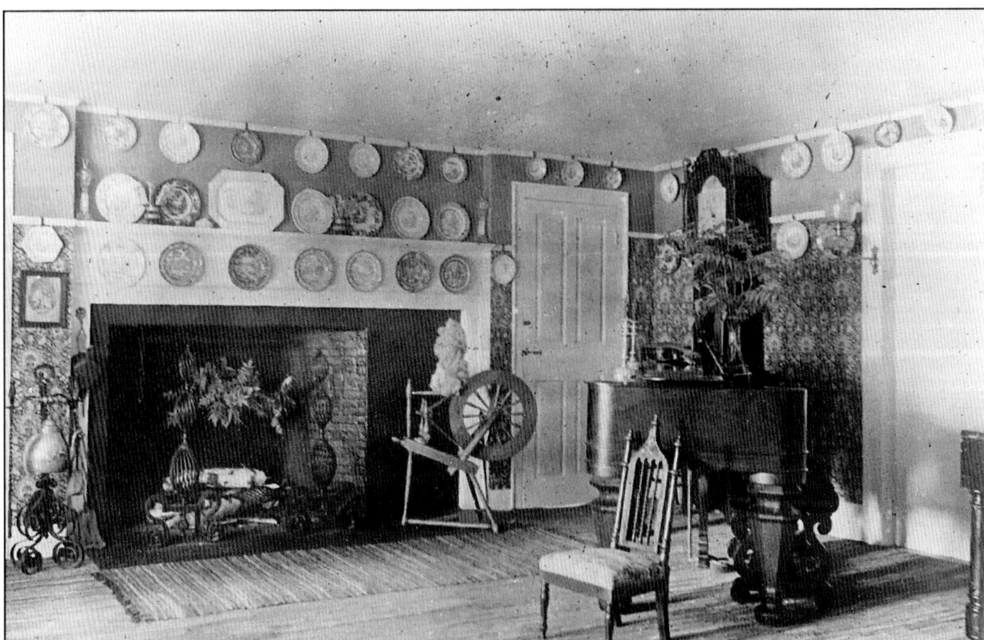

The seven-doored sitting room at Quillcote in the early 1900s.

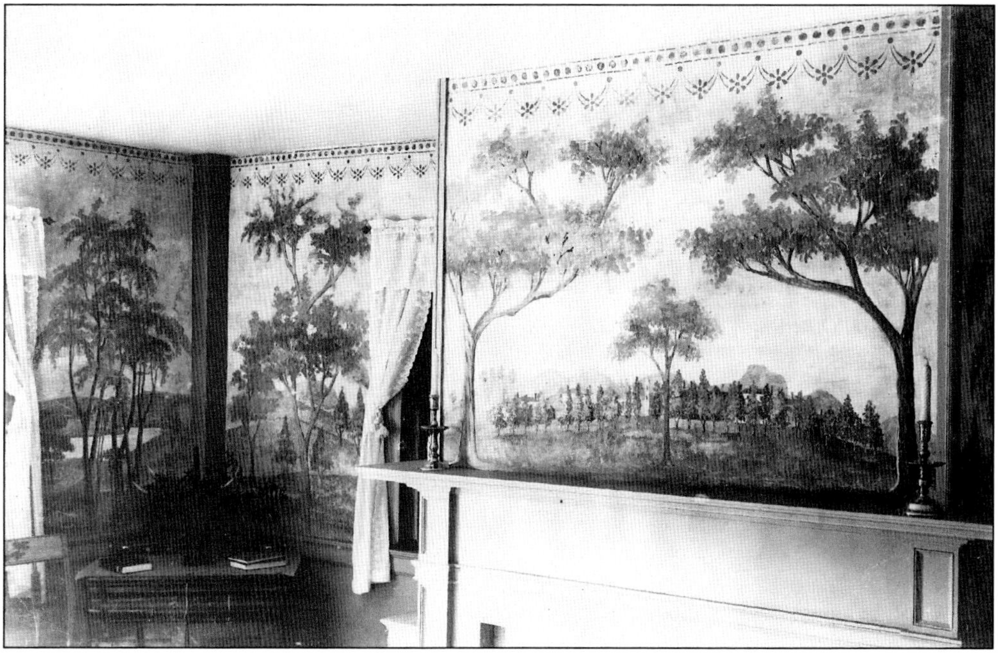

The famous painted room at Quillcote. Kate found these paintings after having five layers of paper removed. They were reportedly done by Rufus Porter.

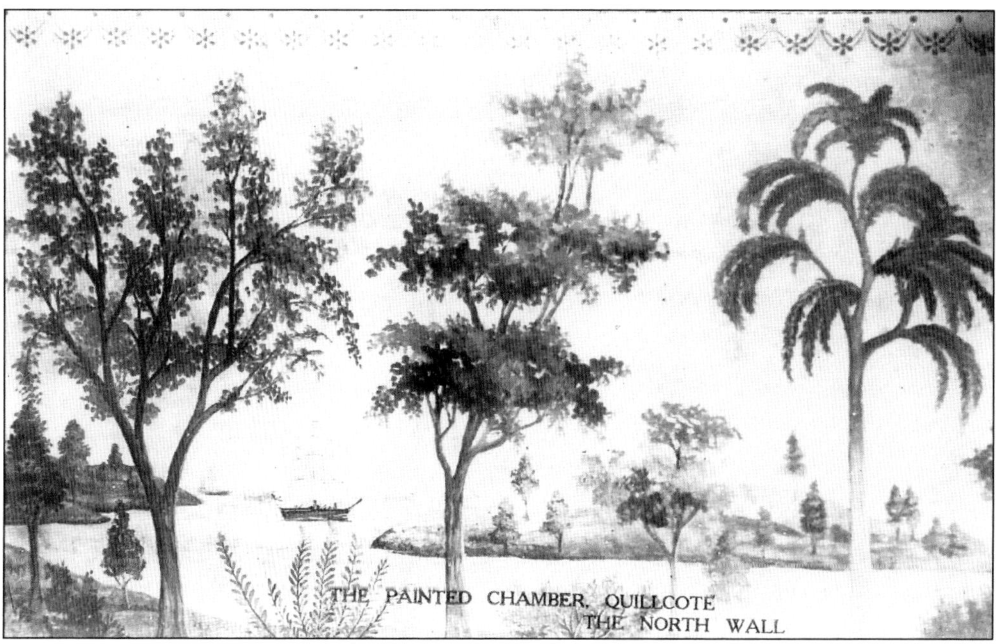

The north wall of the painted chamber at Quillcote around the 1900s or 1910s.

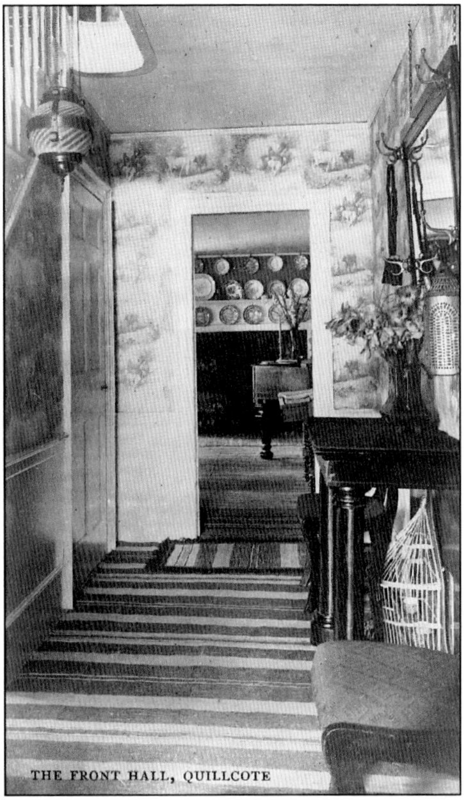

The front hall at Quillcote in Hollis, c. 1918.

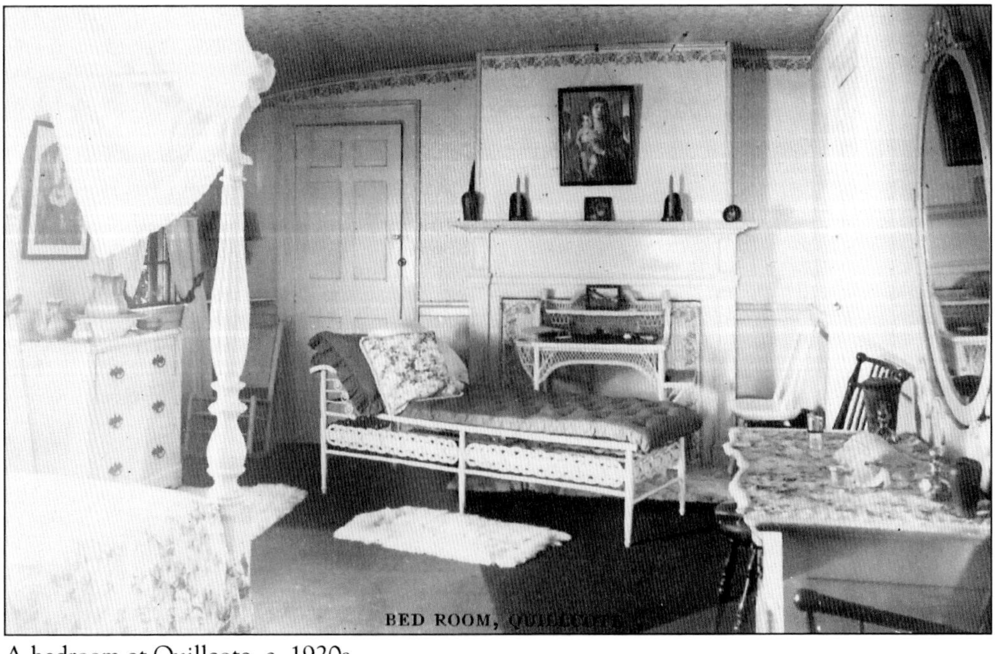

A bedroom at Quillcote, c. 1920s.

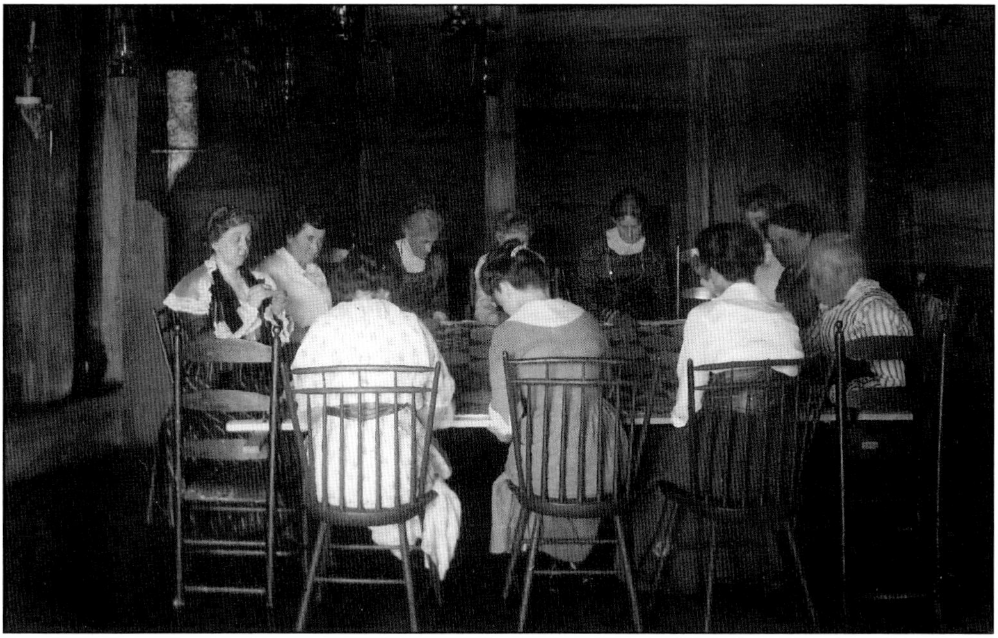

A group, probably from the Dorcas Society, at Quillcote, *c.* 1900s. The Dorcas Society of Buxton and Hollis was founded November 23, 1897, and is still going strong. Kate Douglas Wiggin was the first honorary president and a force behind the founding. *Dorcas Doings* was edited by her sister, Nora Archibald Smith. There are still Dorcas fairs. The first, at Quillcote, drew about 1,200 people.

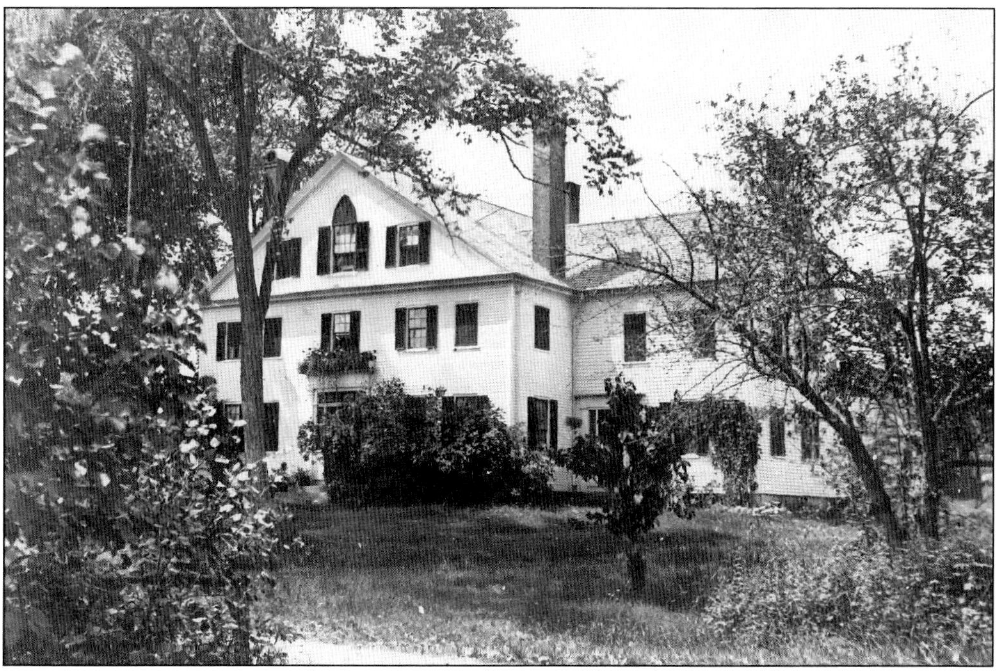

Quillcote itself, *c.* 1900s. The author was very proud of the improvements she made to the house, including a new roof and a back staircase. After her mother married Dr. Albion Bradbury, Kate had lived and gone to school in Hollis and Buxton.

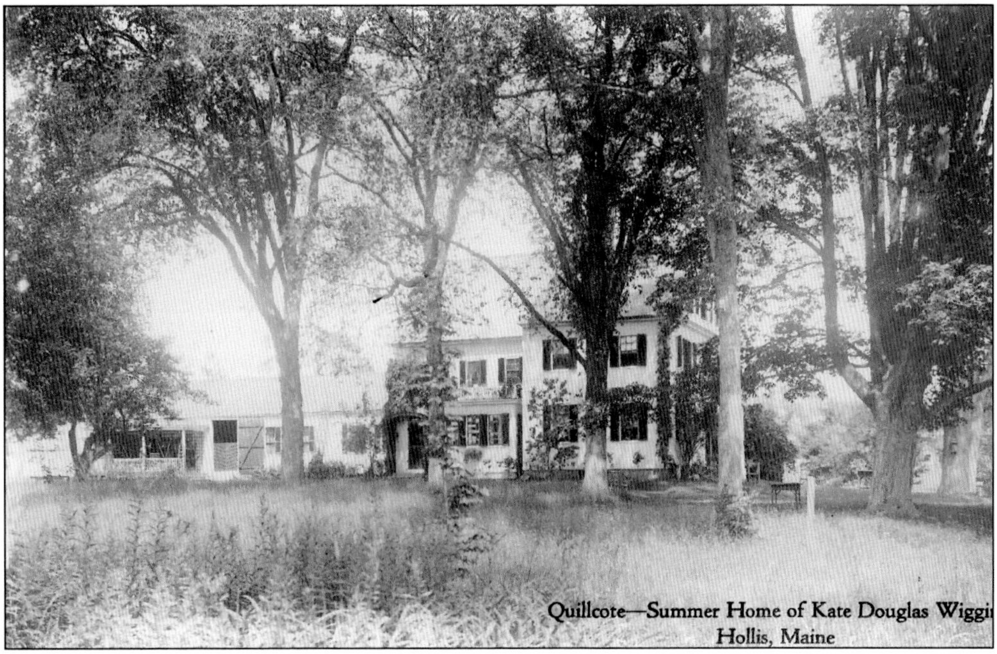

Quillcote in the 1930s.

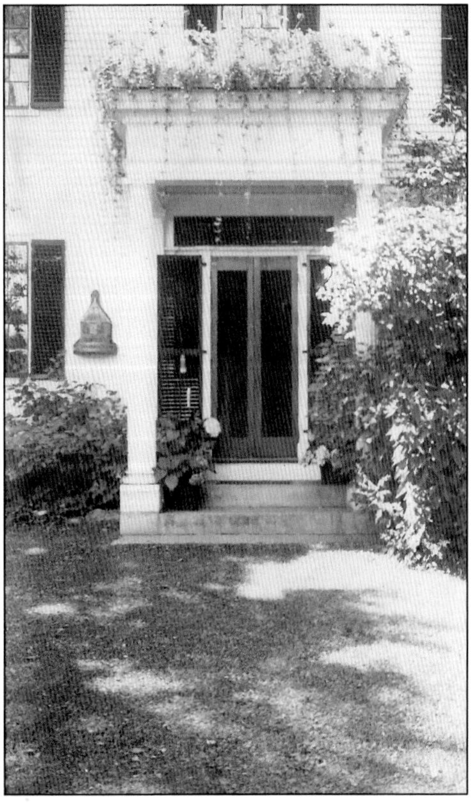

A door at Quillcote, *c.* 1918. All sorts of functions were held here while Kate Douglas Wiggin was in residence.

A corner of Quillcote, September 15, 1918. The author's *Rebecca of Sunnybrook Farm* was made into a silent movie starring Mary Pickford and a sound movie starring Shirley Temple.

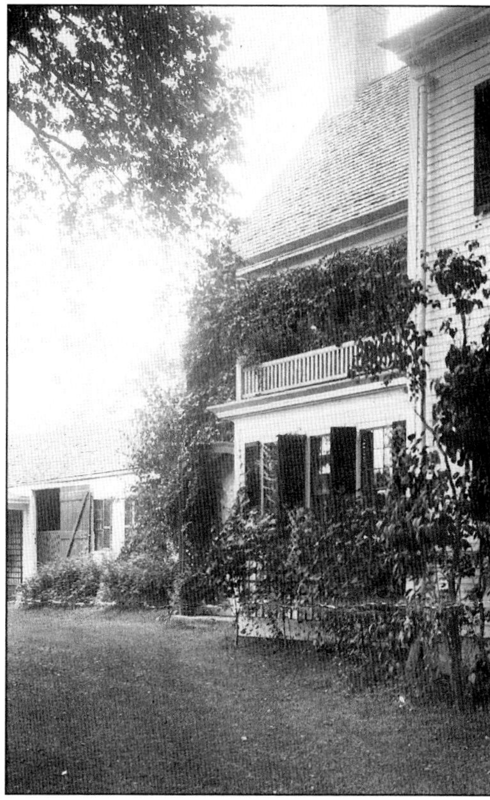

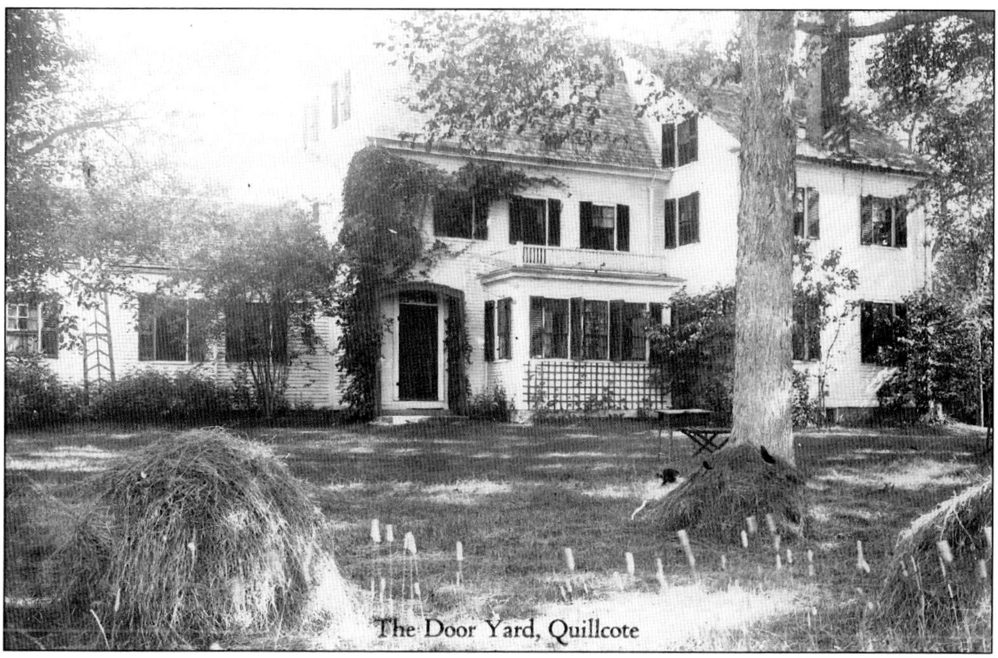

The dooryard at Quillcote, *c.* 1918. This is the spot where almost innumerable functions were held.

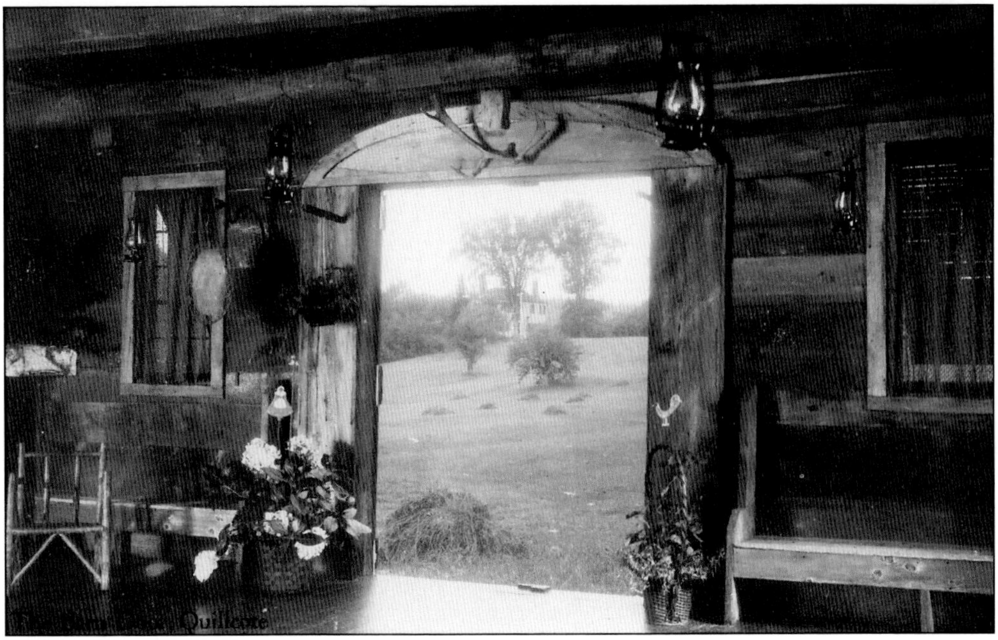

A view through the barn door at Quillcote, *c.* 1910s.

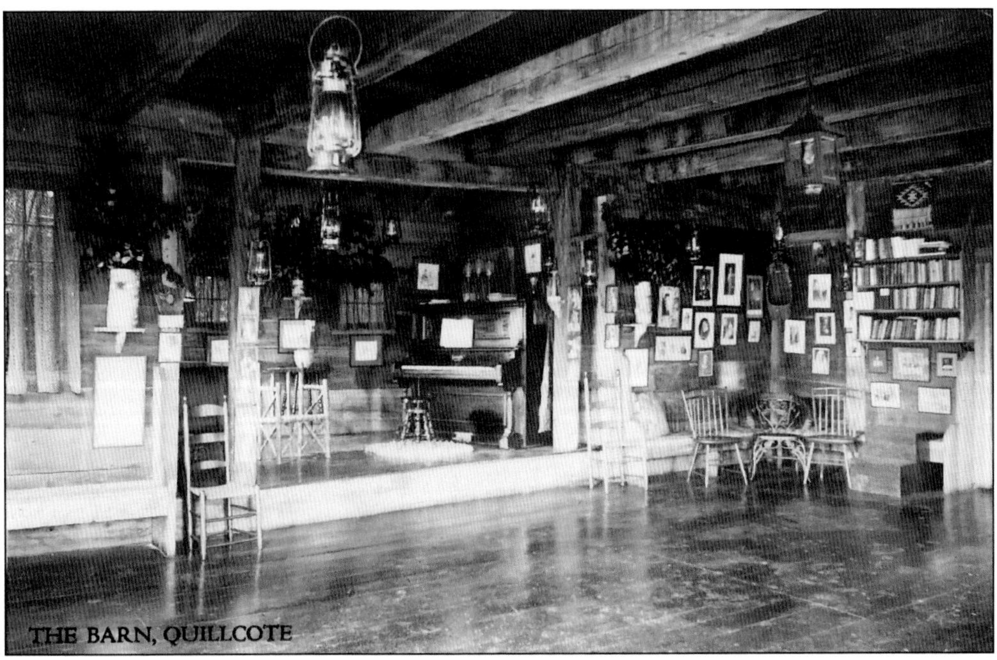

The barn itself, *c.* 1910s. It's not too surprising that Kate received good ideas for her writings from her environment, both at home and in the towns.

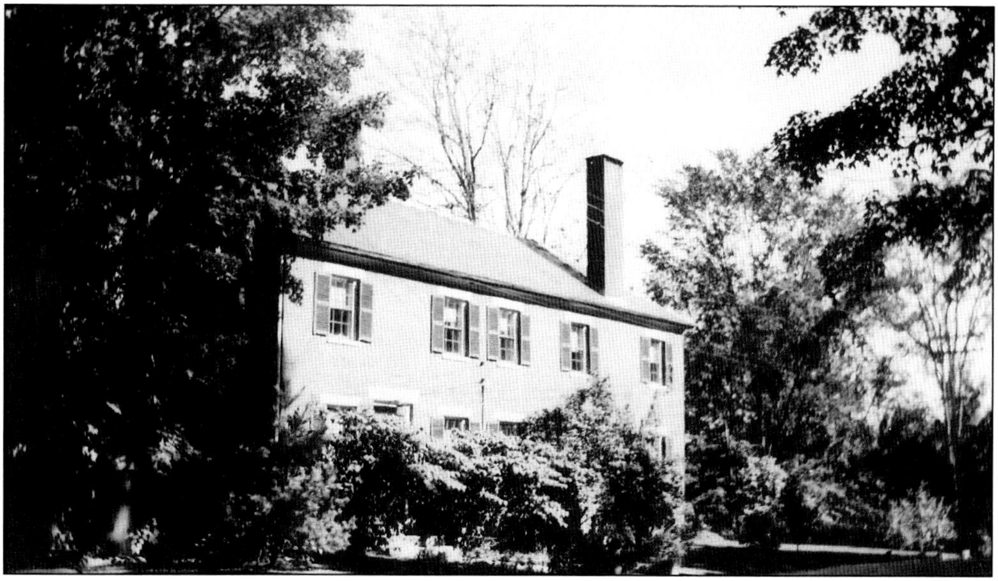

The house opposite Quillcote at Salmon Falls, August 28, 1940. It was the subject of her book *The Village Watch Tower*.

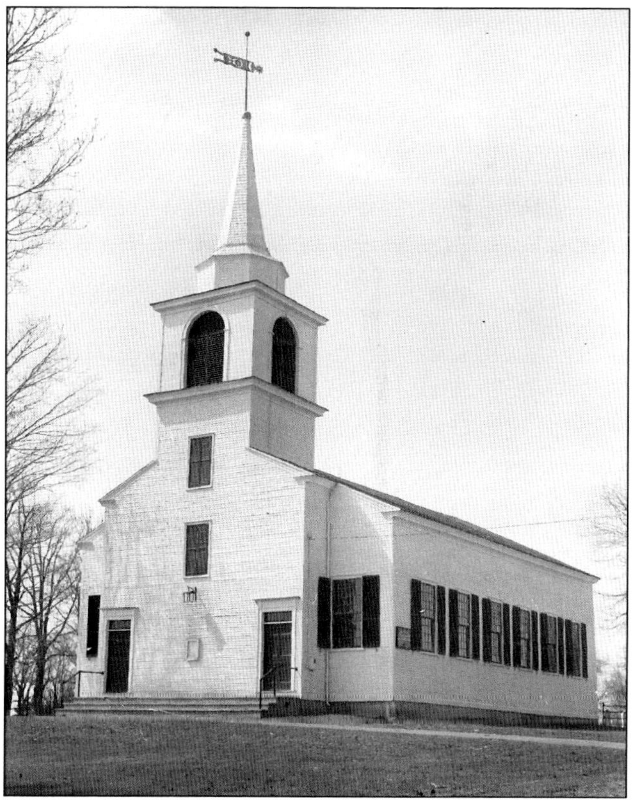

The Tory Hill Meeting House (First Congregational Church) where Kate Douglas Wiggin's *Old Peabody Pew* is given once each year.

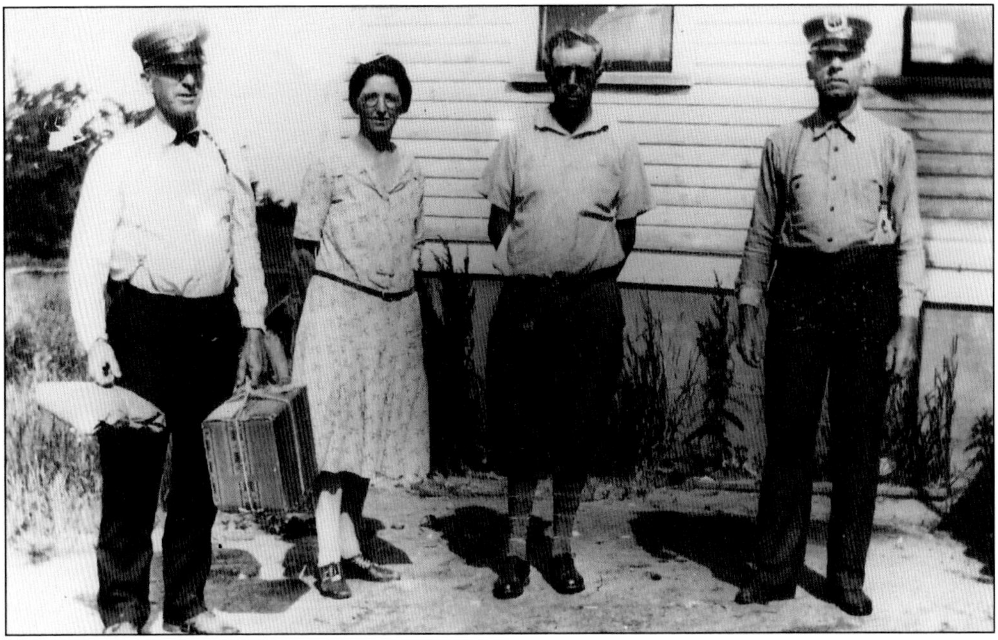

The U.S. Postal Service at Hollis Center, *c.* 1920s or 1930s. From left to right are Guy Smith, Marion Prescott, Scott Prescott, and George Meserve. The burden on the Hollis Post Office was heavier while Kate was alive because of her popularity.

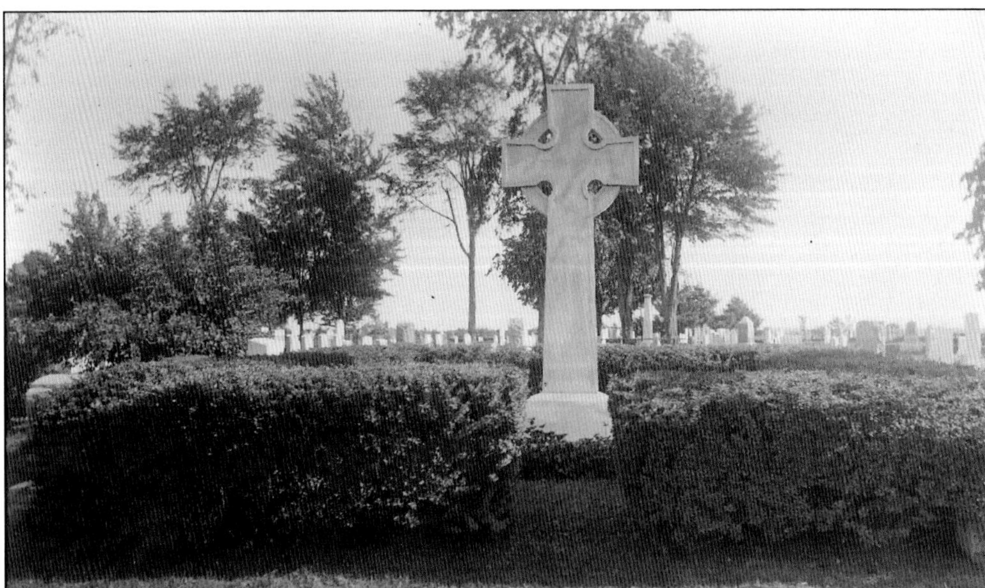

Kate Douglas Wiggin's grave, *c.* 1930s. The author died August 25, 1923. Her ashes were spread on the Saco River, but this monument to her was erected in the Tory Hill Cemetery in Buxton.

Eight

The Bradburys

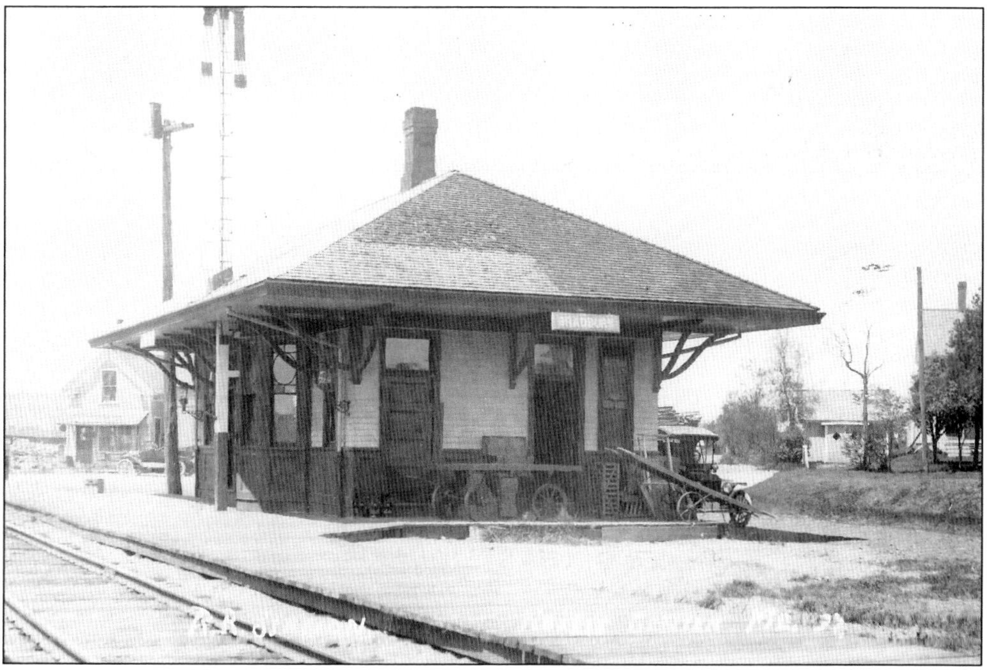

Bradbury Railroad Station in Hollis, named after the eminent and widespread Bradbury family of Buxton and Hollis, *c.* 1920s.

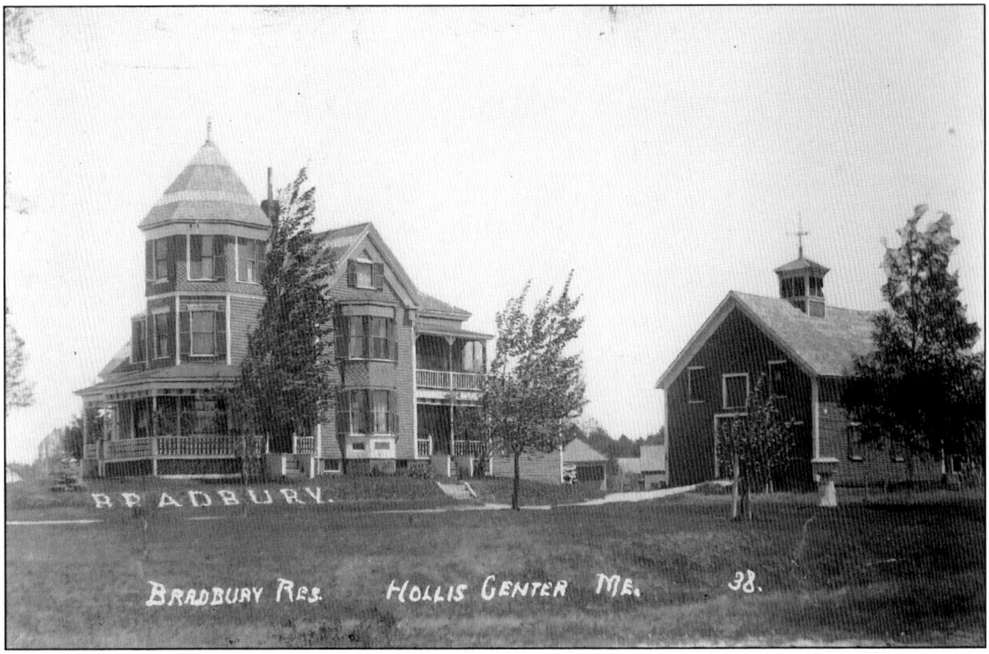

The Bradbury residence at Hollis Center, *c.* 1938. It was later the Aaron Burnham House.

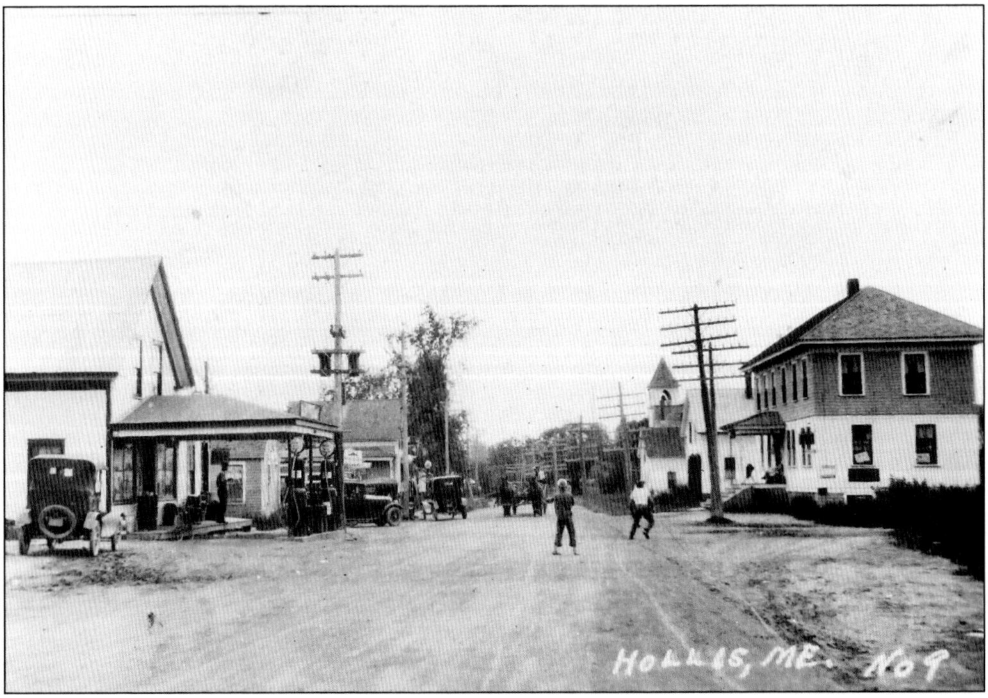

Looking west on Main Street, Hollis Center, *c.* 1930. The store on the left-hand side of the photograph was originally owned by Harrington Bradbury. In 1910 Brice Bradbury and Wilbur (Jib) Brown bought the store, but in 1911 Wilbur bought out Brice. The store continued in operation until 1936.

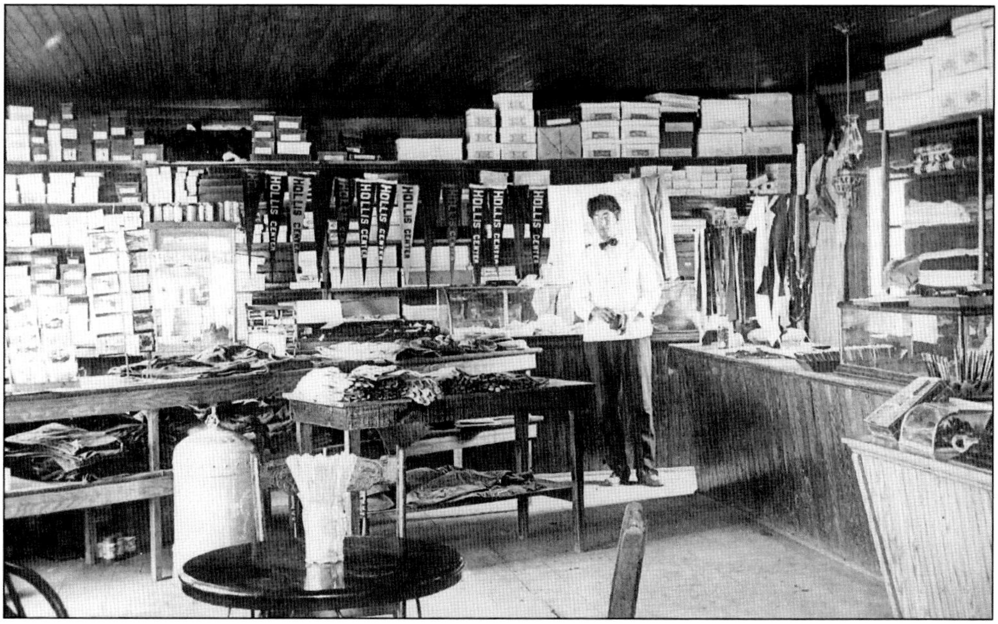

Lester Bradbury in his store at Hollis Center before World War I. Hollis Center pennants can be seen in the rear.

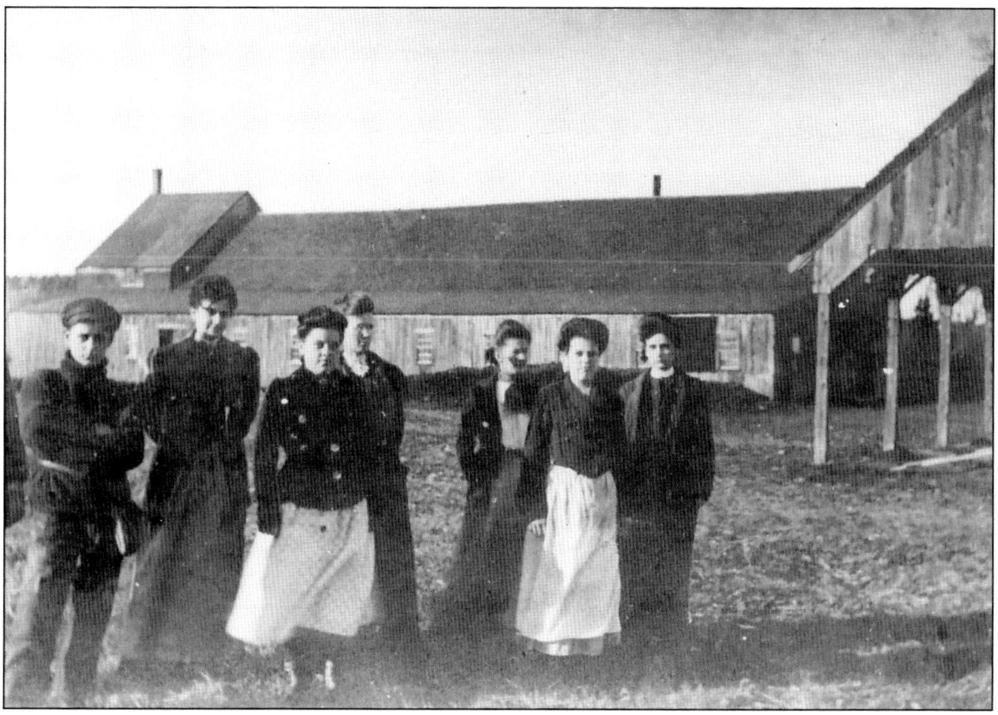
A labeling crew at the corn shop in Hollis Center, *c.* 1906. From left to right are Frank Sanborn, Billie Bradbury, Edna Bradbury, Annie Strom (?), Sarah Strom, Stella Bradbury, and Emma Sanborn. The shop burned in the 1930s. This is just an example of how the Bradburys were just about everywhere.

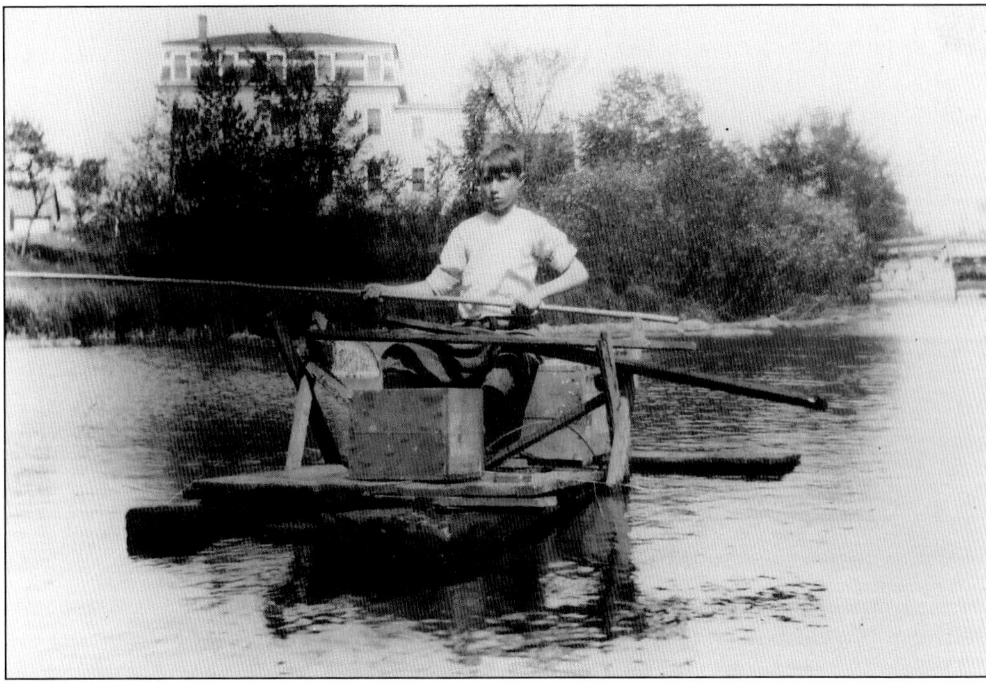

Ivory Bradbury (born in 1898) and his "foot-powered raft" in the brook at Hollis Center. The Knights of Pythias Hall is in the background of this c. 1910 photograph.

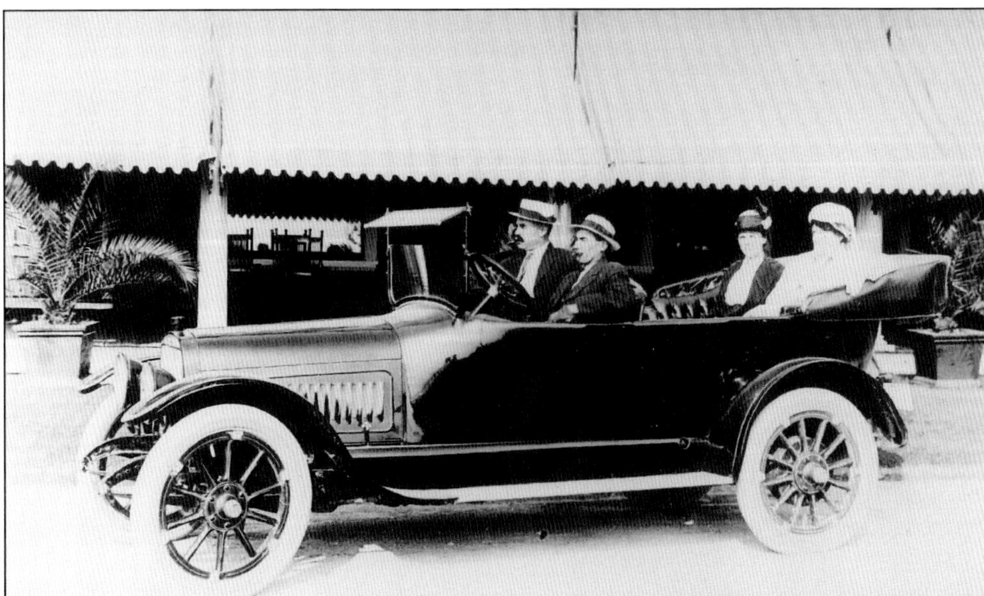

Lindley L. Bradbury, Mr. Locke, Alice Bradbury, and Evangeline Locke in a large sports car, c. 1910s.

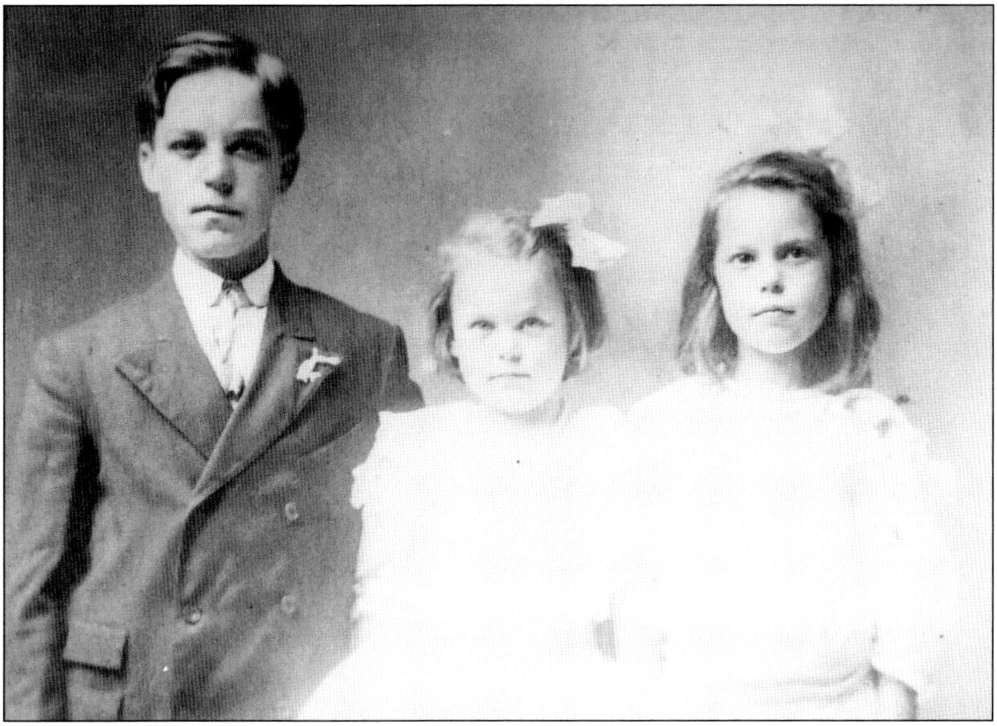

Everett, Florence, and Mildred Bradbury, in a photograph taken on April 16, 1935. These are the children of Lindley L. Bradbury, who died in the 1919 flu epidemic.

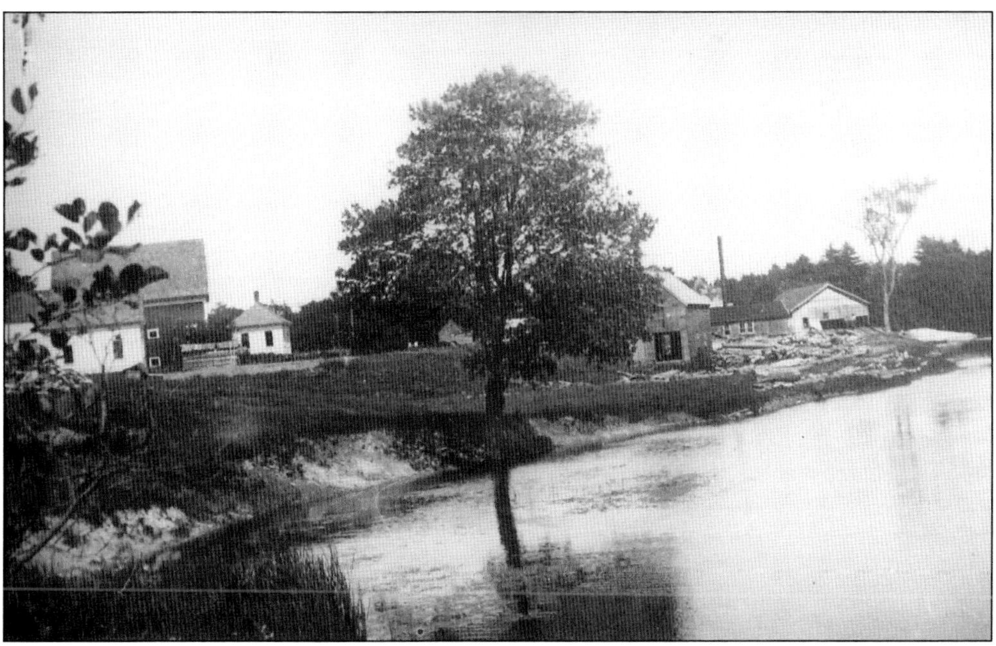

The Bradbury mill pond, *c.* 1920s.

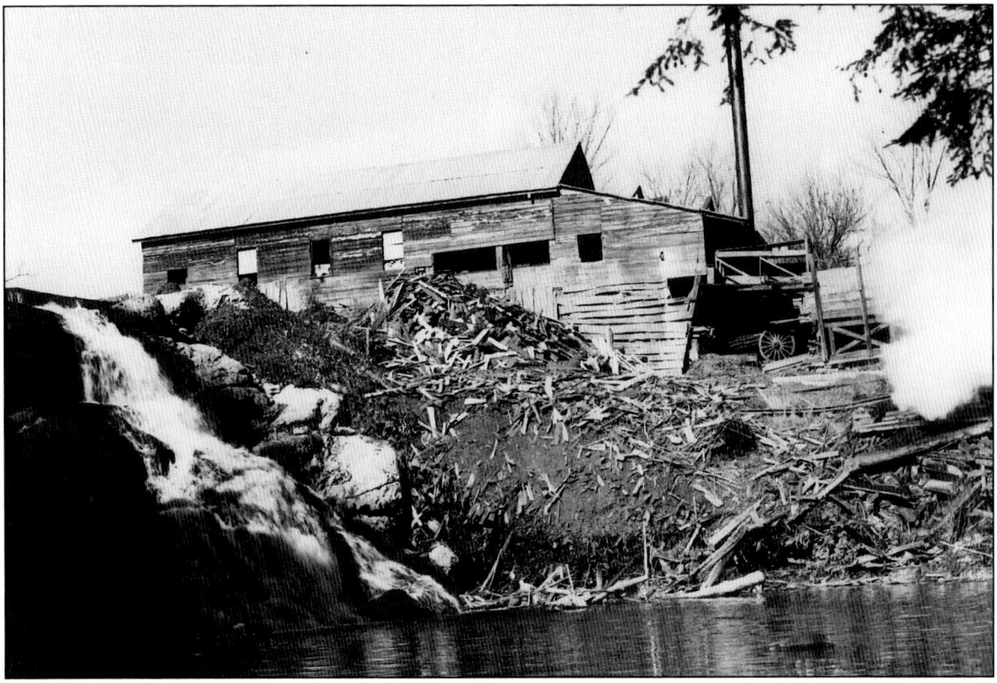

The L.L. Bradbury Lumber Corporation, Hollis Center, *c.* 1945.

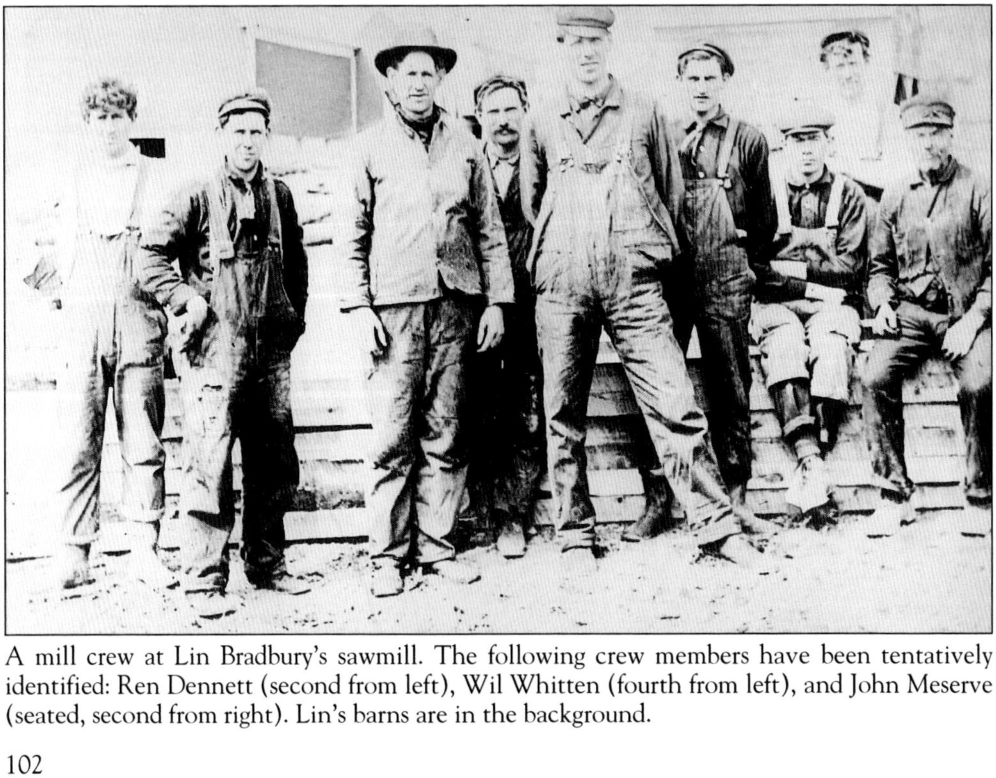

A mill crew at Lin Bradbury's sawmill. The following crew members have been tentatively identified: Ren Dennett (second from left), Wil Whitten (fourth from left), and John Meserve (seated, second from right). Lin's barns are in the background.

Louise Moulton Berry Bradbury, who took some of the photographs here about 1900. Dana Smith of Tenant's Harbor (once of Buxton and Hollis) borrowed her glass negatives and made contact prints in 1948 or 1949. Louise was born in 1868, the daughter of William and Elizabeth Hanson Moulton. Her first husband was Orrington Berry; after being widowed, she remarried to Lewis Bradbury. She died at age ninety-five.

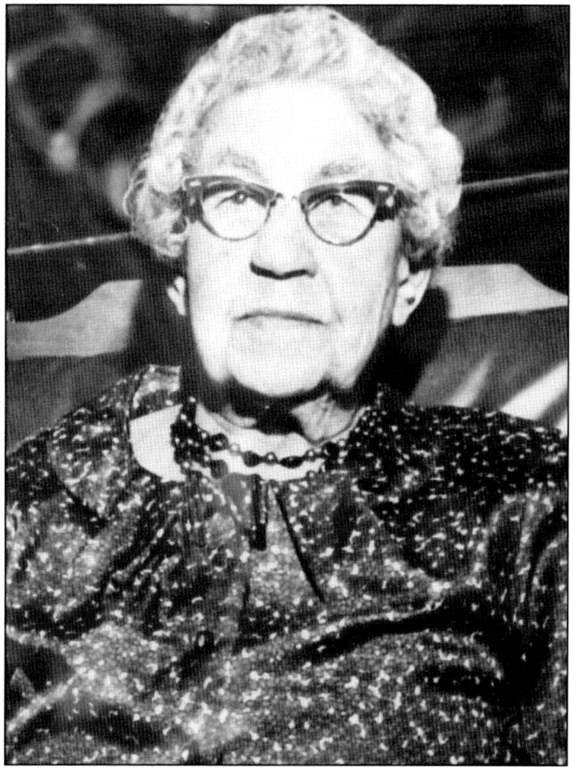

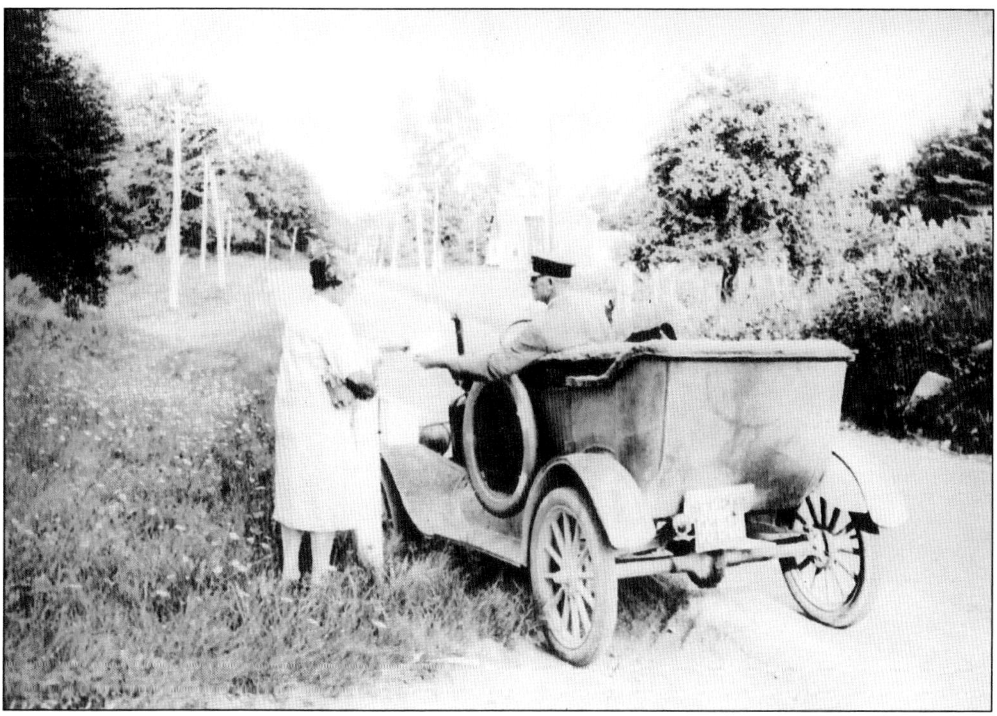

George Meserve delivering the mail to Louise Bradbury in 1930. Oz Bradbury's house is in the background.

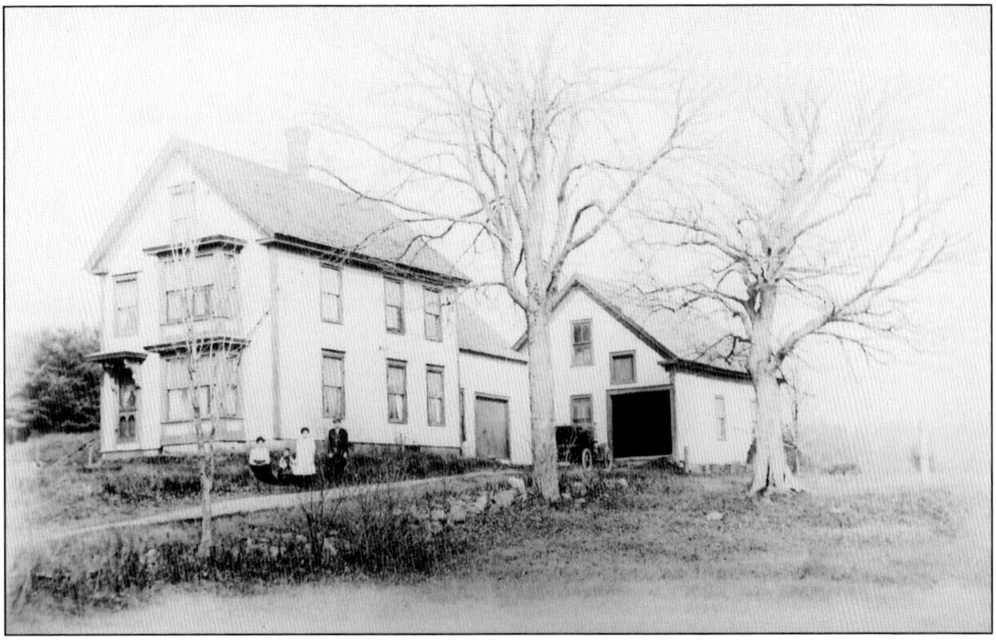

The Orrington Berry house, *c.* 1900. It burned many years later. Berry, Louise Bradbury's first husband, was a blacksmith.

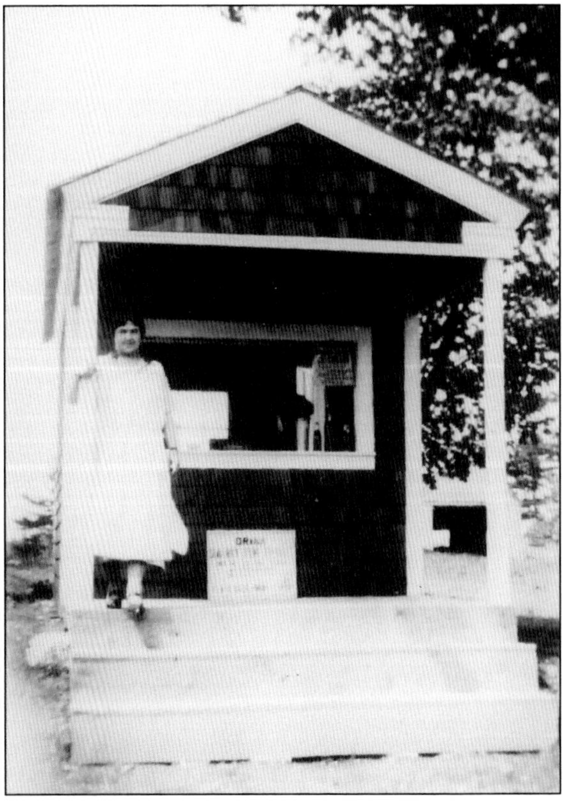

Gladys Berry at her refreshment stand, *c.* 1910. When Gladys was about nine years old, Lew Bradbury (father of Kenneth, Bernice, and Lester) became her stepfather. Lew made Gladys this refreshment stand near the Bradbury house, and Gladys later added a gas pump.

Gladys Berry and Bernice Bradbury on a snow roller, *c*. 1900s.

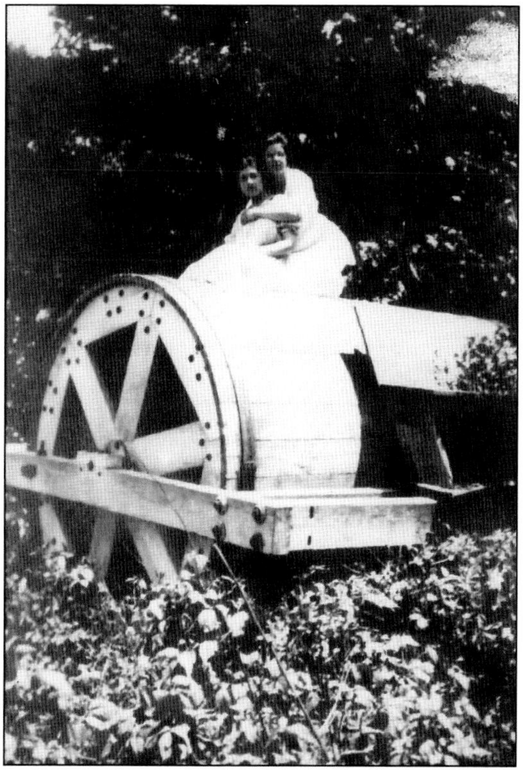

A group of ladies in the neighborhood in Hollis who called themselves "The Silver Greys," *c*. 1900. From left to right are: (front row) Louise Berry Bradbury, Amanda Garrett, Elnora Vittum, and Georgia Bradbury; (back row) Blanche Bradbury, Susie Smith, Lillian Moulton Allen, Orilla Meserve, Addie Bradbury, and Ella Palmer.

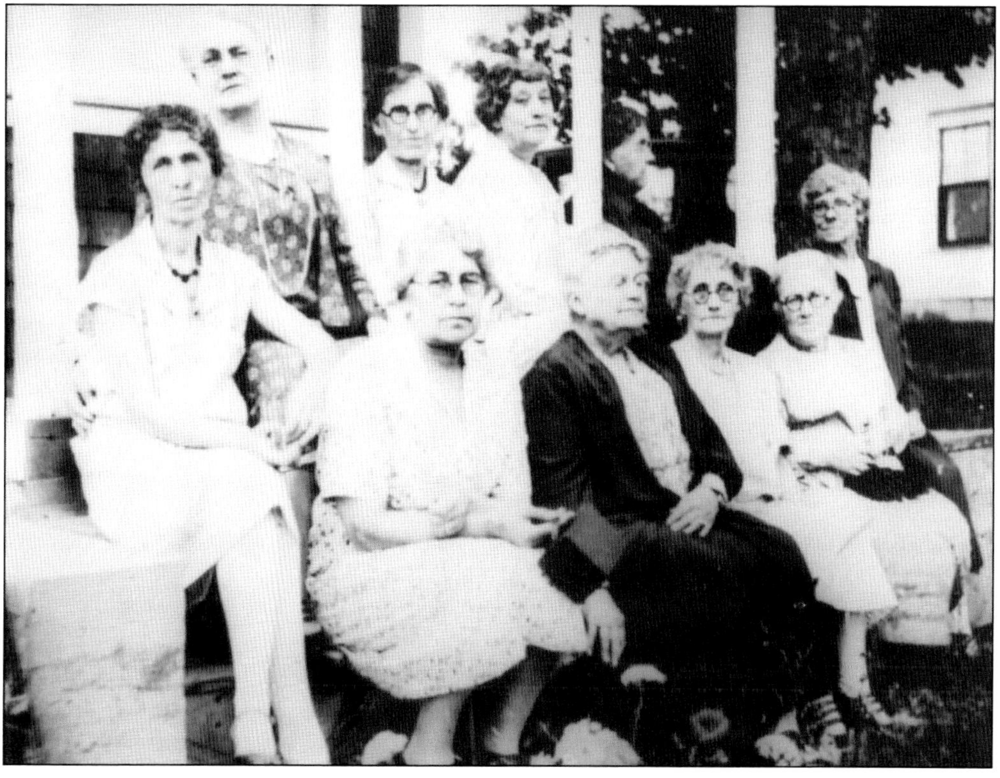

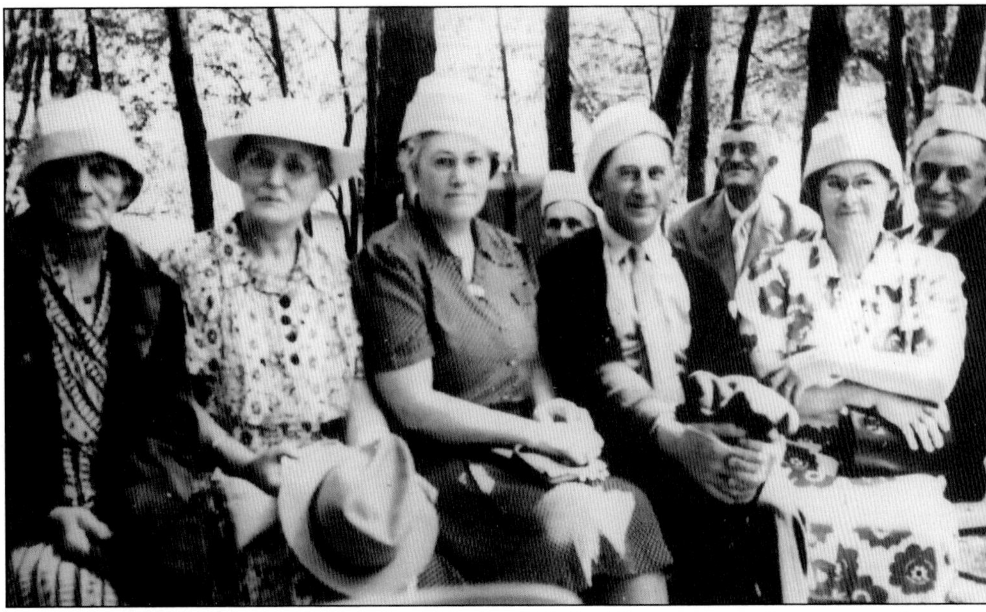

Former students of Fannie McDaniel, *c.* 1930s or 1940s. The group used to get together once in awhile. From left to right are Lizzie Whitten, Alice Barnes Fluent, Esther Bradbury Doe, Miles Bradbury, Frank Guilford, Sarah Guilford, and Oz Bradbury. The partially hidden person remains unidentified.

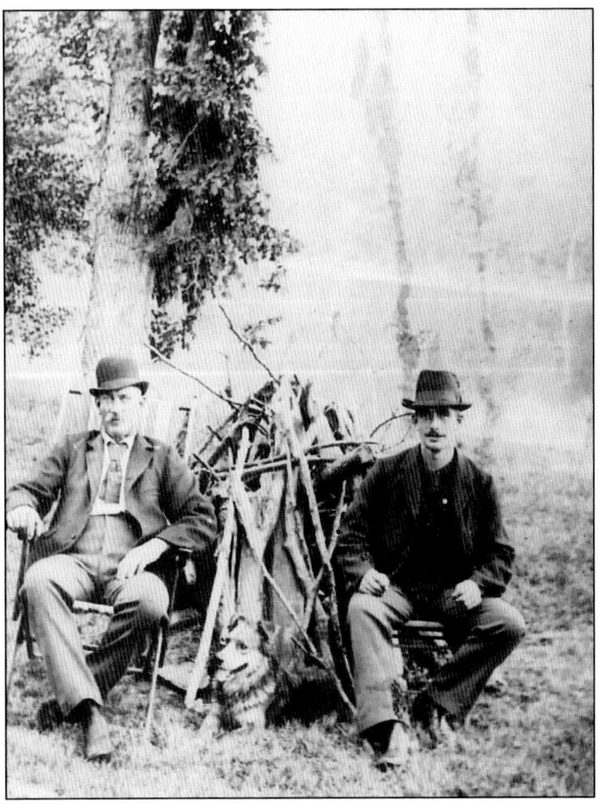

Fred Barnham Bradbury and Ivory Stevens (Frank Stevens' brother), September 3, 1898.

Nine

Doers and Shakers

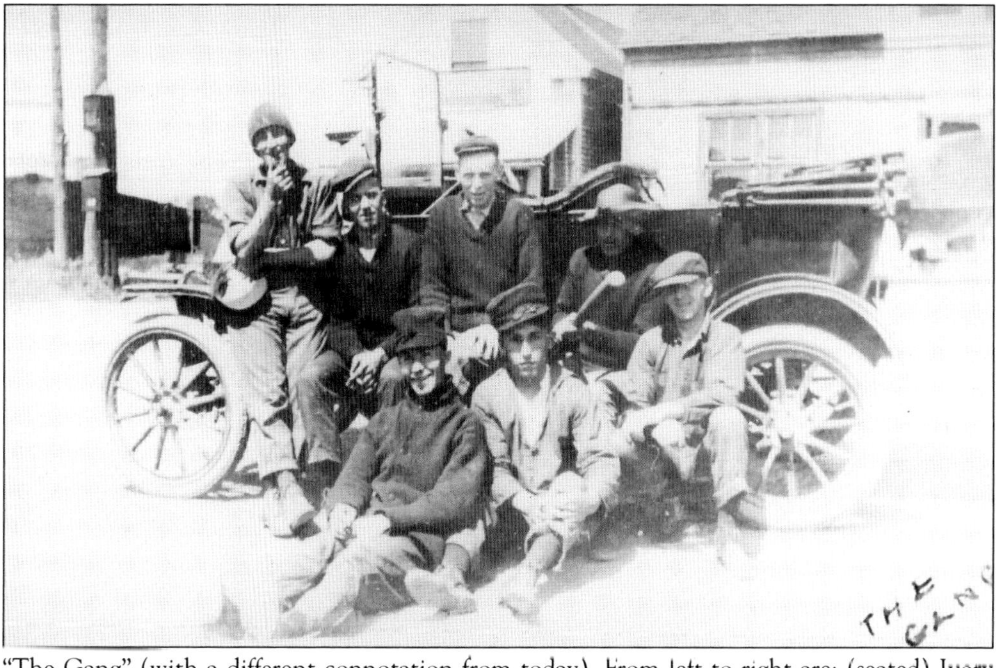

"The Gang" (with a different connotation from today). From left to right are: (seated) Ivory Bradbury, unknown, and unknown; (back row) Ernest Carter, Gene Moore, Millard Tripp, and unknown, *c.* 1920s. They are sitting on a Ford convertible.

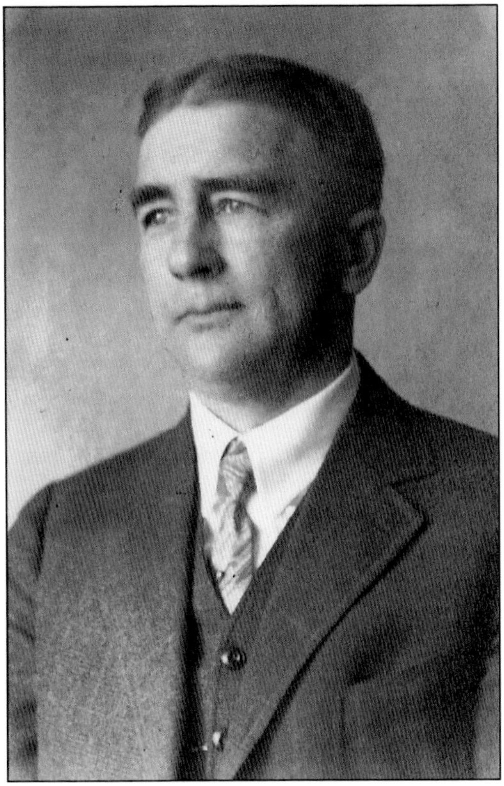

William Soule, the Buxton farmer who had his farm opposite John Henry Harmon's farm, *c.* 1910–30.

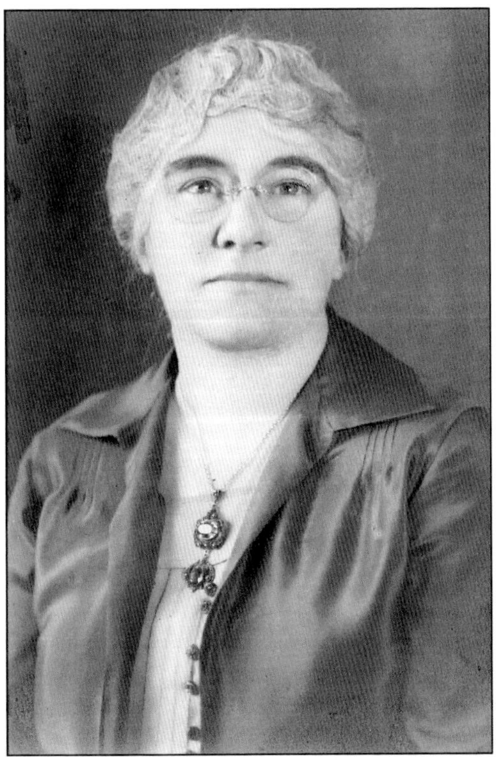

Mrs. Helen Soule, wife of William Soule.

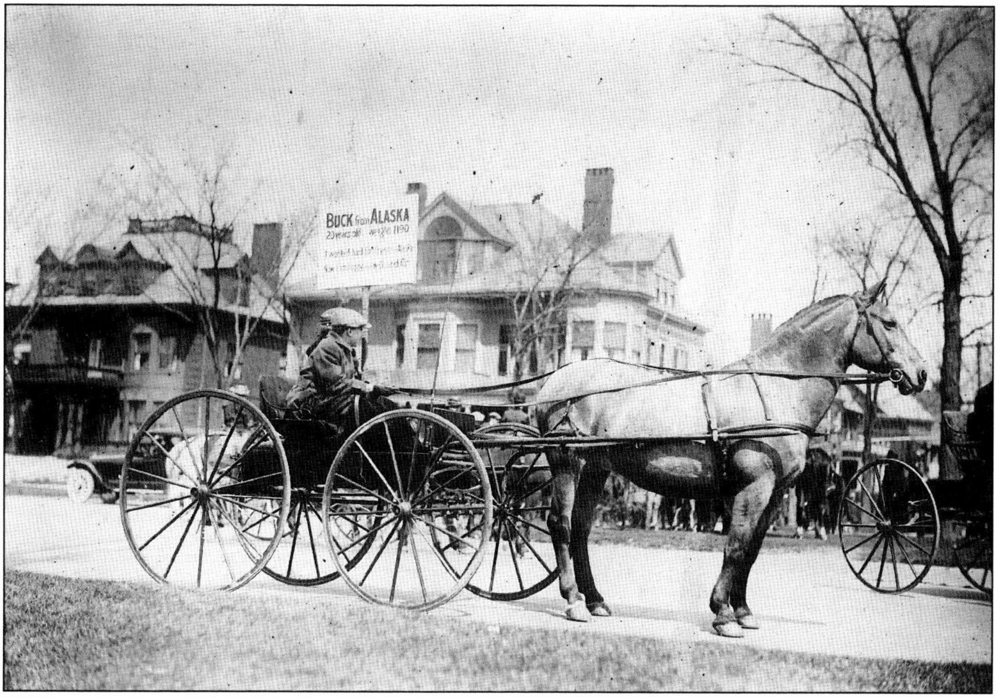

William Soule and his horse Buck. This twenty-year-old horse was from Alaska and weighed 1,190 pounds. He had worked hard many years in Alaska and was now taking it easy, *c.* 1920s.

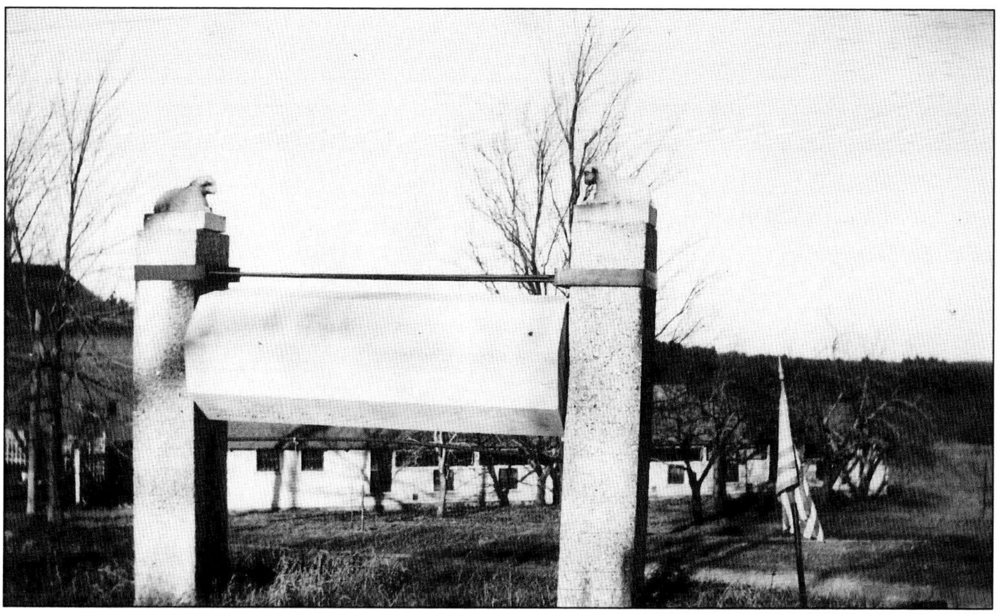

The Elwell tomb, around December 1939. This octagonal marble roller between granite pillars marks the ancient tomb in Buxton near the powder house. The tomb is off Route 22. Over the years, the Elwell family has been very prominent in the area.

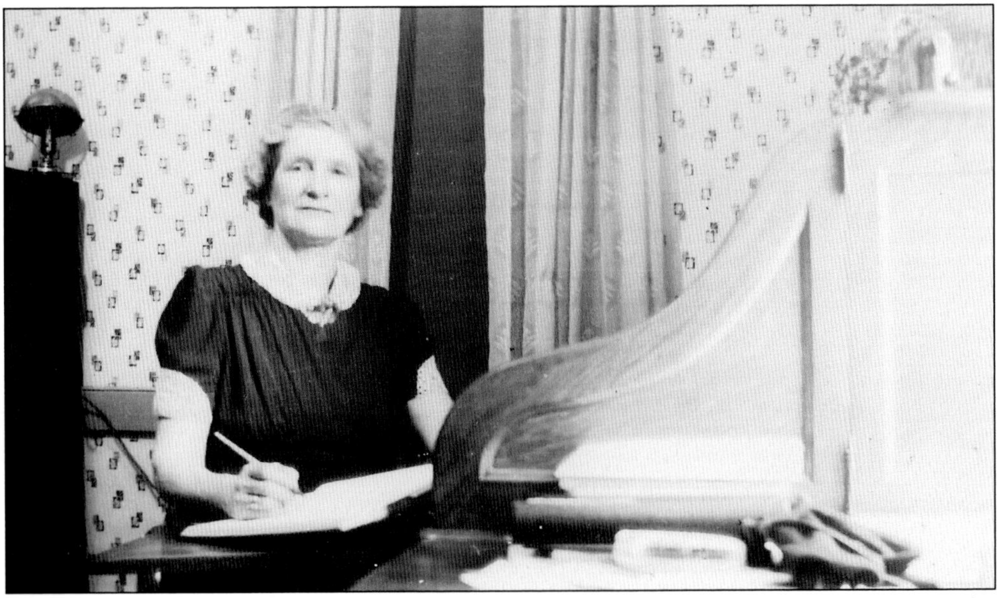

Mrs. R. Blanche Dean of Buxton, reportedly the first female town clerk in Maine, *c.* 1941. She was re-elected for her 14th term on March 10, 1941. Her office was at her West Buxton home.

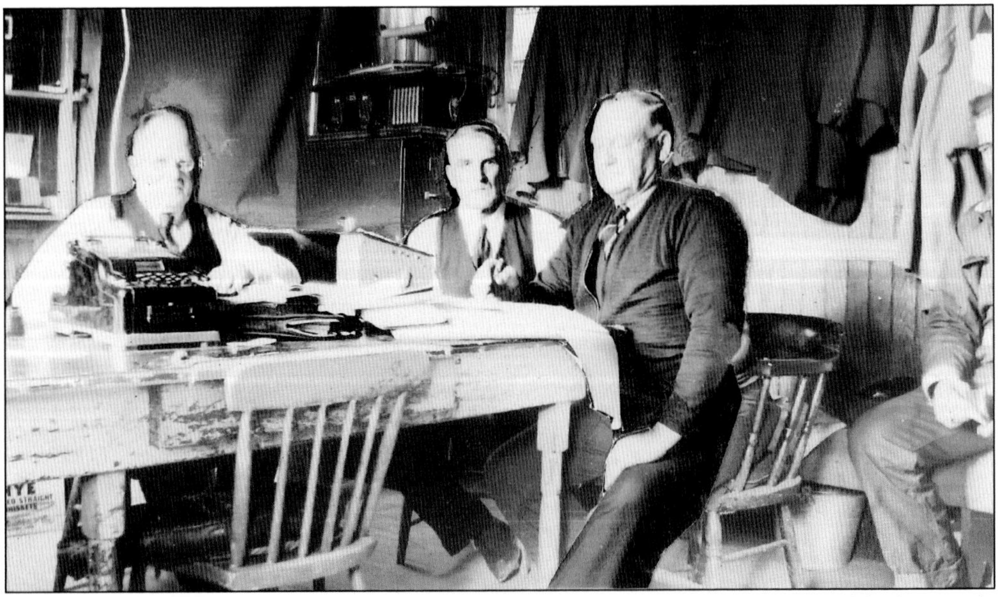

Buxton town fathers trying to balance the budget. From left to right are Nat Lord (selectman), Amos L. Towle (selectman), and A.F. Flint (town treasurer). This was March 1, 1941, in the town hall, Buxton Center. But one has to be a bit suspicious of this photograph because all three heads appear to have been pasted on the bodies. Anyone know why?

Edwin C. Brown, age seventy, of Hollis, crier in the York County Superior Court, at his desk in the court room at Alfred in December 1940.

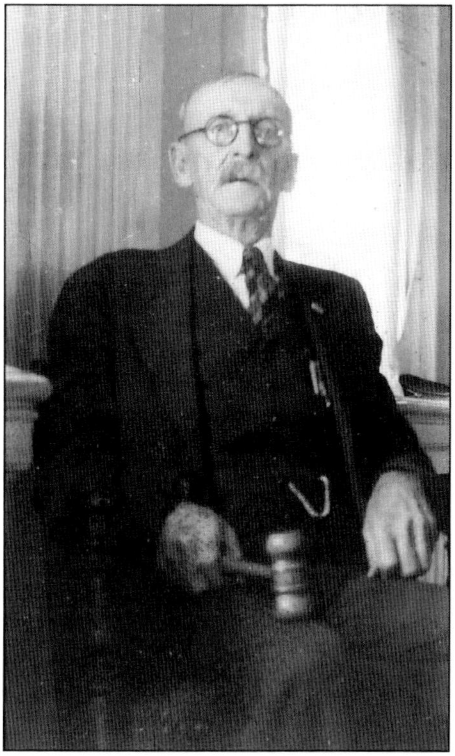

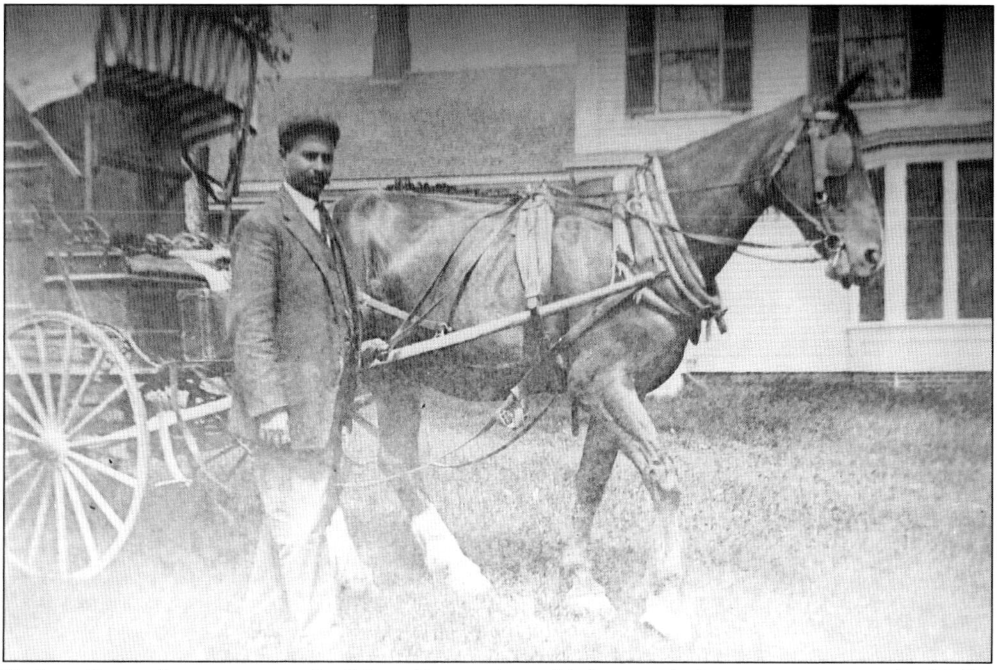

"Salem Carter," more correctly Salim Catir, who sold dry goods for many years in the Hollis area. This was taken at Sumner Haley's house, *c.* 1910s or 1920s. He began as a peddler on foot, carrying his goods with him. He then progressed to horse and wagon and, eventually, to a truck. His sons operated a store in Portland, but Catir continued to sell from his truck.

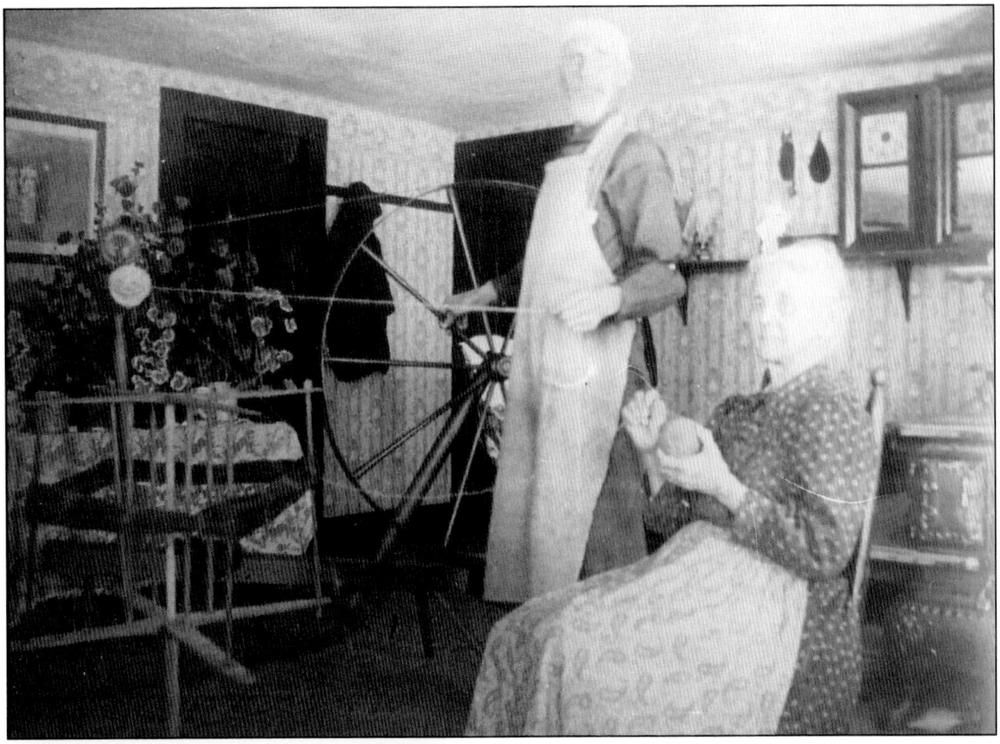

Colby and Nancy Bean of West Buxton with a spinning wheel, *c*. 1940s.

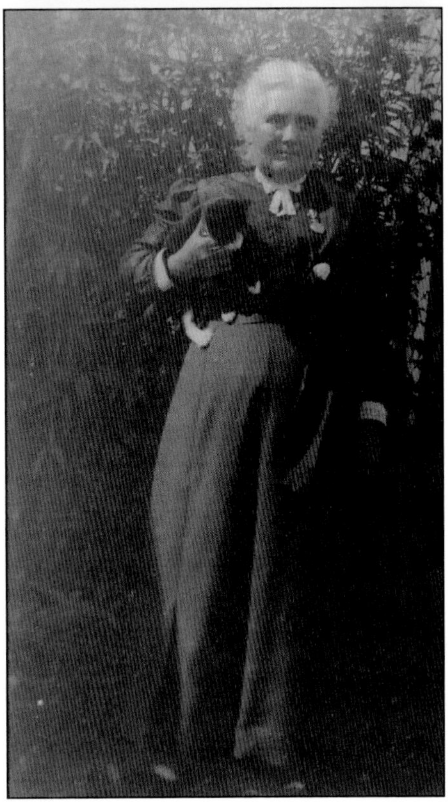

Martha Abigail Littlefield (Marth Abby) kept house for Algie Hanson and smoked a clay pipe.

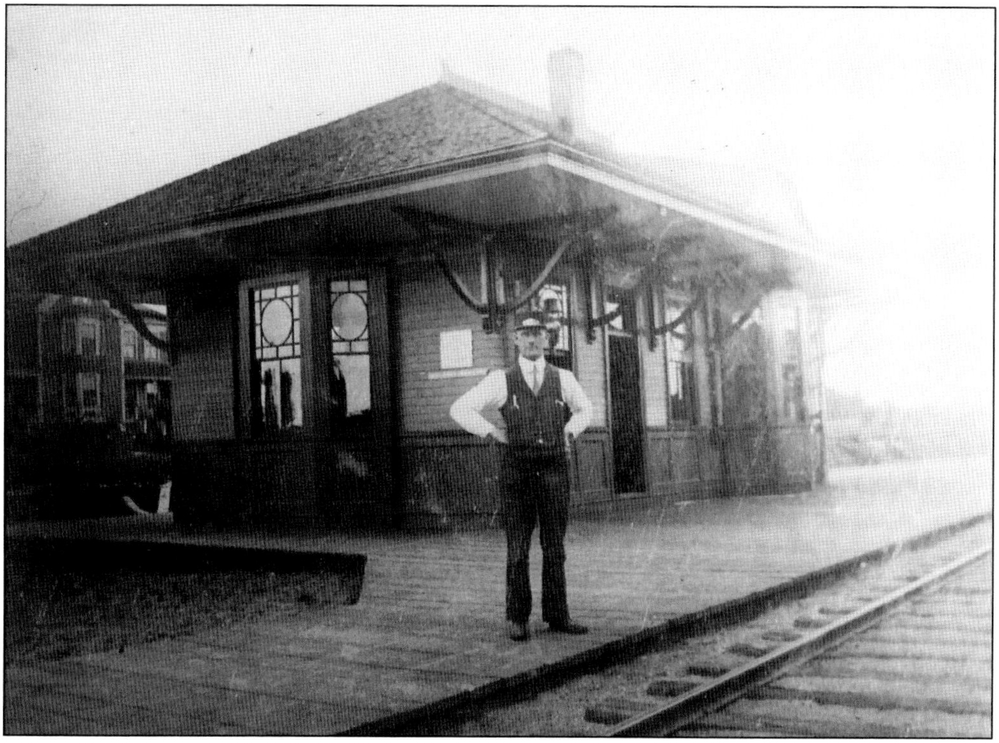

Leroy Eaton Miles (known to his friends as "Roy) at Bradbury Station, Hollis Center, *c.* 1920s. Roy is shown here posing in front of the station.

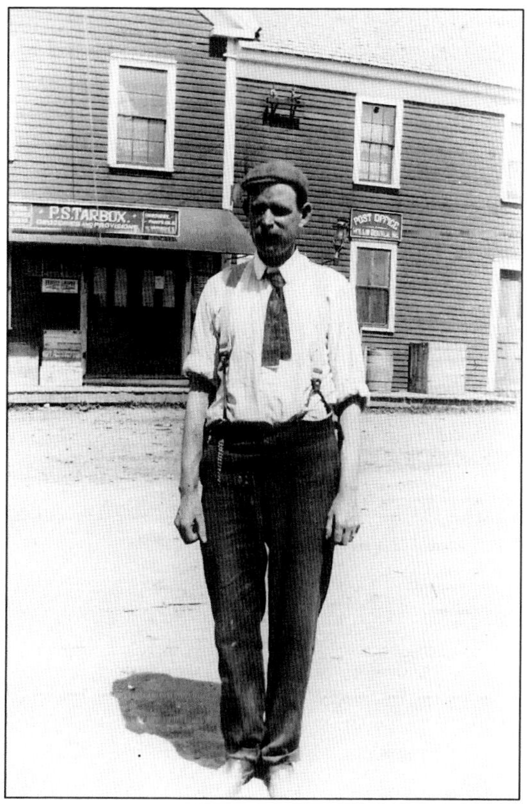

Clarence E. Cousens, *c.* 1920s or 1930s. He helped to run C.E. Cousens in Hollis Center, which carried, among other things, family groceries, choice teas, pure coffees, spices, butter, cheese, and eggs.

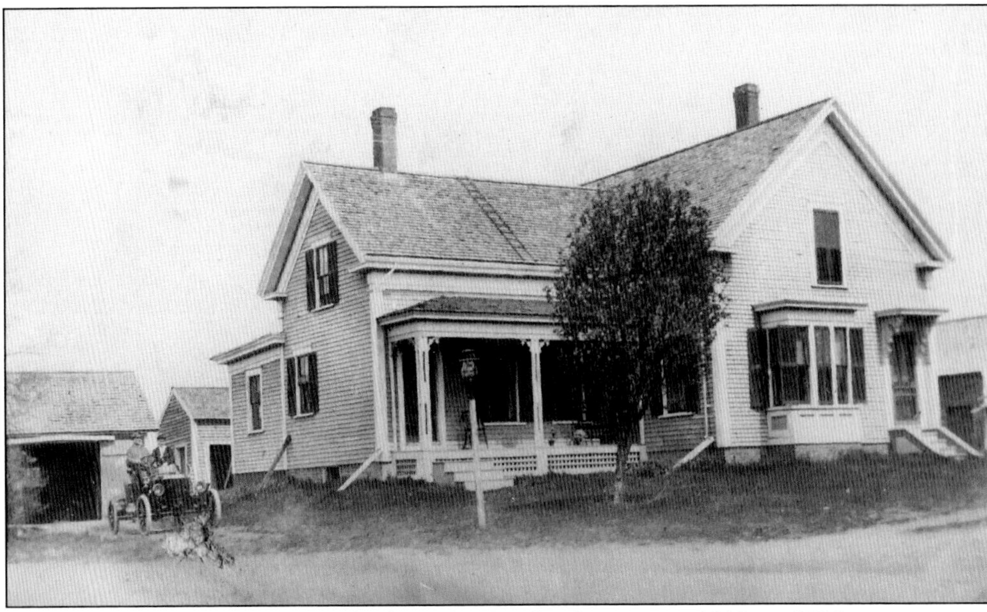

Charles Colcough's home with Charles in his Stanley Steamer, *c.* 1910s or 1920s.

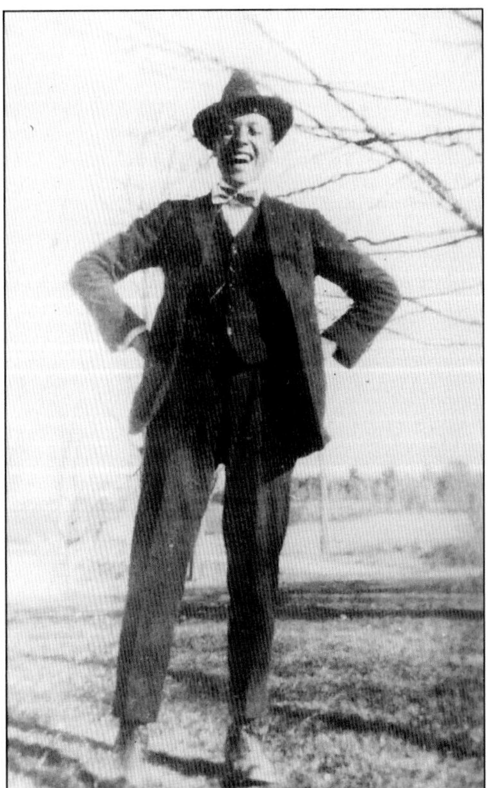

Jimmy Mack, one of the few blacks ever to reside in Hollis Center. He lived with the Hal Bradbury family a few years before World War I. It was said he was from a family of blacks who lived in the brick house at the Hollis end of the Bar Mills bridge but wasn't their child. Jimmy got a motorcycle, buzzed around awhile, and then left town. Reports were he joined the Canadian army.

Joe Dennett and Frank Stevens at traverse jury, May 1925.

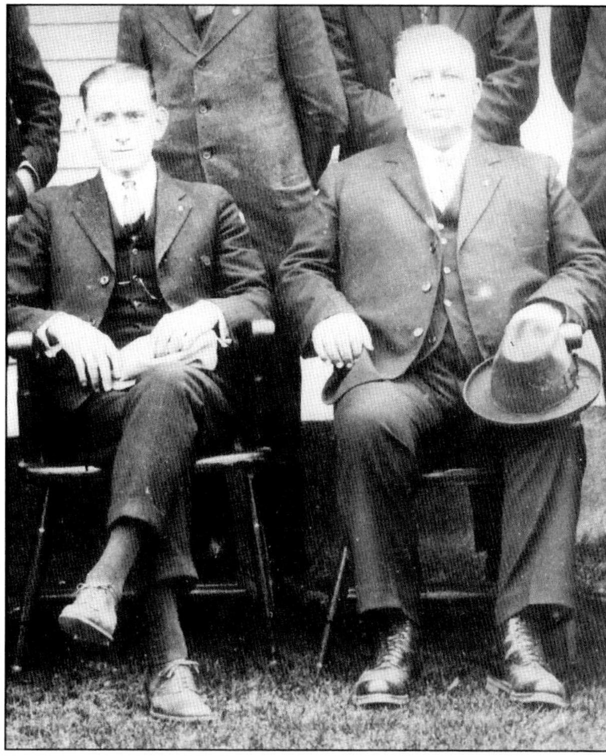

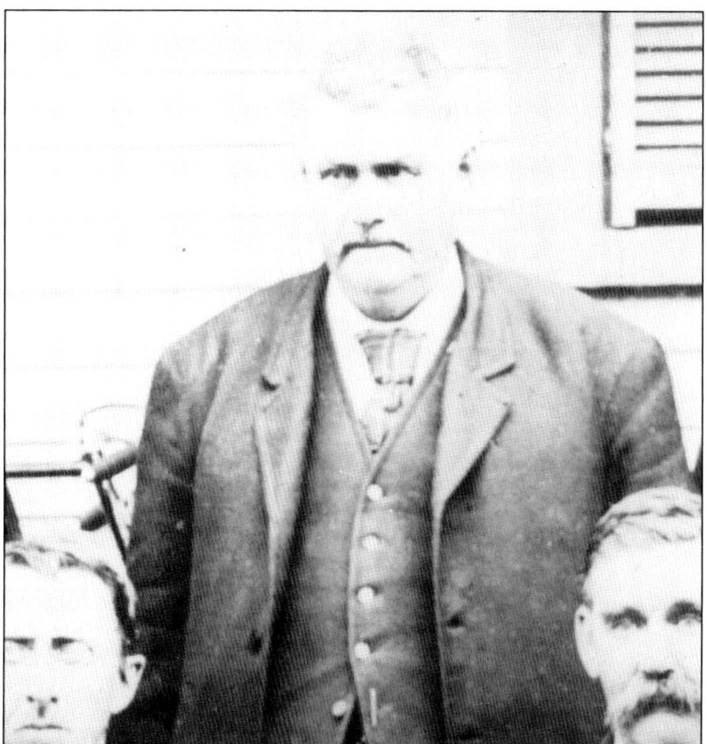

Nathaniel Stevens (Frank's father), *c.* 1900. They were involved in Stevens Bros. natural milk, Hollis Center.

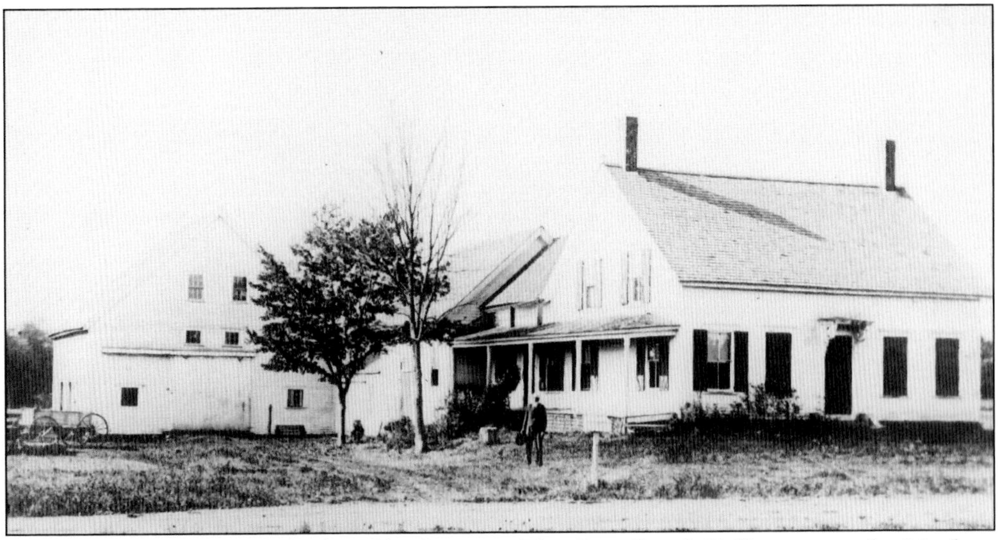

John Berry (Orrington's father) and his home on The Cape Road, Hollis, next to the Moulton house, *c.* 1900s. The house is gone.

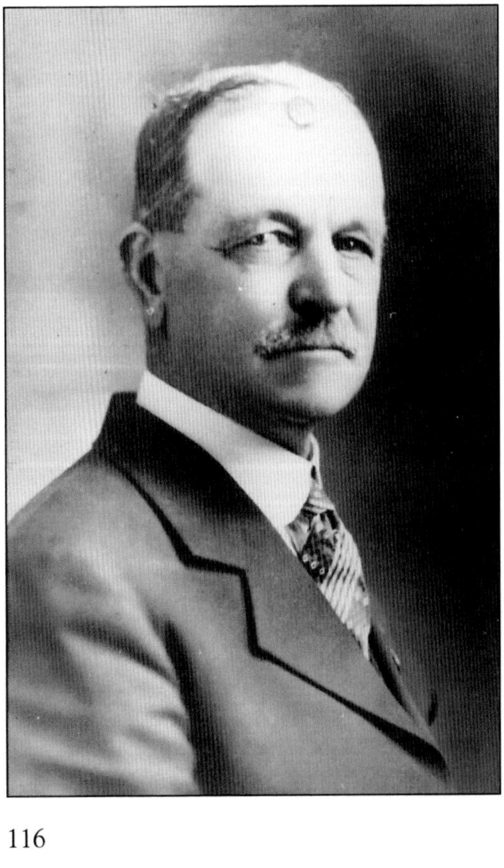

William "Will" Deering, *c.* 1910s.

Jim Burnham at age ninety-one, August 14, 1924.

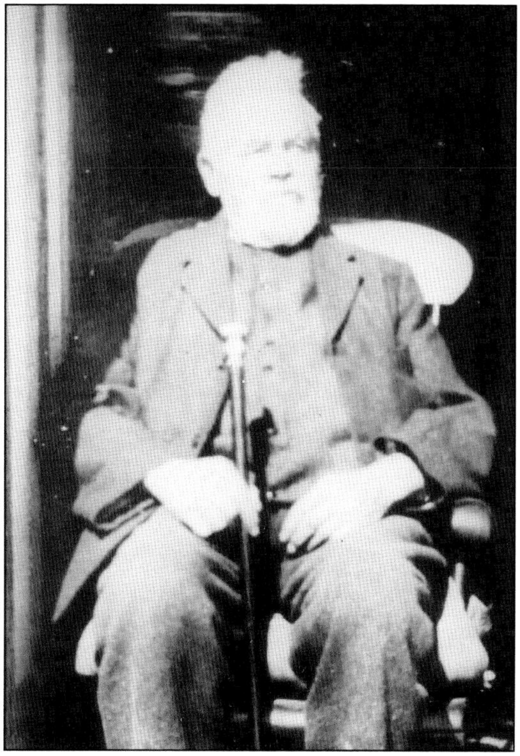

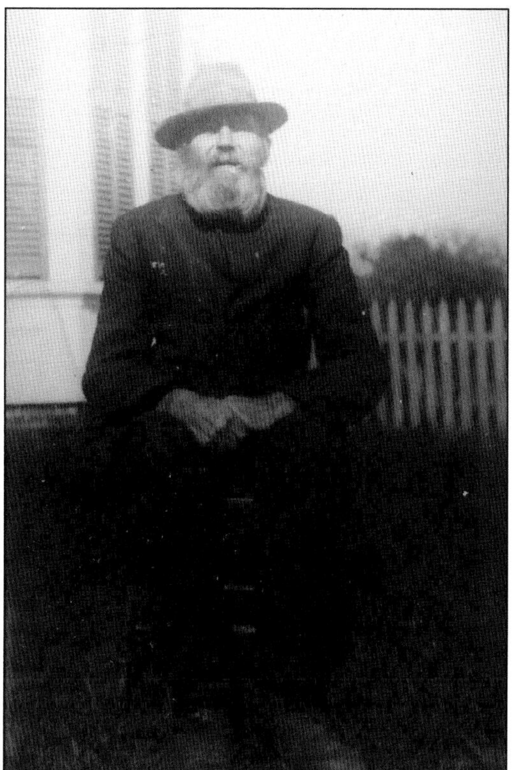

William Kimball, who lived at Sumner Haley's in Hollis, *c.* 1900s.

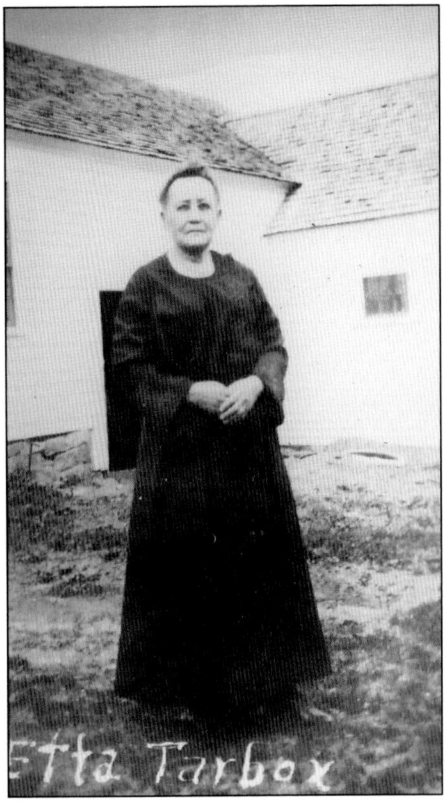

Etta Tarbox, 1913. The Tarboxes were another of the area's leading families.

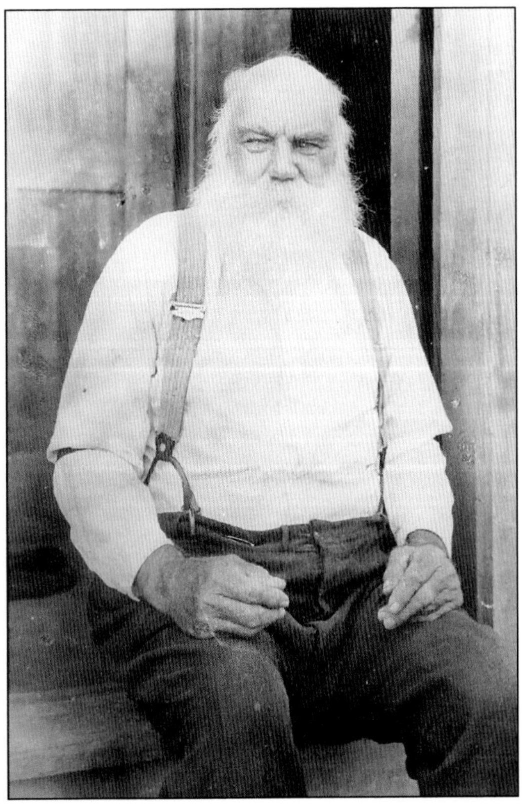

Josiah York, a familiar sight with his oxen at the end of The Cape Road, c. 1932.

John Johnson, herb doctor. Many today would consider him to be a quack.

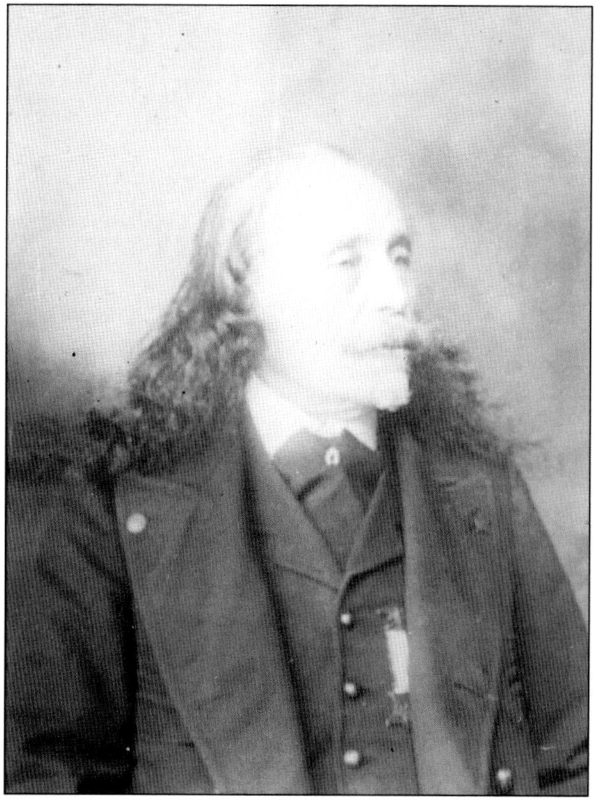

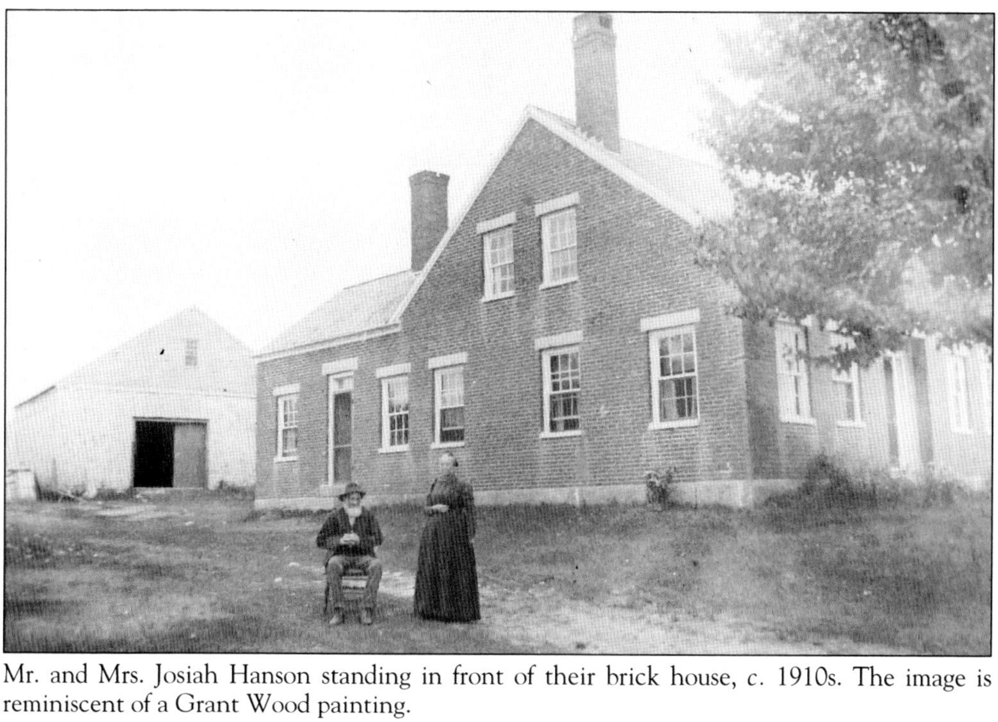

Mr. and Mrs. Josiah Hanson standing in front of their brick house, c. 1910s. The image is reminiscent of a Grant Wood painting.

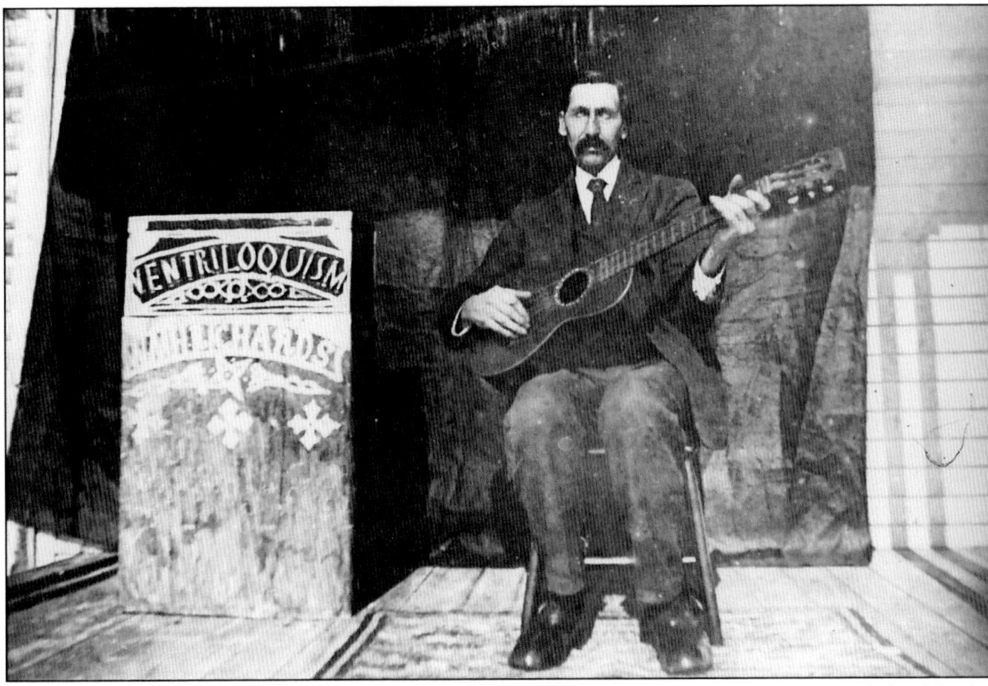

Will Richards, who lived (for the most part) at the beginning of Foss's Lane. He did odd jobs, such as haying and cutting wood in the neighborhood, often living wherever he was employed. He would put on "shows" at the River Road School, one or two evenings a year. Families would bring their lanterns for lights and pay in nickels and dimes. Will would play his guitar, do some "magic," and perform his ventriloquist act.

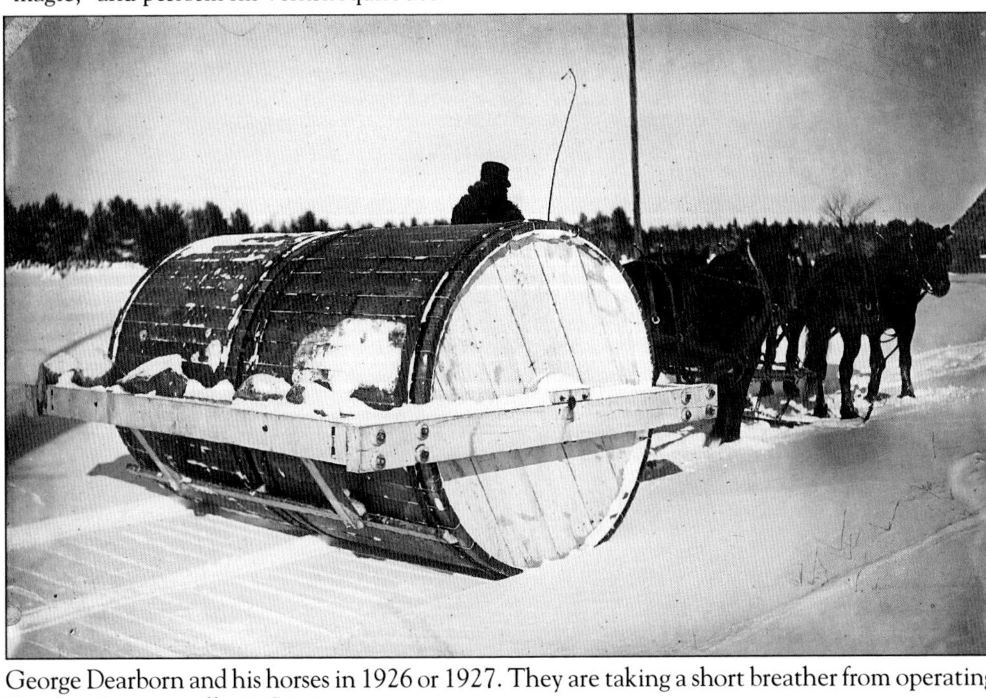

George Dearborn and his horses in 1926 or 1927. They are taking a short breather from operating Dearborn's snow roller in Limington.

Silas Hubbard, founder of Hubbard Lumber Co., and his wife on their 45th wedding anniversary at Limington. Her nickname was Nanny.

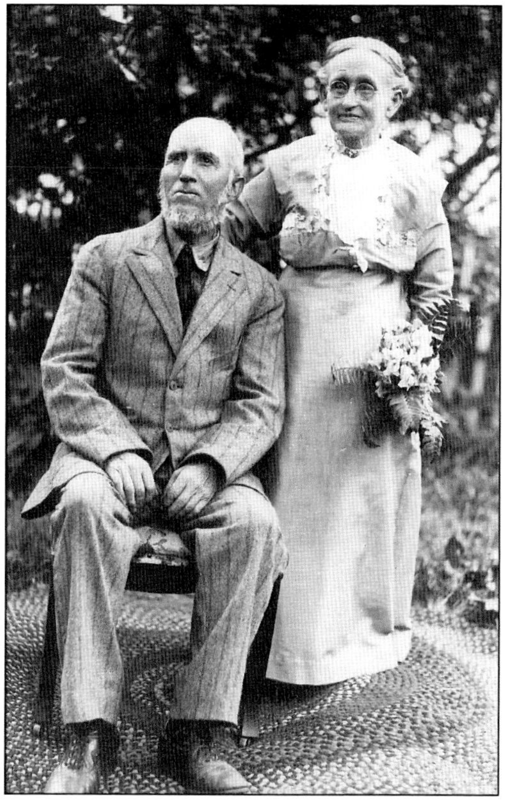

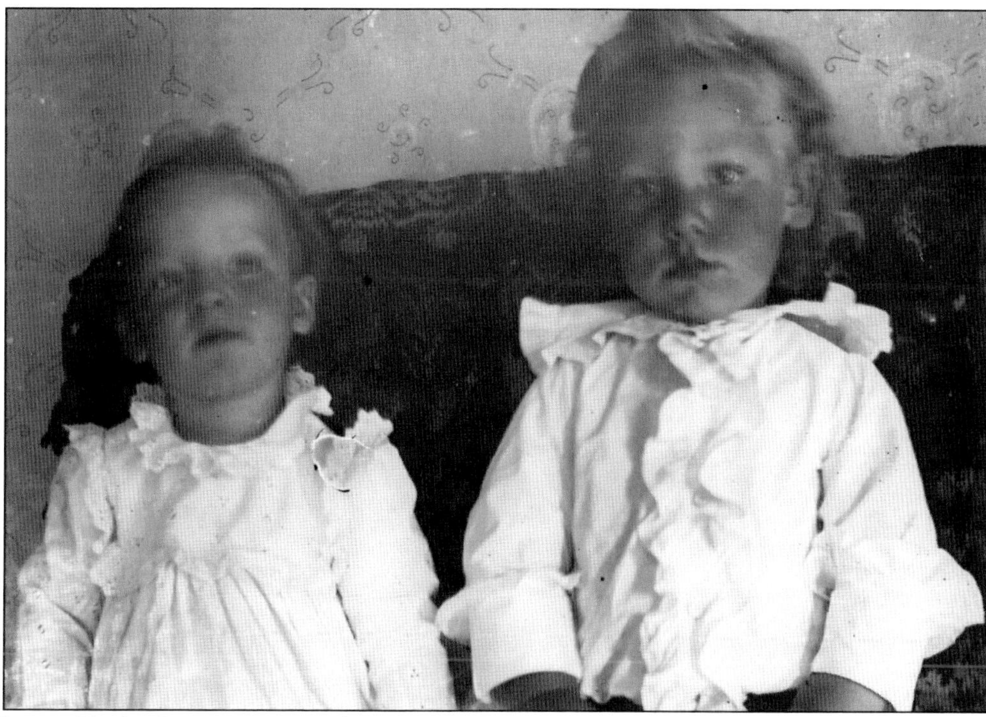

Lester Chick, about age one, and George E. Chick, about age two, of Limington, *c.* 1899.

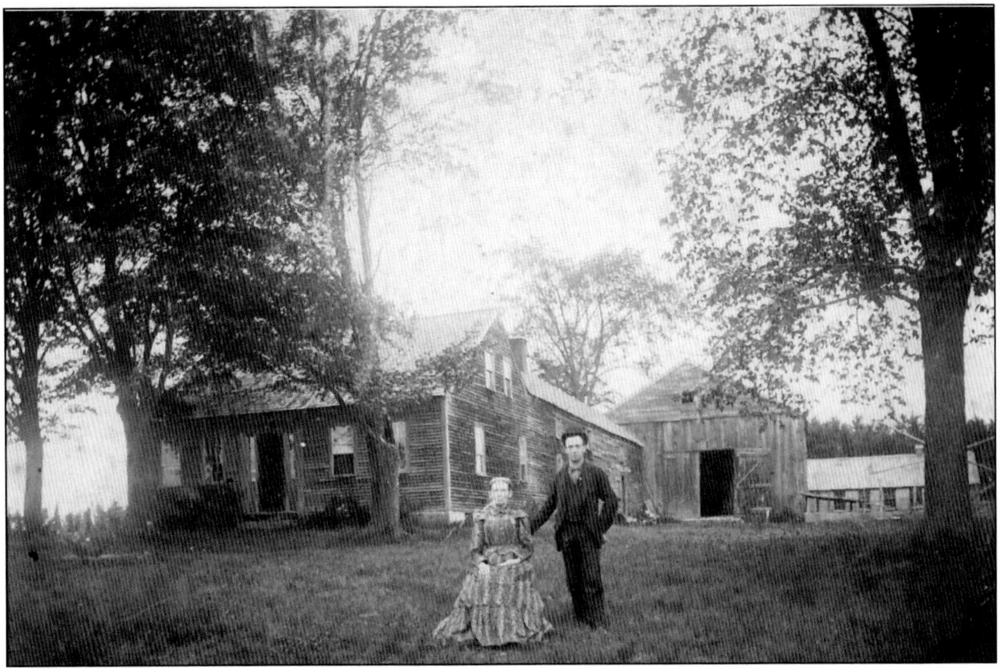

Amelia Chick and her son, Ed Peter Chick, in front of their Limington home about 1900.

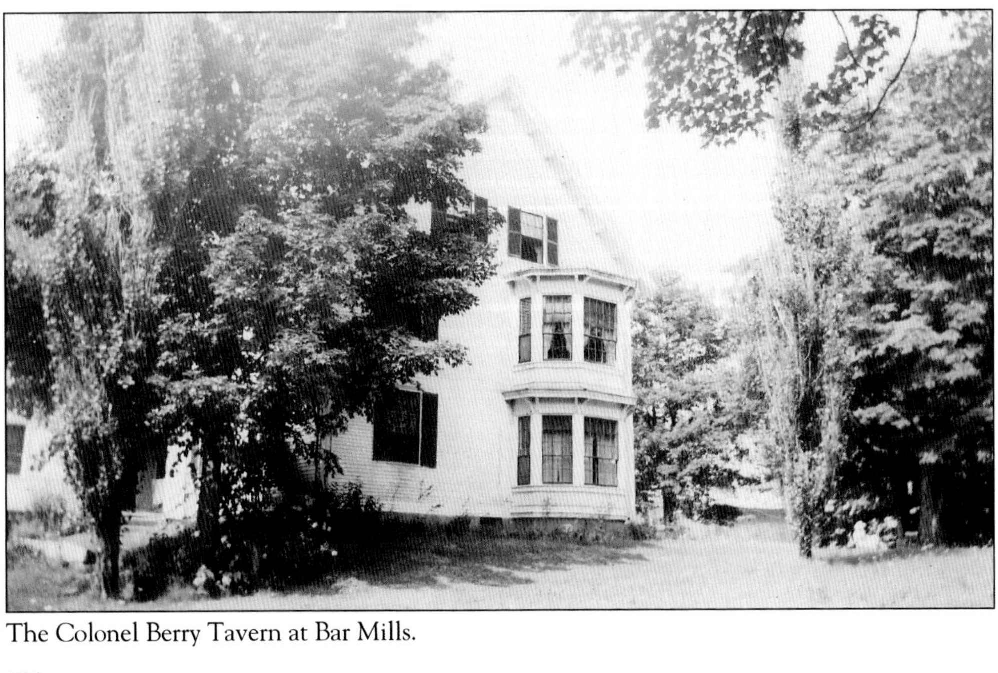

The Colonel Berry Tavern at Bar Mills.

Florence Marilla Flood of West Buxton, ten months old, November 26, 1894.

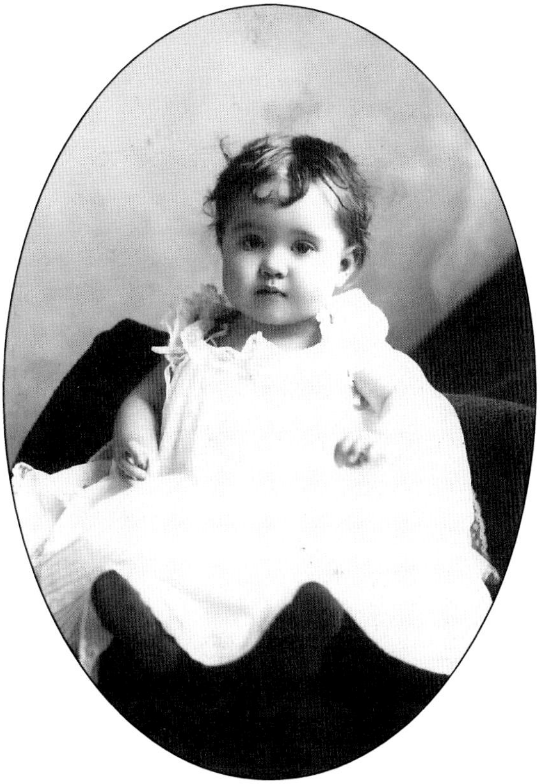

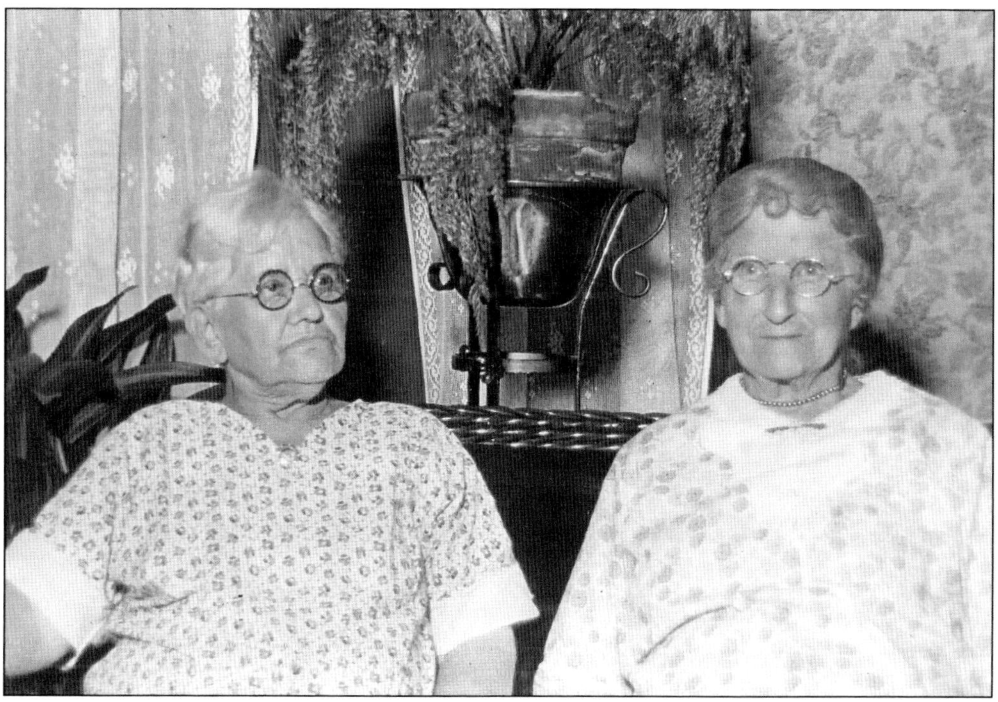

Bessie Milliken and Ella Harmon of West Buxton, May 23, 1931. These are strong faces of the Maine countryside.

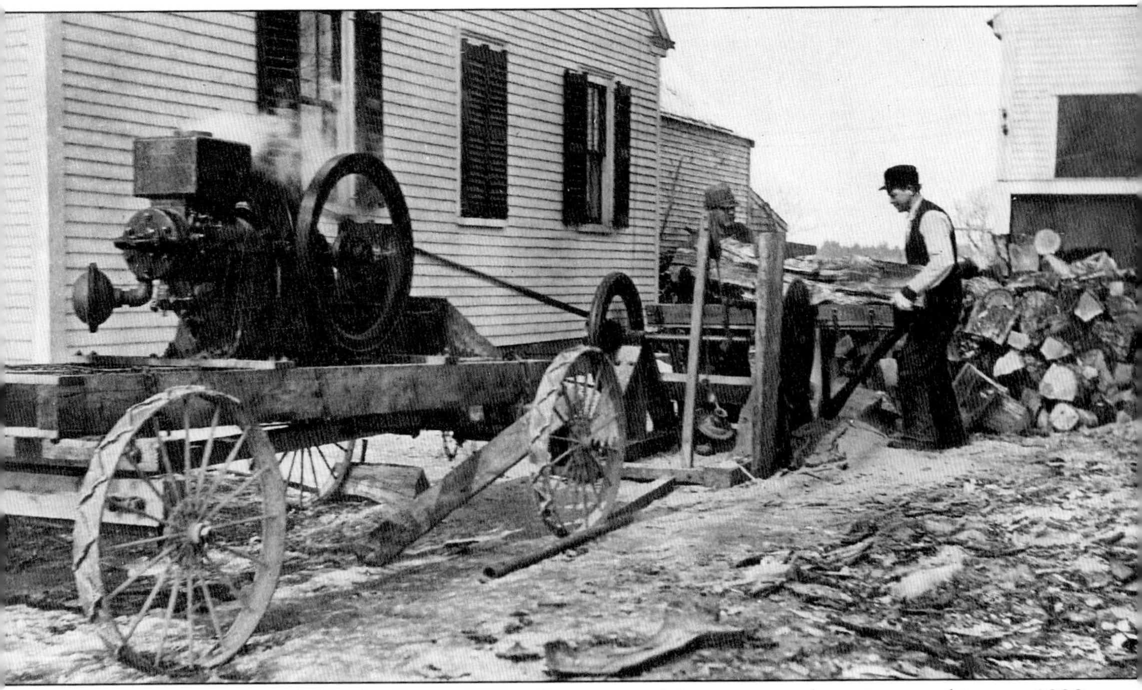

Oscar Harmon and Charles Fogg of West Buxton working at a wood cutting machine, *c.* 1890s or 1900s. There were all kinds of lumber manufacturing skills in this area. The varieties of skills that the early settlers needed were often carried over into later generations. With the disappearance of many of the sawmills and the growing importance of the three communities as bedroom towns for the Greater Portland area, some of these skills are beginning to disappear or become rare.

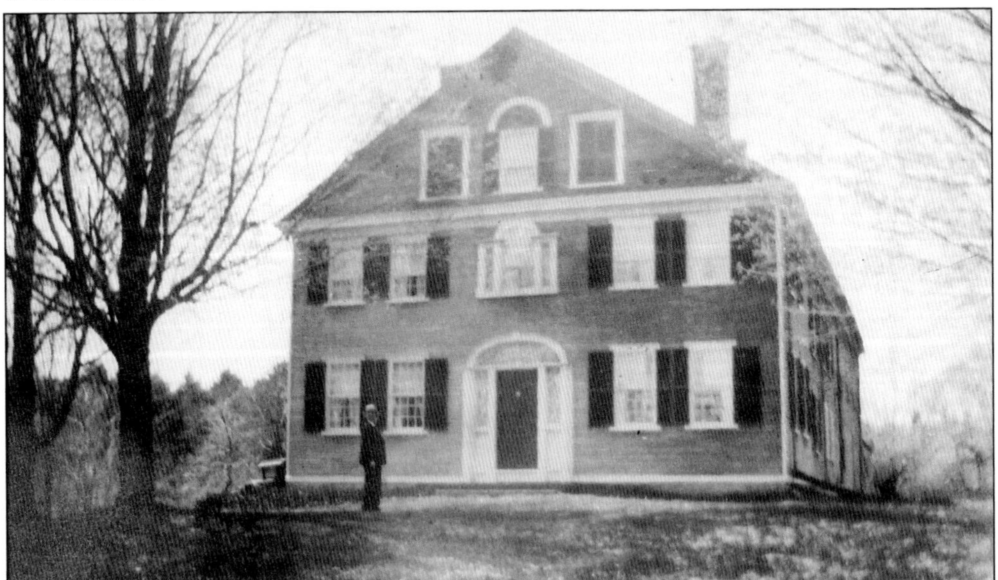

The Captain Moses Davis house, built in 1820, at Salmon Falls, Hollis, August 4, 1941. There was a ballroom in the ell. It was owned later by Mrs. Estrella Frothingham and her daughter, Mrs. Dexheimer, descendants of the captain.

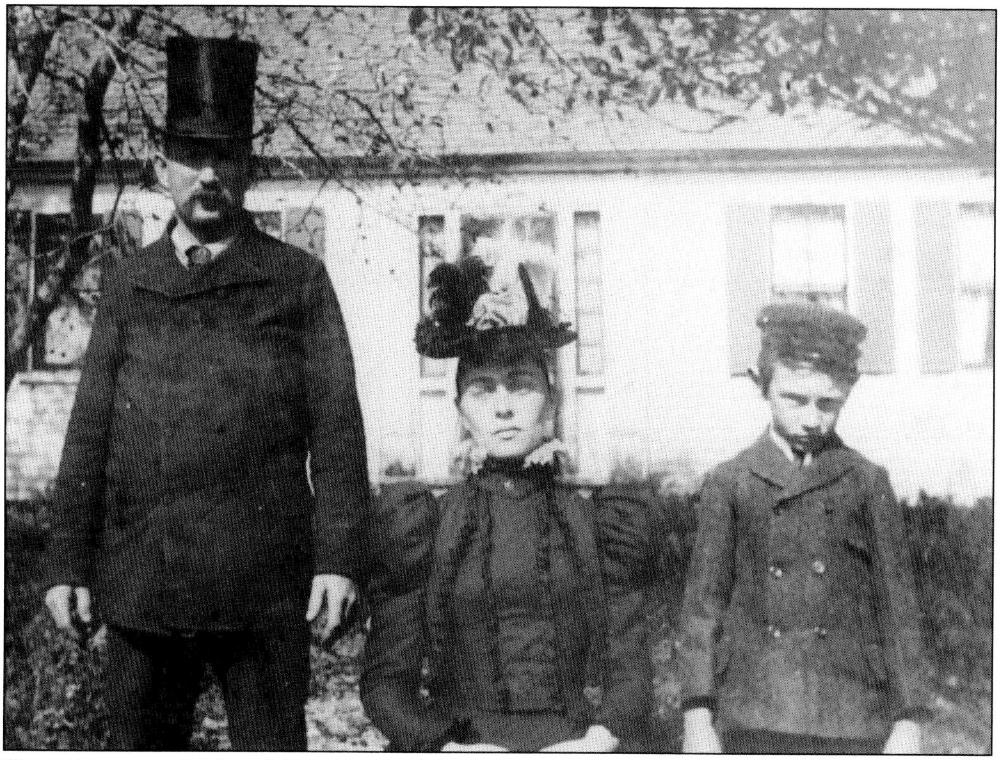

Eben, Annie, and Albert Hanson, *c.* 1896.

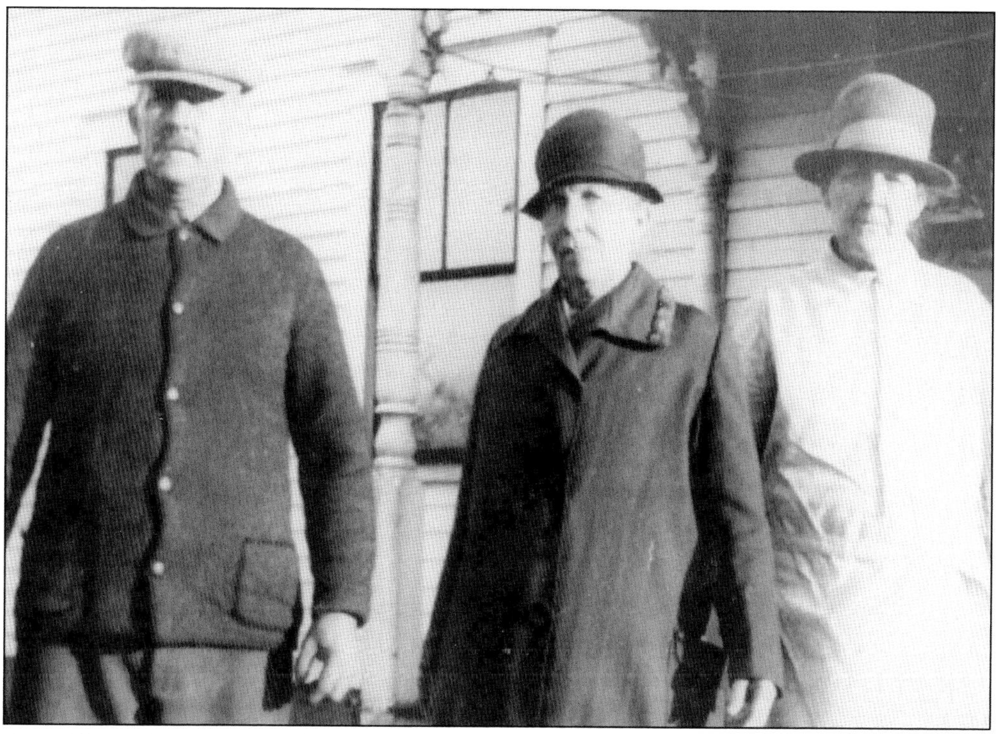

Granville, Sadie, and Emma Hanson, *c.* 1942.

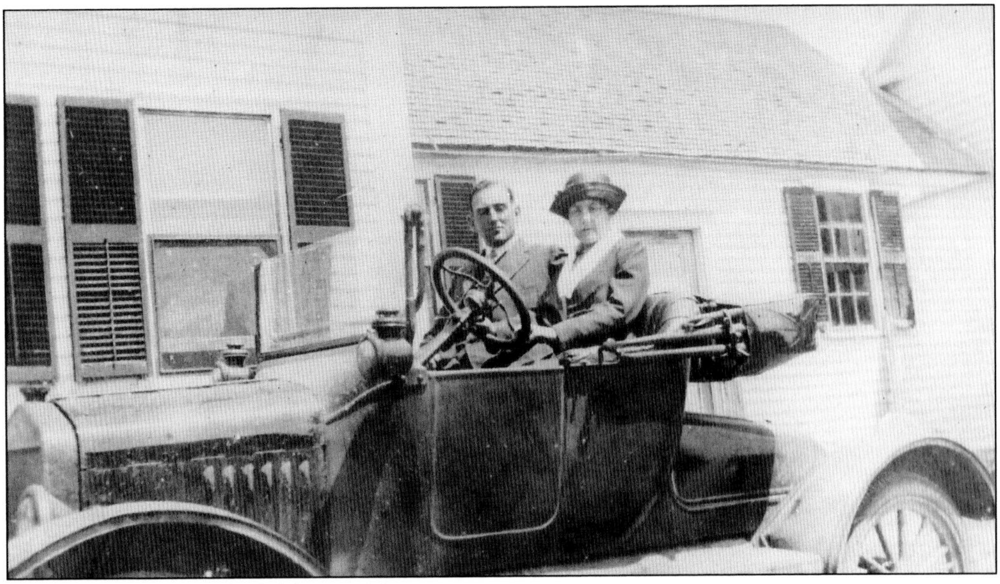

Walter and Susie Wakefield, *c.* 1920s.

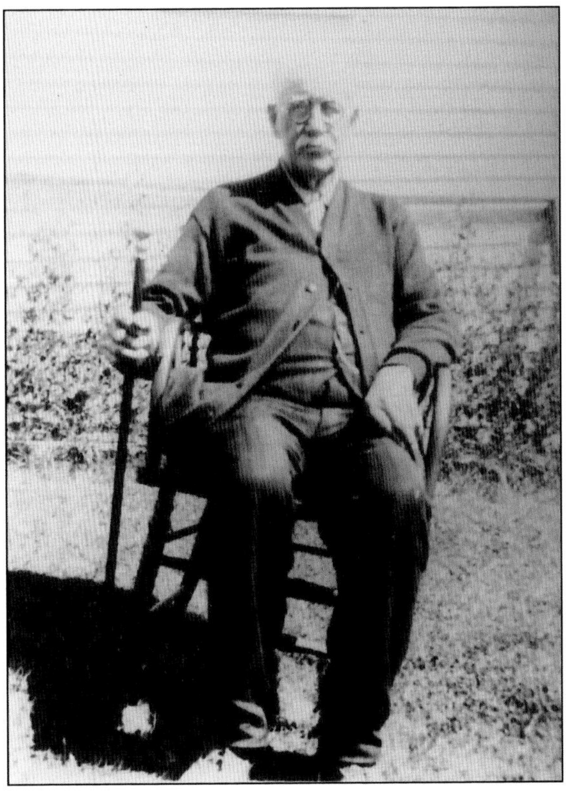

Collins Hanson, *c.* 1910s.

Mr. and Mrs. Scammon and their daughter Alta, River Road, Hollis, *c.* 1920s.

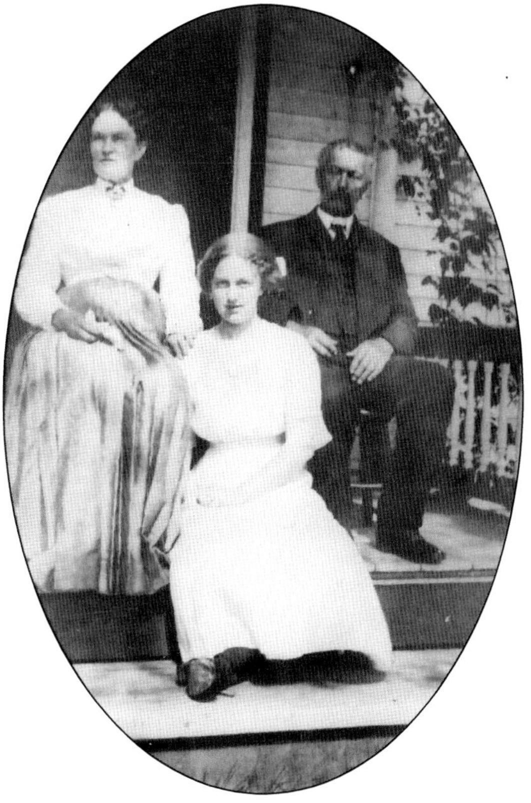

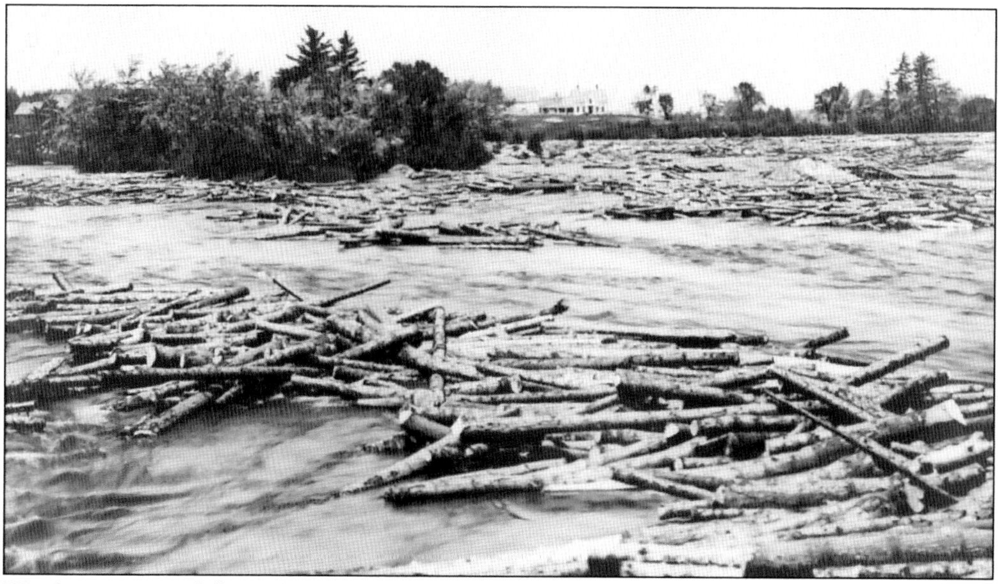

We have come full circle, back to the river. This photograph, taken from the bridge at East Limington, shows the log-laden Saco River, and serves as a reminder that the river was a dominant factor in the community until the late 1940s.

Acknowledgments

The man who really got me started on this three-town area and who was a great help throughout was Major General (Ret.) Stephen Nichols of West Buxton who, among his many other duties, is president of the Buxton-Hollis Historical Society. From him, we move to Mrs. Sylvia Smith, one of the Hollis selectmen, who had a good number of old photographs available. Dana Smith of Tenant's Harbor had taken or made copies of those photographs and gave me carte blanche to use them.

Steve Nichols opened the historical society to me, letting me pick through a mass of material which hasn't yet been used. As usual, Earl Shettleworth of the Maine Historic Preservation Commission provided some excellent photographs.

After I underwent an operation in the midst of preparing this book, I had help from a number of people in its completion. In Limington, Town Clerk Marilyn Webb was very helpful. Mrs. Marion Foss and her husband, Frank, were great help at the last moment, as were John Hubbard and Mrs. Elsie Boothby, all of Limington. Also helpful near the end of compiling the photographs were Mrs. Arlene Woodward (and her daughter Jean), Mrs. Ruth Johnson, Mrs. Barbara Anderson (president of the Dorcas Society), and Pat Packard, all of Buxton. Mrs. Arthur Gannett came through with good information at a crucial point. Mrs. Rose Taylor of Danville Junction was of huge, rapid assistance.

Mrs. Glenys L. Tarlow of Somers, New York, who is probably the leading authority on Kate Douglas Wiggin, supplied good material as did David Wise of Northeast Historic Film in Bucksport. All books that could be found in the Maine State Library on the three towns were read.

Once again, I'd like to thank the people at Arcadia, my publishers. Included are Sarah Maineri, my editor, who has moved to greener and warmer pastures, Jim Burkinshaw, Michael Guillory, Aaron Faulkner, Jamie Carter, and Paige Rosella. I hope I'll be able to keep the flow coming.

Frank H. Sleeper